An Introduction to Hindu Philosophy of Religion

An Introduction to Hindu Philosophy of Religion

U.S. Shaji

CYBER TECH PUBLICATIONS
4264/3, Ansari Road, Daryaganj, New Delhi-110002 (India)
Ph.: 011-23244078. Fax: 011-23280028
E-Mail: cyberpublicationsdelhi@yahoo.com

AN INTRODUCTION TO HINDU PHILOSOPHY OF RELIGION

U.S. Shaji

First Edition 2009

Published by :

G.S. Rawat for **Cyber Tech Publications**
4264/3, Ansari Road, Daryaganj, New Delhi-110002 (India)
Ph.: 011-23244078. Fax: 011-23280028
E-Mail: cyberpublicationsdelhi@yahoo.com

Printed at : Asian Offset Printers

Preface

Hinduism originates from the ancient Vedic tradition and other indigenous beliefs, incorporated over time. Due to its diversity Hinduism can only be defined in terms of peoples and places. It is possible to find Hindu groups whose beliefs have nothing in common and it is impossible to identify any universal belief of practice. Prominent themes in Hinduism include Dharma (ethics and duties), Samsara (The continuing cycle of birth, life, death and rebirth), Karma (action and subsequent reaction), and Moksha (liberation from the cycle of samsara). Buddhism, Jainism and Sikhism share traits with Hinduism, because these religions originated in India and focus on self-improvement with the general aim of attaining personal (first hand), spiritual experiences. They along with Hinduism are collectively known as Dharmic religions.

This book is meant specially for the people who are keen to know more about the Hinduism. I hope that readers will find interesting to go through the text. Any kind of suggestions and complaints are always welcome.

—Author

CONTENTS

1

Introduction

Hinduism (known as Hindu Dharma in some modern Indian languages) is a religion that originated in the Indian subcontinent. In contemporary usage Hinduism is also referred to as Sanatana Dharma, a Sanskrit phrase meaning "eternal law". With its origins in the Vedic civilization it has no known founder, being itself a conglomerate of diverse beliefs and traditions. It is the world's oldest extant religion, and has approximately a billion adherents, of whom about 905 million live in India and Nepal, placing it as the world's third largest religion after Christianity and Islam. Other countries with large Hindu populations include Sri Lanka, Bangladesh, Indonesia, Malaysia, Fiji, Suriname, Guyana and Trinidad and Tobago.

Hinduism contains a vast body of scriptures. Divided as revealed and remembered and developed over millennia, these scriptures expound on a broad of range of theology, philosophy and mythology, providing spiritual insights and guidance on the practice of dharma (religious living). Among such texts, Hindus consider the *Vedas* and the *Upanishads* as being among the foremost in authority, importance and antiquity. Other major scriptures include the Tantras and the sectarian Agamas, the *Puranas* and the epic *Mahabharata* and *Ramayana*. The *Bhagwad Gita*, a treatise excerpted from the *Mahabharata*, is sometimes called a summary of the spiritual teachings of the *Vedas*.

ETYMOLOGY

The Persian term *Hindu* comes from the Sanskrit *Sindhu*, *i.e.* the Indus River. The Rig Veda mentions the land of the

Indo-Aryans as *Sapta Sindhu* (the land of the seven rivers in northwestern South Asia, one of them being the Indus). This corresponds to *Hapta Hindu* in the *Avesta* (*Vendidad or Videvdad: Fargard* 1.18)—the sacred scripture of Zoroastrianism. The term was used for those who lived in the Indian subcontinent on or beyond the "Sindhu".

BELIEFS

Core Concepts: Hinduism originates from the ancient Vedic tradition and other indigenous beliefs, incorporated over time. Due to its diversity Hinduism can only be defined in terms of peoples and places. It is possible to find Hindu groups whose beliefs have nothing in common and it is impossible to identify any universal belief of practice. Prominent themes in Hinduism include *Dharma* (ethics and duties), *Samsara* (The continuing cycle of birth, life, death and rebirth), *Karma* (action and subsequent reaction), and *Moksha* (liberation from the cycle of *samsara*). Buddhism, Jainism and Sikhism share traits with Hinduism, because these religions originated in India and focus on self-improvement with the general aim of attaining personal (first hand), spiritual experiences. They along with Hinduism are collectively known as *Dharmic* religions.

CONCEPT OF GOD

Hinduism is sometimes considered to be henotheistic, but such a view tends to oversimplify a diverse system of thought with beliefs spanning monotheism, polytheism, pantheism, monism and even atheism. For instance, the Advaita Vedanta school holds that there is only one causal entity (Brahman), which manifests itself to humans in multiple forms while many scholars consider the Samkhya school of thought to have had atheistic leanings.

Brahman

According to the monistic/panentheistic theologies of Hinduism, Brahman (the greater Self or God) is in the highest sense One and nondifferentiated from the world and its beings (hence 'nondualist'). In connoting Brahman's absolutely unparalleled nature, it is also called *Parambrahman*, where the Sanskrit prefix *param*-denotes "ultimate". Brahman is also sometimes seen as synonymous with the concept of *Paramatma* (Supreme Spirit).

Beyond time and space, both immanent and transcendent, *Brahman* is often described succinctly as *Sacchidananda*, meaning 'Truth-Consciousness-Bliss', not only possessing the qualities but also being their very essence. Advaita philosophy declares that ultimately Brahman (the impersonal God) is beyond mere intellectual description and can be understood only through direct spiritual experience, where the 'knower' and the 'known' are subsumed into the act of 'knowing'. The goal is to "wake up" and realize that one's *atman*, or soul, is really identical to Brahman, the uber-soul.

On the other hand, monotheistic (for example, Dvaita Vedanta) and other devotional (bhakti) schools, understand Brahman as a Supreme Being who possesses personality. In these conceptions, Brahman is associated with Vishnu, Shiva or Shakti depending on the sect. Brahman is seen as fundamentally separate from its reliant souls (humanity) so, in achieving liberation, individual beings experience God as an independent being, a living personality, and retain their individual identities.

Ishvara

When God is viewed as the supreme personal being (rather than as the infinite principle) God is called *Ishvara* ("The Lord";), *Bhagvan* ("The Auspicious One";), or *Parameshwara* ("The Supreme Lord"). *Ishvara* thus refers to the personal aspect of God in general; it is not specific to a particular deity. *Ishvara* transcends gender, yet can be looked upon as father, mother, friend, child, or even as sweetheart. Some schools of Hindu philosophy do not believe in *Ishvara*, while others interpret *Ishvara* in different ways. Some schools do not distinguish between *Ishvara* and *Brahman*. The Dvaita school holds that *Ishvara* is not incorporeal, but is infinite and a personal being.

Devas and Devis

The Hindu scriptures refer to many celestial entities, called *Devas* ("The heavenly or shining ones", also called *devatas*).

Devas may be translated into English as gods, demigods, deities, celestial spirits or angels. The feminine of *deva* is *devi*.

The *Vedas* and *Puranas* depict the devas in their mythological stories. The latter lauds the Trimurti of *Mahadevas* ("Great Gods"), which are the three aspects of God, Brahma, Vishnu and Shiva. Other devas have been worshipped throughout Hinduism's history. The *devas* are an integral part of Hindu culture and are depicted in art, architecture and through icons. Hindus can primarily worship one of these deities, known as their *isma devata*, or chosen ideal. The particular form of God worshipped as one's chosen ideal depends on individual preference and needs, influenced by regional and family traditions.

Avatars

Krishna (left), the eighth incarnation (avatar) of Vishnu, with his consort Radha. Many denominations of Hinduism teach that from time to time God descends to Earth in corporeal form to help humans along in their struggle towards liberation from rebirth (known as *moksha*) in the form of *bhakti* and restore dharma in society. Such an incarnation of God is an avatar. The most famous avatars are of Vishnu, the two most popular being Rama, whose life is depicted in the Ramayana, and Krishna, who is a central figure in the Mahabharata and whose life is depicted in the Srimad Bhagavatam.

Atheism

Mainstream Hindu philosophy talks about the existence of God, being heavily influenced by the Vedanta school, the dominant philosophical school of Hinduism. Nonetheless, there were earlier atheistic schools such as Samkhya, which did not acknowledge the existence of God.

Atman

Most Hindus believe that the spirit or soul, the true "self" of every person, called the atman, is eternal; as is Brahman, which may be seen as either the greater Self or as God, depending on the outlook. According to the Advaita (non-dualist) schools of philosophy, the individual self and greater Self are not fundamentally distinct. They argue that the core spirit, or "Self", of every individual person is identical with the greater Spirit. Referring to 'Brahman' unequivocally as God may reveal problems of semantics, where certain traditions understand God to be a motivating agency with personality and others that it is without personality and form, beyond any sort of definition and thus non-equivalent to the 'God' as understood by dualist schools of Hinduism or Abrahamic understandings of God.

According to the Upanishads, whoever gains insight into the depths of his own nature and becomes fully aware of the atman as the innermost core of his own Self will realize his identity with Brahman and will thereby reach Moksha. According to the Dvaita (dualist) school, (often associated with Vaishnavism), the atman is not identical with Brahman, which is seen as being God with personality (though not limited); instead, the atman is dependent on God. Moksha depends on love towards God and on God's grace.

Karma, Samsara and Moksha

Karma translates literally as action, work or deed and is often described as the "moral law of cause and effect". According to the Upanishads, an individual, known as the *jiva-atma*, develops samskaras (impressions) from actions, whether physical or mental. The "linga sharira", a body more subtle than the physical one, but less subtle than the soul, retains impressions, carrying them over into the next life, establishing a unique trajectory for the individual. Thus, the concept of a universal, neutral and never-failing karma intrinsically relates to reincarnation as well as one's personality, characteristics and family. Karma threads together the notions of free will and destiny.

This cycle of *action, reaction, birth, death, and rebirth* is a continuum called samsara. The notion of reincarnation and karma is a strong premise in Hindu thought. The Bhagwad Gita states that:

> *As a person puts on new clothes, discarding old and torn clothes, similarly an embodied soul enters new material bodies, leaving the old bodies.*

Samsara provides ephemeral pleasures, which lead people to desire rebirth to enjoy the pleasures of a perishable body. However, escaping the world of samsara through moksha (liberation) is believed to ensure lasting happiness and peace. It is thought that after several reincarnations, an *atman* eventually seeks unity with the cosmic spirit (Brahman/ Paramatman).

The ultimate goal of life, referred to as *moksha*, *nirvana* or *samadhi*, is described as the realization of one's union with God; realization of one's eternal relationship with God; realization of the unity of all existence; perfect unselfishness and knowledge of the Self; liberation from ignorance; attainment of perfect mental peace; or detachment from worldly desires. Such a realization liberates one from *samsara* and ends the cycle of rebirth.

The exact conceptualization of moksha differs among the various Hindu schools of thought. For example, Advaita Vedanta holds that after attaining moksha an atman no longer identifies itself with an individual but as part of Brahman. The followers of dualistic schools such as dvaita on the other hand, expect to spend eternity in a loka, or heaven, in the company of their chosen form of *Ishvara*. Thus, it is said, the followers of *dvaita* wish to "taste sugar," while the followers of Advaita wish to "become sugar."

Yoga

Hatha Yoga traditionally includes meditation, pranayama, and right action—unlike the popular modern approach in the West that emphasizes the physical aspect.

In whatever way a Hindu defines the goal of life, there are several methods (yogas) that sages have taught for reaching that goal. Someone who practices yoga is called a *yogi*. The chief texts dedicated to Yoga are the Bhagwad Gita, the Yoga Sutras, the Hatha Yoga Pradipika and, as their philosophical and historical basis, the Upanishads. Paths one can follow to achieve the spiritual goal of life (moksha, samadhi, or nirvana) include:

- Bhakti Yoga (the path of love and devotion),

- Karma Yoga (the path of right action),
- Raja Yoga (the path of meditation) and
- Jnana Yoga (the path of wisdom).

An individual may prefer one yoga over others according to his or her inclination and understanding. For instance some followers of the Dvaita school hold that Bhakti ("devotion") is the only practical path to achieve spiritual perfection for most people, based on their belief that the world is currently in the age of *Kaliyuga* (one of four epochs part of the Yuga cycle). Practice of one yoga does not exclude others. Many schools believe that the different yogas naturally blend into and aid other yogas. For example, the practice of *jnana yoga*, is thought to inevitably lead to pure love (the goal of *bhakti yoga*), and vice versa. Someone practicing deep meditation (such as in *raja yoga*) must embody the core principles of *karma yoga*, *jnana yoga* and *bhakti yoga*, whether directly or indirectly.

Bhakti Yoga

The bhakti traditions emphasize cultivation of love and devotion for God as the path to perfection. Followers of bhakti typically worship God as a divine personal being or avatar, such as Rama or Krishna. Followers of the bhakti path strive to purify their minds and activities through the chanting of God's names (japa), prayer, devotional hymns (bhajan) and treating all living creatures with compassion. Bhakti followers seek to enjoy a loving relationship with God, rather than to merge their consciousness with Brahman.

Karma Yoga

Swami Vivekananda, shown here practicing meditation, was a Hindu *guru* (teacher) recognized for his inspiring lectures on topics such as yoga.

Followers of karma yoga seek to achieve freedom by acting without attachment to the results of their actions. According to Hinduism, action is inevitable, and has one great disadvantage—any act done with attachment to its fruits generates karmic or psychological bondage. Followers of karma yoga follow the injunction in the Bhagwad Gita:

Without being attached to the fruits of action, one should act as a matter of duty; for by working without attachment, one attains the Supreme.

Many followers of karma yoga offer the results of every action to God, thus combining karma yoga with bhakti yoga. Karma yoga is supposed to bring purification of the heart, freedom from bondage to the ego, humility, and the growing understanding that Brahman is in all people.

Raja Yoga

Followers of Raja yoga seek to experience the spiritual truth directly through meditation. Raja yoga is based on the Yoga Sutras of Patanjali, which has eight 'limbs' that describe the stages a yogi must pass through to reach the goal of *samadhi*. The eight limbs begin with right action (*yamas* and *niyamas*) and perfect meditative posture (*asana*), and continue with control of the body's life force (*pranayama*). From there, the yogi practices techniques of meditation that take him through the progressive stages of interiorization (*pratyahara*), concentration (*dharana*) and meditation (*dhyana*). The final goal of the raja yogi—and the eighth limb of Patanjali's Sutras—is *samadhi*, or oneness with Brahman.

Jnana Yoga

Jnana yoga is the path of wisdom, or true knowledge, and appeals to people with an intellectual nature. The jnana yogi typically practices the four interrelated means to liberation:

1. *Viveka*: discriminating between what is real (the immortal Atman, or true self), and unreal (the physical universe)
2. *Vairagya*, dispassion for material pleasures
3. *Shad-Sampat*, the *six virtues*, which bring about mental control and discipline.
4. *Mumukshutva*, intense desire for liberation.

These practices lead to the unfoldment of wisdom (intuitive perception), rather than mere intellectual knowledge. Through discrimination and introspection, the jnana yogi eventually realizes the highest truth, that "I am Brahman, the pure, all-pervading Consciousness."

HINDUISM

Hinduism, commonly called Sanatana Dharma by Hindus, is the oldest major world religion still practised today and first among Dharma faiths. Hinduism is characterized by a diverse array of belief systems, practices and scriptures. It has its origin in ancient Vedic culture at least as far back as 2000 BC. It is the third largest religion with approximately 890 million followers worldwide, 96% of whom live in the Indian subcontinent.

Perhaps the Hindu spirit, inspired by no one man or woman in particular, is best captured in a line from the ancient Rig Veda, the "oldest religious scripture in the world.":

"Truth is One, though the Sages know it as Many."

The Rig Veda (Book I, Hymn CLXIV, Verse 46)

Essentially, any kind of spiritual practice followed with faith, love and persistence will lead to the same ultimate state of self-realization. Thus, Hindu thought distinguishes itself by strongly encouraging tolerance for different beliefs since temporal systems cannot claim sole understanding of the one transcendental Truth.

To the Hindu, this idea has been an active force in defining the 'Eternal Dharma.' It has been for Hinduism what the infinite Divine Self of Advaita is to existence, remaining forever unchanged and self-luminous, central and pervasive, in spite of all the chaos and flux around it.

In general, Hindu views are broad and range from monism, dualism, pantheism, panentheism, alternatively called monistic theism by some scholars, and strict monotheism, but are not polytheistic as outsiders perceive the religion to be. Hinduism has often been confused to be polytheistic as many of Hinduism's adherents are monists, and view multiple manifestations of the one God or source of being. Hindu monists see one unity, with the personal Gods, different aspects of only One Supreme Being, like a single beam of light separated into colours by a prism, and are valid to worship.

Some of the Hindu aspects of God include Devi, Vishnu, Ganesha, and Shiva. One of the most prominent Hindu monists is the great saint, Ramakrishna whose preferred form of God is Devi and reiterated traditional Hindu beliefs, that aver devotees can invoke God, in whatever form a devotee prefers, (or as monists prefer to call, Ishta Devata, *i.e.*, the preferred form of God) and ask for God's grace in order to attain Moksha, end of the cycle of rebirth.

However, like Judaeo-Christian religions which believe in angels, Hindus also believe in less powerful entities, such as devas.

Contemporary Hinduism is now divided into four major divisions:

- Vaishnavism,
- Shaivism,
- Shaktism,
- and Smartism.

Just as Jews, Christians, and Muslims all believe in the same one God but differ in their conceptions of Him, Hindus all believe in one God but differ in their conceptions. The two primary form of differences are between the two monotheistic religions of Vaishnavism which conceives God as Vishnu and Shaivism, which conceives God as Shiva. Other minor forms are aspects of Vishnu or Shiva.

A BRIEF OVERVIEW

Hinduism rests on the spiritual bedrock of the Vedas, hence Veda Dharma, and their mystic issue, the Upanishads, as well as the teachings of many great Hindu gurus through the ages. Many streams of thought flow from the six Vedic/Hindu schools, Bhakti sects and Tantra Agamic schools into the one ocean of Hinduism, the first of the Dharma religions.

The great debate between followers among the major Hindu philosophical school, Vedanta, from followers of Advaita philosophy on one hand and the strict theistic schools such as those of Ramanuja and Madhva on the other, focused on the true nature of Brahman, on whether Brahman was essentially attributeless or with attributes, *i.e.*, a personal Supreme Being.

The Eternal Way

"The Eternal Way", or the "Perennial Philosophy/Harmony/Faith", is the one name that has represented Hinduism for many thousands of years. According to Hindus, it speaks to the idea that certain spiritual principles hold eternally true, transcending man-made constructs, representing a pure science of consciousness.

But this consciousness is not merely that of the body or mind and intellect, but of a supramental soul-state that exists within and beyond our existence, the unsullied Self of all. Religion to the Hindu is the native search for the divine within the Self, the search to find the One truth that in actuality never was lost. Truth sought with faith shall yield itself in blissful luminescence no matter the race or creed professed. Indeed, all existence, from vegetation and beasts to mankind, are subjects and objects of the eternal Dharma. This inherent faith, therefore, is also known as Arya/Noble Dharma, Veda/Knowledge Dharma, Yoga/Union Dharma, Hindu Dharma or, simply, the Dharma.

What can be said to be common to all Hindus is belief in Dharma, reincarnation, karma, and moksha (liberation) of every soul through a variety of moral, action-based, and meditative yogas. Still more fundamental principles include ahimsa (non-violence), the primacy of the Guru, the Divine Word of Aum and the power of mantras, love of Truth in many manifestations as Gods and Goddessess, and an understanding that the essential spark of the Divine (Atman/Brahman) is in every human and living being, thus allowing for many spiritual paths leading to the One Unitary Truth. An example of the pervasiveness of this paramount truth-seeking spirituality in daily life is the bindi (seen left), which is a common marker for Hindu women.

It symbolizes the need to cultivate supramental consciousness, which is achieved by opening the mystic "third eye." Hindus across the board stress meditative insight, an intuition beyond the mind and body, a trait that is often associated with the ascetic god Shiva. Men, too, will bear on their foreheads the equivalent tilak mark, usually on religious occasions, its shape often representing particular devotion to a certain main deity: a 'U' shape stands for Vishnu, a group of three horizantal lines for Shiva. It is not uncommon for some to meld both in an amalgam marker signifying Hari-Hara (Vishnu-Shiva indissoluble).

The Four Major Sects of Hinduism

Contemporary Hinduism is traditionally divided into four major divisions: Shaivism, Shaktism, Vaishnavism, and Smartism.

Hinduism is a very rich and complex religion. Each of its four sects shares rituals, beliefs, traditions and gods with one another, but each sect has a different philosophy on how to achieve life's ultimate goal (moksha, liberation) and on their views of the Gods. Each sect fundamentally believes in different methods of self-realization and in different aspects of the One Supreme God. However, each sect respects and accepts all others, and conflict of any kind is rare.

Some sects of Hinduism believe in a monotheistic ideal of Vishnu (often as Krishna), Shiva, or Devi; this view does not exclude other gods, as they are understood to be aspects of the chosen ideal (*e.g.*, to many devotees of Krishna, Shiva is seen as having sprung from Krishna's creative force). Often, the monad Brahman is seen as the one source, with all other gods emanating therefrom. Thus, with all Hindus, there is a strong belief in all paths being true religions that lead to one God or source, whatever one chooses to call the ultimate truth.

Shaivism: Also known as Shaivism, Shaivism is a branch of Hinduism that worships Shiva as the Supreme God. Followers of Shaivism are called Shaivites.

Shaivism is a monotheistic faith. Shaivites believe that there is only one God, who simultaneously permeates all creation and exists beyond it, being both immanent and transcendent. The concept is in contrast with many Semitic religious traditions, where God is seen as transcendent only. As all other Hindu denominations, Shaivism acknowledges the existence of many lower Gods under the Supreme One. These Gods are encompassed by Him, seen as either as manifestations of the Supreme Being or as powerful entities who are permeated by

Him, as is all Creation. This type of Monotheism is called Panentheism or Monistic Theism.

Shaivism is a very deep, devotional and mystical sect of Hinduism. It is considered the oldest of the Hindu denominations, with a long lineage of sages and saints who have outlaid practices and paths aimed at self-realization and the ultimate goal of moksha, liberation. As a very broad religion, Shaivism encompasses philosophical systems, devotional rituals, legends, mysticism and varied yogic practices. It has both monistic and dualistic traditions.

Shaivites believe God transcends form, and devotees often worship Shiva in the form of a lingam, symbolizing all universe. God Shiva is also revered in Shaivism as the anthropomorphic manifestation of Shiva Nataraja.

Originated in India, Shaivism has appeal all over India and is particularly strong in South India (especially, Tamil Nadu) and the island of Sri Lanka. Some traditions credit the spreading of Shaivism into southern India by the great sage, Agastya, who is said to brought Vedic traditions as well as the Tamil language.

There can be found almost innumerable Saivite temples and shrines, with many shrines accompanied as well by murtis dedicated to Ganesha, Lord of the Ganas, followers of Shiva, and son of Shiva and Shakti.

Benares is considered the holiest city of all Hindus and Shaivites. A very revered Saivite temple is the ancient Chidambaram, in South India. One of the most famous hymns to Shiva in the Vedas is Shri Rudram. The foremost Saivite Vedic Mantra is Aum Namah Shivaya.

Major theological schools of Shaivism include Kashmir Shaivism, Shaiva Siddhanta and Virashaivism.

Shaktism: Shaktism is a denomination of Hinduism that worships Shakti, the Divine Mother, in all of her forms whilst not rejecting the importance of masculine and neuter divinity.

Shaktism as we know it today developed between the 4th and the 7th centuries CE in India. It was during this development that the many religious texts, known as the Tantras, were written.

One may consider themselves a Shakta (a devotee of Shakti), a Shaiva (a devotee of Shiva), and a Vaishnava (a devotee of Vishnu) all at the same time.

This form of Hinduism, known as is strongly associated with Vedanta, Samkhya and Tantra Hindu philosophies and is ultimately monist, though there is a rich tradition of Bhakti yoga associated with it. The feminine energy (Shakti) is considered to be the motive force behind all action and existence in the phenomenal cosmos in Hinduism. The cosmos itself is Brahman, the concept of the unchanging, infinite, immanent and transcendent reality that is the Divine Ground of all being, the "world soul". Masculine potentiality is actualized by feminine dynamism, embodied in multitudinous goddesses who are ultimately reconciled in one. The keystone text is the Devi Mahatmya which combines earlier Vedic theologies, emergent Upanishadic philosophies and developing tantric cultures in a laudatory exegesis of Shakti religion. Demons of ego, ignorance and desire bind the soul in maya (illusion) (also alternately ethereal or embodied) and it is Mother Maya, shakti, herself, who can free the bonded individual.

The immanent Mother, Devi, is for this reason focused on with intensity, love, and self-dissolving concentration in an effort to focus the shakta (as a Shakti worshipper is sometimes known) on the true reality underlying time, space and causation, thus freeing one from karmic cyclism. A common hymn describing the 1000 names of Devi is the Lalitha sahasranama.

Vaishnavism: Vaishnavism is the branch of Hinduism in which Vishnu or one of his avatars (*i.e.*, incarnations) is worshipped as the supreme God and is a monotheistic faith.

Major branches of Vaishnavism include Srivaishnavism, (espoused by Ramanuja) who advocated Vishishtadvaita, Dvaita (espoused by Shri Madhvacharya) and Gaudiya Vaishnavism (espoused by Shri Chaitanya Mahaprabhu adhered by ISKCON).

The distinction between this branch and others is made by those who study religion. However it may not always be clear to practising Hindus who often take freely from the practices of the different branches. It is likely that a majority (75-80%) of today's Hindus would consider themselves Vaishnava, if pressed to make a distinction. Of the remainder, most would probably consider themselves Shaivites.

Vishnu and Shiva are sometimes visualized as a single divinity named Harihara.

Smartism: Smartism is a denomination of the religion of Hinduism and is closely affiliated with the Advaita tradition. Smartism is monist in theological belief.

Smartas (followers of Smartism) accept and worship all major forms of God, (Ganesha, Shiva, Shakti, Vishnu, Surya and Skanda). Following a meditative, philosophical path, the denomination is generally considered to be liberal and non-sectarian.

In Smartism, devotees pray to whatever form of God a devotee prefers, (or as monists prefer to call, Ishta Devata, *i.e.*, the preferred form of God) and ask for God's grace in order to achieve Moksha, end of the cycle of rebirth.

Notably, Shakti is worshipped to reach Shiva, whom for Shaktas is the impersonal Absolute. Additionally, Shaivites and Vaishnavites often regard Surya as an aspect of Shiva and Vishnu, respectively. For example, the sun is called Surya Narayana by Vaishnavites. In Saivite theology, the sun is said to be one of eight forms of Shiva, the Astamurti. Additionally, Ganesha and Skanda for them, would be aspects of Shiva and Shakti. Hence, it appears to be the case that most Hindus worship Saguna Brahman as Vishnu or Shiva.

Hinduism Origins, Nomenclature and Society

In a 1966 ruling, the Supreme Court of India defined the Hindu faith as follows for legal purposes:

- Acceptance of the Vedas with reverence as the highest authority in religious and philosophic matters and acceptance with reverence of Vedas by Hindu thinkers and philosophers as the sole foundation of Hindu philosophy.

- Spirit of tolerance and willingness to understand and appreciate the opponent's point of view based on the realization that truth is manysided.
- Acceptance of great world rhythm—vast periods of creation, maintenance and dissolution follow each other in endless succession—by all six systems of Hindu philosophy.
- Acceptance by all systems of Hindu philosophy of the belief in rebirth and pre-existence.
- Recognition of the fact that the means or ways to salvation are many.
- Realization of the truth that numbers of Gods to be worshipped may be large, yet there are Hindus who do not believe in the worshipping of idols.

DHARMA IN ORTHODOX HINDU CASTE SOCIETY

According to one view, the Caste system shows how strongly many have felt about each person following his or her dharma, or destined path. A perversion, according to many Hindus, of dharma's true meaning, caste still plays a significant role in Hindu society; however, post Independence, caste is rapidly losing favour in India and caste-based discrimination has been illegitimised.

The British Raj and the subsequent governments have used the caste based politics effectively to divide and conquer for their own personal political gains. The Vedas do not condone discrimination of any sort. The four 'varna's (literally, 'colour') or castes, were based upon the duties to society and worked together towards the welfare of the society. They had equal standing in the society.

However over a period of time this division of labour was misunderstood and exploited. This became more ingrained over centuries until social mobility all but became a thing of the past. In spite of centuries of numerous reform movements, notably within Vedanta, bhakti yoga and Hindu streams of Tantra, and reformers, with recent stalwarts like Swami Vivekananda and Mahatma Gandhi, caste is so deeply ensconced in the Indian consciousness that even Christian converts have been known to separate church meetings for different castes. A number of Muslim communities have retained caste practices as well. What was first an injunction to living one's dharma in surrender to God became an oppressive mandate to surrender to Man. See caste for more.

THE SIX VEDIC SCHOOLS OF THOUGHT

Six Schools: The six Astika or orthodox (accepting the authority of the Vedas) schools of Hindu philosophy are Nyaya, Vaisheshika, Samkhya, Yoga, Purva Mimamsa (also called just 'Mimamsa'), and Uttara Mimamsa (also called 'Vedanta'). The non-Vedic schools are called Nastika, or heterodox, and refer to Buddhism, Jainism and Lokayata. The schools that continue to affect Hinduism today are Purva Mimamsa, Yoga, and Vedanta. See Hindu philosophy for a discussion of the historical significance of Samkhya, Nyaya, and Vaisheshika.

Purva Mimamsa: The main objective of the Purva ("earlier") Mimamsa school was to establish the authority of the Vedas. Consequently this school's most valuable contribution to Hinduism was its formulation of the rules of Vedic interpretation.

Its adherents believed that revelation must be proved by reasoning, that it should not be accepted blindly as dogma. This empirical and eminently sensible manner of religious application is key to the Sanatana/Hindu Dharma and was especially championed by rationalists like Adi Shankara and Swami Vivekananda. For greater depth, please see Purva Mimamsa.

Yoga: Sadhus (Hindu ascetic) are often seen meditating in padmasana (lotus pose). The Yoga system is generally considered to have arisen from the Samkhya philosophy. The yoga referred to here, however, is specifically Raja Yoga (or meditational union). It is based on the sage Patanjali's extremely influential text entitled the Yoga Sutra, which is essentially a compilation and systematization of meditational Yoga philosophy that came before. Upanishads and Bhagwad Gita are also indispensable literature in the study of Yoga.

The most significant difference from Samkhya is that the Yoga school not only incorporates the concept of Ishvara (a personal God) into its metaphysical worldview but also that it holds Ishvara as the ideal upon which to meditate. This is because Ishvara is the only aspect of purusha (the infinite Divine Ground) that has not become entangled with prakrti (the temporal creative forces). It also utilizes the Brahman/ Atman terminology and concepts that are found in depth in the Upanishads, adopting Vedantic monist concepts. Realization of the goal of Yoga is known as moksha or samadhi. It, like the Upanishads, seeks realization of the Atman as being nothing other than the infinite Brahman through ethical (mind), physical (body) and meditational (soul) practices of one-pointedness on the 'one supreme truth.'

Uttara Mimamsa: The Three Schools of Vedanta: The Uttara ("later") Mimamsa school is perhaps one of the cornerstone movements of Hinduism and certainly was responsible for a new wave of philosophical and meditative inquiry, renewal of faith, and cultural reform. Primarily associated with the Upanishads and their commentary by Badarayana, the Vedanta Sutras, Vedanta thought split into three groups, initiated by the thinking and writing of Adi Shankara.

Most Hindu thought today in some way relates to changes affected by Vedantic thought, which focused on meditation, morality and centeredness on the one Self rather than on rituals and societal distinctions like caste. The great debate between followers among the major Hindu philosophical school, Vedanta, from followers of Advaita philosophy on one hand and the strict theistic schools such as those of Ramanuja and Madhva on the other, focused on the true nature of Brahman, on whether Brahman was essentially attributeless or with attributes, *i.e.*, a personal Supreme Being.

PURE MONISM: ADVAITA

Advaita literally means "not two"; thus this is what we refer to as a monistic (or non-dualistic) system, which emphasises oneness. Its consolidator was Shankara (788?-820?). Shankara expounded his theories largely based on previous teachings of the Upanishads and his own guru Govinda

Bhagwadpada. By analysis of experiential consciousness, he exposed the relative nature of the world and established the non-dual reality of Brahman in which Atman (the individual soul) and Brahman (the ultimate reality) are identified absolutely. It is not merely philosophy, but a conscious system of applied ethics and meditation, all geared towards attaining peace and understanding of truth. Adi Shankara denounced caste and meaningless ritual as foolish, and in his own charismatic manner, exhorted the true devotee to meditate on God's love and apprehend truth.

To Advaitists (nondualists) Ultimate Truth is best expressed as Nirguna Brahman, or God without form, or God without personal attributes; indeed, some might go so far as to say it is not 'God' but something beyond. However, even that definition can be limiting. Nirguna Brahman can never be described as that as It transcends all definitions. All personal forms of God such as Vishnu or Shiva are different aspects of God in personal form or God with attributes, Saguna Brahman.

God's energy is personified as Devi, the Divine Mother. For Vaishnvaites who follow Ramanuja's philosophy, Devi is Lakshmi, who is the Mother of all and who pleads with Vishnu for mankind who is entrenched in sin. For Shaivites, Devi is Parvati. For Shaktas, who worship Devi, Devi is the personal form of God to attain the impersonal Absolute, God, *i.e.*, Shiva. For them, Shiva is personified as God without attributes.

QUALIFIED MONISM: VISHISTADVAITA

Ramanuja (1040-1137) was the foremost proponent of the concept of Sriman Narayana as the supreme Brahman. He taught that Ultimate reality had three aspects: Isvara (Vishnu), chit (soul) and achit (matter). Vishnu is the only independent reality, while souls and matter are dependent on God for their existence. Because of this qualification of Ultimate reality, Ramanuja's system is known as qualified non-dualism.

Dualism: Dvaita

Like Ramanuja, Madhva (1199-1278) identified God with Vishnu, but his view of reality was purely dualistic in that he understood a fundamental differentiation between the ultimate

Godhead and the individual soul, and the system is therefore called Dvaita (dualistic) Vedanta.

Alternative Cultures of Worship

The Bhakti schools-The Bhakti (Devotional) school takes its name from the Hindu term that signifies a blissful, selfless and overwhelming love of God as the beloved Father, Mother, Child, or whatever relationship finds appeal in the devotee's heart. The philosophy of Bhakti seeks to tap into the universal divinity through personal form, which explains the proliferation of so many Gods and Goddesses in India, often reflecting the singular inclinations of small regions or groups of people. Seen as a form of Yoga, or union, it seeks to dissolve the ego in God, since consciousness of the body and limited mind as self is seen to be a divisive factor in spiritual realization. Essentially, it is God who effects all change, who is the source of all works, who acts through the devotee as love and light. 'Sins' and evildoings of the devotee are said to fall away of their own accord, the devotee shriven, limitedness even transcended, through the love of God.

The Bhakti movements rejuvenated Hinduism through their intense expression of faith and their responsiveness to the emotional and philosophical needs of India. They can rightly be said to have affected the greatest wave of change in Hindu prayer and ritual since ancient times.

The most popular means of expressing love for God in the Hindu tradition has been through puja, or ritual devotion, frequently using the aid of a murti (statue) in conjunction with the singing or chanting of meditational prayer in the form of mantras. Devotional songs called bhajans (written primarily from the 14th-17th centuries), kirtan (praise), and arti (a filtered down form of Vedic fire ritual) are sometimes sung in conjunction with performance of puja. This rather organic system of devotion attempts to aid the individual in connecting with God through symbolic medium. It is said, however, that the bhakta, through a growing connection with God, is eventually able to eschew all external form and is immersed entirely in the bliss of undifferentiated Love in Truth.

Shri Ganesha is the son of Shiva and Parvati; beloved by many Hindus, he is widely worshipped as Vignesh, the remover of obstacles. Altogether, bhakti resulted in a mass of devotional literature, music and art that has enriched the world and given India renewed spiritual impetus, one eschewing unnecessary ritual and artificial social boundaries.

Tantrism

According to the most famous Western Tantrik scholar, Sir John Woodroffe (pseudonym Arthur Avalon): "The Indian Tantras, which are numerous, constitute the Scripture (Shastra) of the Kaliyuga, and as such are the voluminous source of present and practical orthodox 'Hinduism'. The Tantra Shastra is, in fact, and whatever be its historical origin, a development of the Vaidika Karmakanda, promulgated to meet the needs of that age. Shiva says: 'For the benefit of men of the Kali age, men bereft of energy and dependent for existence on the food they eat, the Kaula doctrine, O auspicious one! is given' (Chap. IX., verse 12). To the Tantra we must therefore look if we would understand aright both ritual, yoga, and sadhana of all kinds, as also the general principles of which these practices are but the objective expression." (Introduction to Sir John Woodroffe's translation of "Mahanirvana Tantra.")

The word "tantra" means "treatise" or "continuum", and is applied to a variety of mystical, occult, medical and scientific works as well as to those which we would now regard as "tantric". Most tantras were written in the late middle ages and sprang from Hindu cosmology and Yoga.

Origins: The earliest evidence for certain (minor) elements of Hinduism date back as far as the late neolithic to the early Harappan period (ca. 5500–2600 BC). The beliefs and practices of the pre-classical era (ca. 1500-500 BC) are called the "Vedic religion". The oldest text of Hinduism is the Rigveda, which is dated to between 1700–1100 BC based on linguistic and philological evidence.

The Vedic Period

Sacred Mount Kailash in Tibet is regarded as the spiritual abode of Shiva.

Modern Hinduism grew out of the Vedas. The earliest of these, the *Rigveda*, centres on worship of deities such as *Indra*, *Varuna* and *Agni*, and on the *Soma* ritual. They performed fire-sacrifices, called *yajna* and chanted Vedic mantras but did not build temples or icons. Buddhist and Jain texts claim that animals were sacrificed in larger *yajnas*. The oldest Vedic traditions exhibit strong similarities to Zoroastrianism and with other Indo-European religions.

Epic and Puranic Periods

The epic poems Ramayana and Mahabharata were composed roughly from 400 BC to 200 CE but were transmitted orally for hundreds of years prior to this period. The Ramayana and Mahabharata contain secular and mythological stories of the rulers and wars of ancient India as well as on the avatars Rama and Krishna respectively.

They are interspersed with treatises on various Hindu philosophical concepts. These include the nature of the atma, karma, dharma, moksha, and the organisation of society and government. The later Puranas recount tales about devas and devis, their interactions with humans and their battles against demons.

The Age of Mahajanapadas

During the Iron Age in India, several schools of thought arose and developed in Hindu philosophy including Samkhya, Yoga, Nyaya, Vaisheshika, Purva-Mimamsa and Vedanta. Three key revolutions underpinned the nascence of a new epoch in Hindu thought.

These were the spiritual upheaval initiated by the Upanishads, and the arrival of Mahavira (founder of Jainism) and the Buddha (founder of Buddhism). Charvaka, the leader of an atheistic materialist school, also came to the fore in North India in the sixth century BC. The Upanishads, Mahavira and Buddha taught that to achieve moksha or nirvana, one did not have to accept the authority of the Vedas or the caste system; the Buddha went a step further and claimed that the existence of a Self/soul or God was unnecessary. In this intellectual ferment, many Hindus became Buddhists and Jains while others were influenced by their teachings. The arrival of new philosophies substantially changed the religion during the Maurya and Gupta periods.

Islam and Bhakti

From the last twelfth century successive waves of armies from Muslim kingdoms invaded and to varying degrees, gained control over North India. During this period Buddhism declined rapidly, and many Hindus converted to Islam. Some Muslim rulers such as Aurangzeb destroyed Hindu temples and otherwise persecuted non-Muslims, while others, such as Akbar, were more tolerant.

Hinduism underwent profound changes due in large part to the influence of the prominent teachers Ramanuja, Madhva, and Chaitanya. Followers of the Bhakti movement moved away from the abstract concept of Brahman, which the philosopher Adi Shankara consolidated a few centuries before, to a focus on the more accessible avataras, especially Krishna and Rama. A new attitude toward God—emotional, passionate love—replaced the old approaches of sacrificial rite and meditation on the formless Brahman.

Indology and Reform Movements

The 19th and 20th centuries saw an unprecedented interaction between Hindu and European thought (in the form of Abrahamic religions and Western Philosophy). This intercultural correspondence catalyzed developments in Indology, formations of new schools of Hindu thought, the global spread of Hinduism and changes within Hindu society. Meanwhile, traditional systems of Hinduism witnessed revivals and new developments that flourished independently.

Indology as an academic discipline of studying Indian culture from a European perspective was established in the 19th century, led by Max Muller and John Woodroffe. They brought much of the Vedic, Puranic and Tantric literature and philosophy to Europe and the United States. At the same time, societies such as the Brahmo Samaj and the Theosophical Society attempted to reconcile and fuse Abrahamic and Dharmic philosophies, endeavouring to institute societal reform.

This period also saw the emergence of movements which, while sometimes highly innovative, were rooted in indigenous tradition, sometimes based on the personalities and teachings of individuals, as with Shri Ramakrishna and Ramana Maharshi. Prominent Hindu philosophers, including Sri Aurobindo and Swami Prabhupada (founder of ISKCON) translated, reformulated and presented Hinduism's foundational texts for contemporary audiences in new iterations, attracting followers and attention in India and abroad. Others such as Swami Vivekananda, Paramahansa Yogananda, B.K.S. Iyengar and Swami Rama have been instrumental in raising the profiles of traditional Yoga and Vedanta in the West.

In the Indian subcontinent, Hinduism is still practised by the majority of India's inhabitants although the number in the areas of modern Pakistan and Bangladesh have dwindled after the Partition of India. Hinduism is the official religion in Nepal, which is the world's only Hindu state.

SCRIPTURES AND THEOLOGY

Hinduism is based on "the accumulated treasury of spiritual laws discovered by different persons in different times." The scriptures were transmitted orally, in verse form to aid memorization, for many centuries before they were written down. Over many centuries, sages refined the teachings and expanded the canon. The majority of the sacred texts are in the Sanskrit language. The texts are collectively referred to as *Shastras* and are classified into two classes: *Shruti* and *Smriti*.

Shruti

The *Rig Veda* is one of the oldest religious texts. This is a Rig Veda manuscript in Devanagari.

Shruti (lit: that which has been heard) refers to the *Vedas* which form the earliest record of the Hindu scriptures. While they have not been dated with much certainty, the most conservative estimates date their origin to 1200 BC or earlier.

Hindus revere the Vedas as eternal truths revealed to ancient sages (*Rishis*) through meditation. Many of these sages were women, called *Rishikas*. Many devotees do not associate the creation of the Vedas with a God or person. They are thought of as the laws of the spiritual world, which would still exist even if they were not revealed to the sages.

There are four Vedas (called *Rig-*, *Sama-Yajur-*and *Atharva*). The *Rigveda* is the first and most important Veda. Each Veda is divided into four parts: the primary one, the *Veda proper*, being the *Samhita*, which contains sacred *mantras*. The other three parts form a three-tier ensemble of commentaries, usually in prose and are believed to be slightly later in age than the *Samhita*. These are: the *Brahmanas*, *Aranyakas*, and the Upanishads. The first two parts were subsequently called the *Karmakanda* (the ritualistic portion), while the last two form the *Jnanakanda* (the knowledge portion).

While the Vedas focus on rituals, the Upanishads focus on spiritual insight and philosophical teachings. They constitute a major portion of the Jnana Kanda. The Upanishads discuss Brahman and reincarnation. While the *Vedas* are not read by most lay Hindus, they are revered as the eternal knowledge whose sacred sounds help bring spiritual and material benefits. Theologically, they take precedence over the *Smriti*, and local custom.

Smriti

The *Naradeya Purana* describes the mechanics of the cosmos. Depicted here are Vishnu with his consort Lakshmi resting on Shesha Nag. The sage Narada and Brahma are also pictured.

Hindu texts other than the *Shrutis* are collectively called the *Smritis* (memory). The most notable of the smritis are the *Itihasa* (epics), which consist of the *Mahabharata* and the *Ramayana*. *Bhagwad Gita* is an integral part of the *Mahabharata* and one of the most popular sacred texts of Hinduism. It contains philosophical teachings from *Krishna*, an incarnation of *Vishnu*, told to the prince Arjuna on the eve of a great war. The *Bhagwad Gita* is described as the essence of the *Vedas*.

The Smritis also include the *Purans*, which illustrate Hindu ideas through vivid mythological narratives. There are texts with a sectarian nature such as *Devi Mahatmya*, the *Tantras* as well as the *Mahanirvana Tantra*, *Tirumantiram*, *Shiva Sutras* and the *Hindu Agamas*. A more controversial text, the *Manusmriti*, is a prescriptive lawbook which epitomizes the societal codes of the caste system.

Most Hindu scriptures are not typically interpreted literally. More importance is attached to the ethics and metaphorical meanings derived from them. Hindu exegesis leans toward figurative interpretations of scriptures rather than the literal.

Many Scriptures, Many Paths

In contrast to the scriptural canons of some religions, the Hindu scriptural canon is not closed. Hindus believe that because the spiritual truths of the Vedas are eternal, they continue to be expressed in new ways. Some Hindus even venerate the scriptures of other religions. One much-quoted verse from the *Rigveda* that emphasizes the diversity of paths to the one goal is:

ekam sad vipra bahudha vadanty

Truth is one, the wise call it in many different ways.
—Rig Veda 1.164.46

This openness means that there is little theological quarrel between Hindu denominations although these denominations may view God and their notions in a different form or sense.

Schools of Philosophy

The six *Astika* or orthodox schools of Hindu philosophy, which accept the authority of the Vedas, are *Nyaya*, *Vaisheshika*, *Samhya*, *Yoga*, *Purva Mimama* (also called *Mimama*), and *Uttara Mimama* (also called *Vedanta*). Although scholars mainly study these philosophies, they influence the beliefs of average Hindus.

Practices

Hindu practices generally involve seeking awareness of God and sometimes also seeking blessings from Devas. Therefore, Hinduism has developed numerous practices meant to help one think of divinity in the midst of everyday life.

According to Swami Vivekananda: "The ideal of man is to see God in everything. But if you cannot see Him in everything, see Him in one thing, in that thing you like best, and then see Him in another. So on you go... Take your time and you will achieve your end."

Puja

Hindus can engage in formal worship (Sanskrit: puja, worship or veneration) either at home or at a temple. At home, Hindus often create a shrine with icons dedicated to the individual's chosen form(s) of God. Veneration may involve offering food, water, or flowers and may be expressed through the burning of incense, lighting of candles or oil-lamps, ringing a bell, waving a fan, or sounding a conch-shell. Other practices of Puja include meditation, chanting mantras, and reciting scriptures. Icons of *devas* and *devis* are an integral part of most Hindu temples. Shown here are icons of Ganesha and Lakshmi, heavily laden with garlands, taken during a Hindu prayer ceremony.

Devotional Singing

Devotional singing is an important part of *bhakti*. Devotional singing occurs in temples, ashrams, on the banks of holy rivers, at home and elsewhere. Hymns are in Sanskrit or in modern Indian languages. Musical instruments accompanying devotional singing include the manjeera, tanpura, harmonium, and tabla. Another form of community worship is Satsang, the practice of gathering for study or discussion of scriptures and religious topics as well as chanting *mantras*.

Yajna

Vedic rites of fire-oblation (yajna) are now only occasional practices although they are highly revered in theory. In a Hindu wedding ceremony however, the presence of sacred fire as the divine witness, the *yajna* and chanting of Vedic mantras is still the norm. The same applies to death rituals.

Worship of God Through Icons: Hindus may perform their worship through icons (murti), such as statues or paintings symbolic of God's power and glory. The icon serves as a tangible link between the worshipper and God. Another view is that the image is a manifestation of God, since God is immanent. The Padma Purana states that the *murti* is not to be thought of as mere stone or wood but as a manifest form of the Divinity. A few Hindu sects, such as the Arya Samaj, do not believe in worshipping God through icons.

Temples

Hindu temples are a place of worship for Hindus. They are usually dedicated to a primary deity along with associated subordinate deities though some commemorate multiple deities. Most temples are constructed as per the *agama shastras* and many are pilgrimage sites. Visiting temples is not obligatory. Many Hindus only go during religious festivals but others visit more regularly. Temples are not used for funerals, or as social hubs but are sometimes used for weddings. Some view the four Shankaracharyas (the abbots of the monasteries in Joshimath, Puri, Shringeri and Dwarka) as the Patriarchs of Hinduism.

HINDU ICONOGRAPHY

Swastika: Hinduism has a developed system of symbolism and iconography to represent the sacred in art, architecture, literature and worship. These symbols gain their meaning from the scriptures, mythology, or cultural traditions. The symbols Om (which represents the *Parabrahman*), Swastika (which symbolizes auspiciousness) have grown to represent Hinduism itself, while other markings such as tilaka identify a follower of the faith. Hinduism associates many symbols, which include the lotus, chakra and veena, with particular deities. These associations distinguish their physical representations in sculptures and pictures and are based on allegorical references in Hindu mythology. While most representations of deities are largely anthropomorphic there are exceptions. For instance the deity Shiva can be worshipped in the form of a pillar-like stone called a *lingam*.

The Guru-disciple Tradition

In many Hindu sects, spiritual aspirants adopt a personal spiritual teacher, called a guru. Traditionally, during brahmacharya a Guru taught a disciple all things necessary to lead a dharmic life. The student is expected to follow the instructions of the guru and to have a spiritual life.

Japa and Mantra

Mantras are prayers that through their meaning, sound, and chanting style help a person focus their mind on holy thoughts or to express devotion to God. Mantras are meant to give courage in exigent times and invoke one's inner spiritual strength. After the pranava or "fundamental" mantra of "Aum", one of the most revered mantras is the Gayatri Mantra. Hindus are initiated into this most sacred mantra at the time of their Upanayanam (thread ceremony). Many Hindus perform morning ablutions at the bank of a sacred river while chanting the Gayatri or Mahamrityunjaya mantras.

Japa (ritualistic chanting) is extolled as the greatest duty for the Kali Yuga (what Hindus believe to be the current age) in the epic Mahabharata. Many Hindu traditions adopt Japa as their primary spiritual practice. The Gaudiya Vaishnava tradition chanting the Hare Krishna mantra is one such example.

Pilgrimage

Pilgrimage is not mandatory in Hinduism though many adherents undertake them. There are many Hindu holy places in India. One of the most famous is the ancient city of Varanasi. Other holy places in India include Kedarnath and Badrinath in the Himalayas, the Jagannath temple at Puri, Rishikesh and Haridwar in the foothills of the Himalayas, Prayag, Rameshwaram in the South and Gaya in the east.

The largest single gathering of pilgrims is during the annual Kumbh Mela fair held in one of four different cities on a rotating basis. Another important "set" of pilgrimages are the 51 "Shakti Peethas," where the Mother Goddess is worshipped, the two principal ones being Kalighat and Kamakhya. Vaishno Devi, the Shakti temple near Katra, Jammu and Kashmir is the second most visited religious shrine in India, after Tirupati Balaji Mandir.

Hindu Festivals

Hinduism has many festivals throughout the year. Their dates are usually prescribed by the Hindu calendar and typically celebrate events from Hindu mythology, often coinciding with seasonal changes and occasions of importance in an agrarian society. There are festivals which are primarily celebrated by specific sects or in certain regions of the Indian subcontinent.

Some widely observed Hindu festivals are:

- Dusshera, or Durga Puja, celebrates events from Hindu mythology symbolizing the triumph of good over evil;
- Diwali, the festival of lights;
- Ganesha Chaturthi, the festival celebrating Ganesha;
- Maha Shivaratri, the festival dedicated to Shiva;
- Ram Navami, celebrates the birth of Rama, the seventh incarnation of Vishnu;
- Krishna Janmashtami, celebrates the birth of Krishna, the eighth incarnation of Vishnu;
- Holi, a spring festival of colours and light;
- Sankranti, a harvest festival of India

Cremation

On death, cremation is considered obligatory for all except *sanyasis*, *hijra*, and children under five. Cremation is typically performed by wrapping the corpse in cloth and burning it on a pyre. Manikarnika Ghat, in Varanasi, is a famous site where bodies are cremated by the side of the river, in full view of the public. Those not cremated may be simply wrapped in cloth, weighted with stones and cast into a river.

Hinduism obliges the closest male relative (son, father, husband, etc.) of the deceased to immerse the cremated remains in the holy river Ganga (Ganges), preferably at the holy city of Haridwar, India. The cremated remains may also be entombed, in case the deceased was a well-known person.

Society

Hinduism has no central doctrinal authority and many practising Hindus do not claim to belong to any particular denomination at all. However, academics categorize contemporary Hinduism into four major denominations: Vaishnavism, Shaivism, Shaktism and Smartism. The denominations differ primarily in the God worshipped as the Supreme One and in the traditions that accompany worship of that God.

Vaishnavas worship *Vishnu*; Shaivites worship *Shiva*; Shaktas worship *Shakti* (power) personified through a female divinity or Mother Goddess, *Devi*; while Smartists believe in the essential sameness of all deities.

There are also many movements that are not easily placed in any of the above categories, such as Swami Dayananda Saraswati's *Arya Samaj*, which rejects image worship and veneration of multiple deities. It focuses on the *Vedas* and the Vedic fire sacrifices (*yajna*). The Tantric traditions in Hinduism have various sects, as Banerji writes in "*Tantra in Bengal*":

> *Tantras are also divided as* astika *or Vedic and* nastika *or non-Vedic. In accordance with the predominance of the deity the* astika *works are again divided as Shakta, Shaiva, Saura, Ganapatya and Vaishna.*

As in every religion, some view their own denomination as superior to others. However, many Hindus consider other denominations to be legitimate alternatives to their own. Heresy is therefore generally not an issue for Hindus.

Ashramas

Traditionally the life of a Hindu was divided into four *Ashramas* ("phases" or "stages"; unrelated meanings include "monastery").

The first part of one's life, *Brahmacharya,* the stage as a student, is spent in celibate, controlled, sober and pure contemplation under the guidance of a Guru, building up the mind for spiritual knowledge. *Grihastha* is the householder's stage, in which one marries and satisfies *kama* and *artha* within one's married and professional life respectively.

The moral obligations of a Hindu householder include supporting one's parents, children, guests and holy figures.

Vanaprastha, the retirement stage, is gradual detachment from the material world. This may involve giving over duties to one's children, spending more time in religious practices and embarking on holy pilgrimages. Finally, in *Sanyasa*, the stage of asceticism, one renounces all worldly attachments to secludedly find the Divine through detachment from worldly life and peacefully shed the body for Moksha.

Monasticism

In their quest to attain the spiritual goal of life, some Hindus choose the path of monasticism (sanyasa). Monastics commit themselves to a life of simplicity, celibacy, detachment from worldly pursuits, and the contemplation of God. A Hindu monk is called a *sanyasi, sadhu*, or *swami*. A female renunciate is called a *sanyasini*. Renunciates receive high respect in Hindu society because their outward renunciation of selfishness and worldliness serves as an inspiration to householders who strive for *mental* renunciation. Some monastics live in monasteries, while others wander from place to place, trusting in God alone to provide for their needs. It is considered a highly meritorious act for a householder to provide sadhus with food or other necessaries. Sadhus strive to treat all with respect and compassion, whether a person may be poor or rich, good or wicked, and to be indifferent to praise, blame, pleasure, and pain.

VARNAS AND THE CASTE SYSTEM

Hindu society has traditionally been categorized into four classes, called *Varnas* (*Sanskrit*: "colour, form, appearance");

- the *Brahmins*: teachers and priests;
- the *Kshatriyas*: warriors, nobles, and kings;
- the *Vaishyas*: farmers, merchants, and businessmen; and
- the *Shudras*: servants and labourers.

Hindus and scholars debate whether the caste system is an integral part of Hinduism sanctioned by the scriptures or an outdated social custom. Although the scriptures contain passages that clearly sanction the *Varna* system, they contain indications that the caste system is not an essential part of the religion, and both sides in the debate can find scriptural support for their views.

The oldest scriptures, the *Vedas,* strongly sustain the division of society into four classes (varna) but place little emphasis on the caste system, mentioning it rarely and in a cursory manner. A verse from the Rig Veda indicates that a person's caste was not necessarily determined by that of his family:

> *"I am a bard, my father is a physician, my mother's job is to grind the corn." (Rig Veda 9.112.3)*

In the Vedic Era, there was no prohibition against the *Shudras* listening to the Vedas or participating in any religious rite, as was the case in the later times. Mobility and flexibility within the varnas challenge allegations of social discrimination in the caste system, as has been pointed out by several sociologists.

Many social reformers, including Mahatma Gandhi and B.R. Ambedkar, criticized caste discrimination. The religious teacher Sri Ramakrishna (1836-1886) taught that

"Lovers of God do not belong to any caste... A Brahmin without this love is no longer a Brahmin. And a pariah with the love of God is no longer a pariah. Through bhakti (devotion to God) an untouchable becomes pure and elevated."

Ahimsa and Vegetarianism

Hindus advocate the practice of *ahimsa* (non-violence) and respect for all life because divinity is believed to permeate all beings, including plants and non-human animals. The term *ahimsa* first appears in the Upanishads, and is the first of the five *Yamas* (eternal vows/restraints) in Raja Yoga.

In accordance with *ahimsa*, many Hindus embrace vegetarianism to respect higher forms of life. While vegetarianism is not a requirement of Hinduism, it is recommended for a *satvic* (purifying) lifestyle. Estimates of the number of lacto vegetarians in India (includes inhabitants of all religions) vary between 20% and 42%. The food habits usually vary with the community and region, with some castes having fewer vegetarians and coastal populations relying on seafood. Some Hindus avoid even onion and garlic, which are regarded as *rajasic* foods. Some avoid meat on specific holy days.

Observant Hindus who do eat meat almost always abstain from beef. The largely pastoral Vedic people and subsequent generations relied heavily on the cow for protein-rich milk and dairy products, tilling of fields and as a provider of fuel and fertilizer. Thus, it was identified as a caretaker and a maternal figure. Hindu society honours the cow as a symbol of unselfish giving. Cow-slaughter is legally banned in almost all states of India.

Conversion

Since the Hindu scriptures are essentially silent on the issue of religious conversion, the question of whether Hindus should evangelize is open to interpretation. Those who see Hinduism mainly as a philosophy, a set of beliefs, or a way of life generally believe that one can convert to Hinduism by incorporating Hindu beliefs into one's life and considering oneself a Hindu. Some view Hinduism as more of an ethnicity than a religion and believe being born a Hindu makes one a Hindu for life. These people tend to believe that there is an assumption that one is Hindu when they come from India. The Supreme Court of India has taken the former view, holding that the question of whether a person is a Hindu should be determined by the person's belief system, not by their ethnic or racial heritage.

There is no formal process for conversion to Hinduism, although in many traditions a ritual called *diksha* ("initiation") marks the beginning of spiritual life. Most Hindu sects do not actively recruit converts because they believe that the goals of spiritual life can be attained through any religion, as long as it is practiced sincerely. Nevertheless, Hindu "missionary" groups operate in various countries to provide spiritual guidance to persons of any religion. Examples include the Vedanta Society, Parisada Hindu Dharma, International Society for Krishna Consciousness, Arya Samaj and the Self-Realization Fellowship.

The History of Hinduism spans more than 9000 years. Hinduism is the world's oldest existing major religion. Worldwide religious tradition based on the Vedas and the beliefs and traditions of the various groups in India, Hinduism's origins include cultural elements of the Indus valley civilisation (c.3300 BC), and the Vedic religion of the Indo-Aryans, and other Indian civilizations. Being highly localised within India, Hinduism has seen many changes throughout the history of the Indian subcontinent. Over time, Hindu philosophy evolved into six schools: Samkhya, Yoga, Nyaya, Vaisheshika, Purva Mimamsa and Vedanta.

Earliest Records

The dates of Hinduism's origins are approximate, based on archaeological evidence and scriptural references:

- Archaeological evidence unearthed at Indus Valley Civilization sites has been dated to circa 3000 BC, suggesting that the Varnashrama system of four classes was adhered to no earlier than that. Seals depicting the deity Shiva in a Yogic posture of meditation also support that approximation. Philological evidence suggests that the earliest Hindu scripture, the Rig Veda, was composed around 1500-1300 BC.
- Astronomical interpretation of Hindu scriptures suggest a date of approximately 3102 BC. This date results from close examination of the Mahabharata, where the positions of the stars were noted at Sri Krishna's birth. Hindus believe Krishna was born 5000 years ago, and using the star locations in the Mahabharata, the exact year was 3228 BC. Sri Rama, according to the Ramayana, lived around 9000-5000 BC.

ANALYSIS OF HISTORIC SOURCES

Early Hinduism is a term used to designate the religious development of India before written history. Two kinds of evidence are available: literature and archeology.

Literature

The earliest literature of Hinduism is made up of the four Vedas, namely the Rig-Veda, Sama-Veda, Yajur-Veda and the

Atharva-Veda. Out of these, the Rig-Veda is considered to be the oldest surviving work of literature. Many Hindus believe that the Vedas were transmitted, via an oral tradition, for perhaps 8000 years (*Fisher*). {Hindus believe that Vedas were orally transmitted or revealed to the Saptha Rishis by the lord himself. We have to go by the Puranas written by the rishis and that is the oldest reference that is available. Puranas talk about various Kalpas and Manvantharas and Yugas as subdivision of each.

The total number of years that has elapsed since the creation of Earth will be in excess of a trillion billion years. Puranas talk about the creation and destruction (Pralaya) of many civilizations. Puranas also talk about life in other galaxies or planets and ability of some life forms to travel from one to the other. They talk about the ability of some Rishis to communicate or establish links between these different worlds or life forms. These cannot be thrown out as pure imagination. The oldest known civilization so far discovered through excavations in Indus valley, exhibits well planned cities with water supply and drainage.

The script used in the inscriptions has not been deciphered yet. This civilization is dating back to 2000 BC. Some bronze statues of Vedic/Hindu Gods (Rudra or Pasupathy) have been excavated from these sites. This indicates that Vedas precede this civilization. Maha Bhagavatham, which was written by Vyasa after completing all other Puranas is supposedly written soon after Swargarohana of Lord Krishna) Western commentators see this as an exaggeration, dating the earliest parts of the Veda, the Rig-Veda Samhita, to oral traditions reaching back to around 1800-1500 BC.

The earliest stage of the Vedas is the Rig-Veda, a collection of poetic hymns used in the sacrificial rites of the Aryan priests. (Rigveda does not prescribe any sacrificial rites. It prescribes worship) Most of the Rig-Veda concerns the offering of Soma-which is both an intoxicant and a god itself-to the gods. The gods in the Rig-Veda are mostly personified concepts, who fall into two categories: the devas, who were gods of nature, such as the weather deity Indra, Agni ("fire"), and Ushas ("dawn") and the asuras, gods of moral concepts, such as Mitra ("contract" or "friend"), Bhaga (guardian of marriage) and Varuna ("the rain god").

The Rigveda is verse narrated by over 12 main rishis. It has 10 Mandalas and there is significant variation in the language and style in the first 8 and the last two namely 9th, 10th mandalas. It is not correct to say that Indra or Varuna are the principal Gods. Rigveda talks about One God (Ekam Sathyam Vipra bahuda Vadanthi. Rigveda talks about the management organization as could be existing.

It assigns functions or roles to each Deva. There are verses in praise of Indra. But the puranas explain that Indra is the name of the post and many persons have occupied that post. Each Manvanthara has a different person as Indra. It is even said that in the next Manvanthara, the Indra will be the same person who was Asura King Mahabali. Hence it is a post with fixed tenure. Same case with other posts. (Veda says that God or Easwara or paramapurusha remains same and constant and has no beginning or end). Indra is head of Devas. Varuna has control over Water and its sources. Vayu has control over Air. There are also others like Agni, Mitra, Yama etc. with assigned roles.

For small or earthly requirements or satisfaction of senses, it is sufficient to pray to these Devas and appease them. Rigveda also talks about origin of sound and also Language. Veda itself says that it was revealed to the rishis by the lord. Rigveda also talks about Vishnu and also Rudra. Purushasooktham is totally in praise of Lord Vishnu and the supreme lord. The Rigveda does not talk about any rivalry between Devas or between Devas and Asuras.)

A rivalry between these two families was already apparent. *Asura* came to mean something like "demon" in later Hinduism, and it is already associated with mischief if not actual malice in the Rig-Veda. Compare this with Iranian Aryan religion, where ahura (*asura*) came to mean "god" and *daava* (cognate to deva) came to mean "evil demon". This theme can be found in other Indo-European religions outside of the Indo-Aryan branch, such as in Norse mythology in the war between the

Aesir and the Vanir. The emerging deprecation of the asuras led to the creation of new categories of gods, such as the adityas. Indra is the king of the gods in the Rig-Veda, although some of the hymns (perhaps representing an older stage) have Varuna as the chief. (However there are no verses in Rig Veda to support this presumption.)

Archaeology

Early Hinduism comprises a period that is hazy in the eyes of archaeologists. The Vedic Aryans, although they left a rich body of hymns, left little material culture behind.

The excavations of the pre-Vedic Indus Valley Civilization, has also not yielded much evidence of religious activity, for example communal temples. However, there is sufficient evidence that the civilization was certainly not purely secular. Only one Indus civilization graveyard has been found and excavated, and has yielded no elaborate royal burials, but the personal possessions buried with the bodies may indicate that these people believed in an afterlife in which they would need these things.

Many figurines of female deities have been discovered. These most probably signified creativity and the origin and continuity of life, and they may have been worshipped as symbolic embodiments of the female principle of creative Energy and Power. In modern Hinduism, the counterpart of these symbols is called Shakti. These "mother Goddess" figurines may have been worshipped in the home rather than in any major state cult, but scholars have seen ancient Dravidian feminine divinity sculptures in groups of seven that date back to the Harappan era which mirror the Hindu belief in a Mother Goddess (Devi) being represented in seven modes.

An Indus Valley seal with the seated figure termed *Pasupathy.*

Figures of a male deity with elaborate horns (or horned headgear) have also been uncovered. He is typically seen surrounded by cattle and is called Pasupathy, (the Protector of Animals), and is seen by some to be the prototype of Hinduism's ascetic God of Destruction, Shiva. Indeed, in modern-day Shaivism, Shiva has absorbed the names, stories and attributes of not only Pasupathy, by which name he is still commonly known, but also the Vedic 'Rudra.' Pasupathy is seen sitting in the meditative posture of yogis, suggesting that yoga or inner contemplation was one of their modes of discovering the secrets of life and creation.

To this day, the Tantric schools of Hinduism know Shiva to be Yogeshwara, Lord of Yoga, and he is said to be the master of Self-knowledge, meditating for centuries at a time. Others see Pasupathy as a form of Brahma.

It is noted by many that the Pasupathy figure is similar to sculptures, paintings and bas-reliefs of horned gods in Europe, stretching as far back as the Paleolithic painting of the "sorcerer" in the cave of Les Trois Frares in France. There exist, in addition, three-headed Pasupathy-statues that seem to resemble the Trimurti (Triple Form) of Brahma-Vishnu-Shiva (Creator-Sustainer-Destroyer) in contemporary Hinduism, and if nothing else, intimate the continuity of religious traditions that have morphed into Hinduism as we know it today from periods as far back as five thousand years ago.

Hindu Mythology

Apart from religious philosophy, mysticism and spiritualism and tales of superhuman heroes and events, Hindu mythology has a strong historical nature and character. It is perhaps the most extensive, although controversial and largely unconfirmable source for the history of ancient India and its peoples.

2

Early Hinduism

Early Hinduism (the historical Vedic religion) consisted not only of aspects inherited from Indo-Iranian religion, but also inherited parts the religious system of the Dravidian peoples, and the Indus Valley Civilization.

INFLUENCES OF THE INDUS VALLEY AND DRAVIDIAN PEOPLES

Interestingly, the Rigvedic deities, like Indra, Agni, Vayu, etc., are not the principal gods of present day Hindus. Those Indo-Aryan gods have equivalents in other Indo-European gods worshipped by other Indo-European speaking peoples. Those gods occupied the highest position until the advent of Christianity in those societies, with little discernible trace remaining of the Pre-Indo-European deities and traditions. However in India the traditions of native groups such as the Dravidians seem to have mingled more fluently with those of the migrants. One view is that this unique mingling is what resulted in modern Hinduism.

VEDIC RELIGION

At the height of the Vedic period, from ca. 800 BC, the inherited mantra texts of the Vedas were extensively commented upon in Brahman literature in many branches (shakhas) throughout India.

EVOLUTION OF HINDU PHILOSOPHY

From prehistoric times of Vedic civilization up to the Gupta Empire era, Hindu philosophy, theology and mythology were constantly evolving.

Socio-Religious Reform Movements

Many orders for religious reform, moksha and religious transformation arose across India.

Hinduism and Jainism

As opposed to Vedic tradition of Hinduism, Jainism follows shramanic tradition and is probably as old as Hinduism. The main disagreement today remains over the rejection of the Vedas, although Hindu society has to a large extent embraced ahimsa and vegetarianism. Over several thousand years, Jain influence on Hindu philosophy and religion have been considerable, while Hindu influence on Jain temple worship and rituals can be observed in some Jain traditions. Jain scriptures are many and varied. Jain scripture rejects both the Hindu Vedas and non-Jain writings as sources of religious authority and practice. The Hindu Vedic (and generally theistic) concepts of divine creation, preservation and destruction are criticised in Jain scriptures such as the *Mahavira Charitam*.

Hinduism and Buddhism

When Mauryan Emperor Ashoka converted to Buddhism, he sponsored the growth of schools and monasteries, and sent missions to Sri Lanka, South East Asia, West Asia and Europe. Following the ascent of the Gupta Dynasty, many communities that had converted to Buddhism returned to Hinduism in India. Also, Hinduism was influenced by many of the teachings promoted by Buddhism and Jainism such as ahimsa and vegetarianism. There was a substantial Buddhist community living in the Indus basin until the Islamic conquest. Later Hindu scriptures, such as the Bhagavata purana, describe the Buddha as an incarnation of Vishnu, effectively reincorporating Buddhism into the Hindu religion, and demonstrating the historical tendency of Hinduism to embrace and absorb many diverse beliefs and traditions. Buddhists themselves, of course, do not necessarily accept this view.

THE GOLDEN AGE

The Gupta dynasty ruled northern India (the north of the Vindhyas), between fourth and sixth centuries of the Common

Era. Though not as vast as Mauryan Empire, Gupta rule has left a deep and wide cultural impact not only in the subcontinent but on the adjacent Asian countries as well. The practice of dedicating temples to different deities came into vogue followed by fine artistic temple architecture and sculpture. Books on medicine, veterinary science, mathematics, astronomy and astrophysics were written.

The famous Aryabhata and Varahamihira belong to this age. The Gupta established a strong central government which also allowed a degree of local control. Gupta society was ordered in accordance with Hindu beliefs. This included a strict caste system, or class system. The peace and prosperity created under Gupta leadership enabled the pursuit of scientific and artistic endeavours.

Adi Shankara and the Establishment of Vedanta

At the time of Adi Shankara's life (c. 788 AE "820 CE), Hinduism had began to decline because of the influence of Buddhism and Jainism. Hinduism had become divided into innumerable sects, each quarrelling with the others. The followers of Mimamsa and Sankhya philosophy were atheists; in so much that they did not believe in God as a unified being. Besides these atheists, there were numerous theistic sects also. Also there were those who rejected the Vedas, like the Charvakas.

Adi Shankara held debates with the leading scholars of all these sects and schools of philosophy to controvert their doctrines. He unified the theistic sects into a common framework of Shanmata system. In his works, Adi Shankara stressed the importance of the Vedas, and his efforts helped Hinduism regain strength and popularity. He travelled on foot to various parts of India to restore the study of the Vedas.

Even though he lived for only thirty-two years, his impact on India and on Hinduism cannot be stressed enough. He reintroduced a purer form of Vedic thought. His teachings and tradition form the basis of Smartism and have influenced Sant Mat lineages. He is the main figure in the tradition of Advaita Vedanta. He is the founder of the *Dashanami Sampradaya* of

Hindu monasticism and *Shanmata* tradition of worship. He travelled all over India (Kerala to Kashmir and Nepal) three times over and was a major cause in the revival and integration of Sanatana Dharma. The mathas he founded are very much active today and form a major guiding force for Hinduism.

Adi Shankara, along with Madhva and Ramanuja, was instrumental in the revival of Hinduism. These three teachers formed the doctrines that are followed by their respective sects even today. They have been the most important figures in the recent history of Hindu philosophy. In their writings and debates, they provided polemics against the non-Vedantic schools of Sankhya, Vaisheshika etc. Thus they paved the way for Vedanta to be the dominant and most widely followed tradition among the schools of Hindu philosophy.

The Vedanta school stresses most on the Upanishads (which are themselves called Vedanta, *End or culmination of the Vedas*), unlike the other schools that gave importance to texts authored by their founders. The Vedanta schools have the belief that the Vedas, which include the Upanishads, are unauthored, forming a continuous tradition of wisdom transmitted orally. Thus the concept of *apaurusheyatva* (being unauthored) came to be the guiding force behind the Vedanta schools. However, along with stressing the importance of Vedic tradition, Adi Shankara gave equal importance to the personal experience of the student also. Logic, grammar, Mimamsa and allied subjects also form main areas of study in all the Vedanta schools.

Cultural Expansion in South-East Asia

During the 1st century, the trade on the overland Silk Road tended to be restricted by the rise in the Middle-East of the Parthian empire, an unvanquished enemy of Rome, just as Romans were becoming extremely wealthy and their demand for Asian luxury was rising. This demand revived the sea connections between the Mediterranean and China, with India as the intermediary of choice. From that time, through trade connection, commercial settlements, and even political interventions, India started to strongly influence Southeast Asian countries. Trade routes linked India with southern Burma, central and southern Siam, lower Cambodia and southern Vietnam, and numerous urbanized coastal settlements were established there.

For more than a thousand years, Indian influence was therefore the major factor that brought a certain level of cultural unity to the various countries of the region. The Pali and Sanskrit languages and the Indian script, together with Theravada and Mahayana Buddhism, Brahmanism, and Hinduism, were transmitted from direct contact and through sacred texts and Indian literature such as the Ramayana and the Mahabharata.

From the 5th to the 13th century, South-East Asia had very powerful empires and became extremely active in Buddhist architectural and artistic creation. The Sri Vijaya Empire to the south and the Khmer Empire to the north competed for influence.

Southeast Asian Hindu Kingdoms

Langkasuka (*-langkha* Sanskrit for "resplendent land"-*sukkha* of "bliss") was an ancient kingdom Hindu located in the Malay Peninsula. The kingdom along with Old Kedah are probably the earliest kingdom founded on the Malay Peninsula. According to tradition the founding of the kingdom happened in the 2nd century. Malay legends claim that Langkasuka was founded at Kedah, and later moved to Pattani.

Pan is a lost Hindu Kingdom believed to be exist around 3rd-5th Century CE somewhere in Kelantan or Terengganu, Malaysia.

Gangga Negara was believed to be a lost Hindu kingdom somewhere in the state of Perak, Malaysia, ruled by Raja Gangga Shah Johan. Researchers believed that the kingdom collapsed after an attack by King Rajendra Chola-I of Coromandel, South India, between 1025 and 1026.

From the 5th-15th centuries Sri Vijayan empire, a maritime empire centred on the island of Sumatra in Indonesia, had adopted Mahayana and Vajrayana Buddhism under a line of rulers named the Sailendras. The Empire of Sri Vijaya declined due to conflicts with the Chola rulers of India, before being destabilized by the Islamic invasion of India from the 13th century.

The Majapahit Empire succeeded the Singhasari Empire. It was one of the last and greatest Hindu empires in the Malay Archipelago.

Funan was a pre-Angkor Cambodian kingdom located around the Mekong delta, probably established by Mon-Khmer settlers speaking an Austro-Asiatic language. According to reports by two Chinese envoys, Kang Tai and Chu Ying, the state was established by an Indian Brahmin named Kaundinya, who in the first century CE, was given instruction in a dream to take a magic bow from a temple and defeat a Khmer queen, Soma. Soma, the daughter of the king of the Nagas, married Kaundinya and their lineage became the royal dynasty of Funan. The myth had the advantage of providing the legitimacy of both an Indian Brahmin and the divinity of the cobras, who at that time were held in religious regard by the inhabitants of the region.

The kingdom of Champa (or *Lin-yi* in Chinese records) controlled what is now south and central Vietnam from approximately 192 through 1697. The dominant religion of the Cham people was Hinduism and the culture was heavily influenced by India. Many Cham towers still stand in central Vietnam. The most significant example of Cham architecture is My Son near the Vietnamese city of Hoi An.

Later, from the 9th to the 13th century, the Mahayana Buddhist and Hindu Khmer Empire dominated much of the South-East Asian peninsula. Under the Khmer, more than 900 temples were built in Cambodia and in neighbouring Thailand. Angkor was at the centre of this development, with a temple complex and urban organization able to support around one million urban dwellers.

HINDUISM IN THE MEDIEVAL AGES

Muslim Invasion

Muslim rulers began to extend their rule across Hindu populated lands in the 8th century CE and Islam began to spread across the Indian-subcontinent over several centuries.

Most converts were from Hinduism or Buddhism; the two dominant local religions.

The prime drivers attributed to the conversions are:-duress by the invaders, political expediency, oppressive legal/legislative climate against Hindus and Buddhists, oppressive caste structure in Hindu society at the time, jizya, Sufi missionaries, intermarriage and immigration from other Islamic lands. Many of the new Muslim rulers looked down upon Hindu Iconodulistic religious practices, and were to various degrees iconoclastic.

In times of conflict they also took the liberty to sack Hindu temples, which were repositaries of significant wealth. In addition, Hindus who were converted to Islam were called "Ajlaf" (the low-born) over the so-called "Arab-descended Ashraf" and subjected to the Caste system among South Asian Muslims

Bhakti Movement

Bhakti movements are Hindu religious movements in which the main spiritual practice is the *fostering of loving devotion to God*, called bhakti. They are monotheistic movements generally devoted to worship of Shiva or Vishnu or Shakti.

The first documented bhakti movement was founded by Karaikkal-ammaiyar. She wrote poems in Tamil about her love for Shiva and probably lived around the 6th century CE.

The twelve Alvars who were Vaishnavite devotees and the sixty-three Nayanars who were Shaivite devotees nurtured the incipient bhakti movement in Tamil Nadu. They constitute South India's 75 Apostles of Bhakti.

During the 12th century CE, the bhakti movement took the form of the Virashaiva movement from Karnataka state inspired by Basavanna, a great Hindu reformer who created the sect of Lingayats or Shiva *bhaktas*. During this time, a unique and native form of Kannada literature-poetry called Vachanas was born. The last Hindu empire of India-The Maratha Empire in 1760.

During the 14th-17th century, the Bhakti movement called the haridasa movement was propagated in Kannada language by great saints of Karnataka like Purandaradasa, Kanakadasa,

Vyasatirtha, guru Raghavendra Swami of Mantralaya, Gopaladasa, Vijayadasa, Jagannathadasa, Narahari tirtha, Sri Kamalesha Vitthala and others. During this time, the teachings of Madhvacharya were propagated through out south India, sowing the seeds of carnatic music and instilling a strong Hindu sentiment at a time when north India was ruled by Muslim Empires.

The Reign of Shivaji

The Hindu Marathas long had lived in the Desh region around Satara, in the western portion of the Deccan plateau, where the plateau meets the eastern slopes of the Western Ghats mountains. They had resisted incursions into the region by the Muslim Mughal rulers of northern India. Under their leader Shivaji, the Maratha freed themselves from the Muslim sultans of Bijapur to the southeast, and became much more aggressive and began to frequently raid Mughal territory, sacking the Mughal port of Surat in 1664. Shivaji was proclaimed Emperor in 1674. The Maratha had spread and conquered much of central India by Shivaji's death in 1680.

Modern Hinduism

Modern Hinduism is the reflection of continuity and progressive changes that occurred in various traditions and institutions of Hinduism during the 19th and 20th centuries. This continuity and adaptation to modern ideas is still a continuing process.

Modern Hinduism has as its values rational thought, modern education and the ideals of humanism, rationalism and religious universalism. This has meant combating the conservative and obscurantist elements, imbibing modernity, modern education compared to classical Sanskritic education system, and countering Christian missionary criticism. The positive consequences of modernity in Hinduism is most visible in the status of women and the dalits. Also, ritualism has declined.

Reform Movements

Brahmo Samaj is a social and religious movement founded in Kolkata, India in 1828 by Raja Ram Mohan Roy. He was influenced by western thought and was one of the first Indians to visit Europe. He died in Bristol, England. The Brahmo Samaj movement thereafter resulted in the Brahmo religion in 1850 founded by Debendranath Tagore AE" better known as the father of Rabindranath Tagore.

Arya Samaj (*Aryan Society* or *Society of Nobles*) is a Hindu reform movement in India that was founded by Swami Dayananda in 1875. He was a sannyasin (renouncer) who believed in the infallible authority of the Vedas. Dayananda advocated the doctrine of karma and reincarnation, and emphasised the ideals of brahmacharya (chastity) and sanyasa (renunciation).

Sri Ramakrishna and his pupil Swami Vivekananda led a reform in Hinduism in late 19th century. Their ideals and sayings have inspired numerous Indians as well as non-Indians, Hindus as well as non-Hindus. Among the prominent figures whose ideals were very much influenced by them were Rabindranath Tagore, Gandhi, Subhas Bose, Satyendranath Bose, Meghnad Saha, and Sister Nivedita.

Converts

Though Hindus have never proselytized, modernity has led to an infusion of newer ideas into the Hindu religion, thereby making it more open, so that we find many non-Asians taking on Hinduism. This is particularly interesting because there is no large-scale proselytising effort in Hinduism.

An important aspect of 20th-century Hinduism has been its spread among non-Indians, who have accepted the religion voluntarily. This perhaps began with the sojourn of Vivekananda to the World Parliament of Religions in Chicago in 1893, where he made a huge impact on the people. He founded the Ramakrishna Mission, which today operates temples, ashrams, charitable hospitals, and schools worldwide. In our times, Transcendental Meditation has become popular. And the International Society for Krishna Consciousness, inspired by the Vaishnavite strand of Bhakti, has established centres around the world. Of late, Pandurang Shastri Athavale a social reformer, philosopher, and spiritual teacher from the Western Indian state of Maharashtra, Guru of Swadhyay Movement, is also a modern spiritual teacher of Hinduism.

The new Hindu communities in Java tend to be concentrated around recently built temples (*pura*) or around archaeological temple sites (*chandi*) which are being reclaimed as places of Hindu worship. An important new Hindu temple in eastern Java is Pura Mandaragiri Sumeru Agung, located on the slope of Mt. Semeru, Java's highest mountain. Mass conversions have also occurred in the region around Pura Agung Blambangan, another new temple, built on a site with minor archaeological remnants attributed to the kingdom of Blambangan, the last Hindu polity on Java, and Pura Loka Moksha Jayabaya (in the village of Menang near Kediri), where the Hindu king and prophet Jayabaya is said to have achieved spiritual liberation (*moksha*).

Another site is the new Pura Pucak Raung in East Java, which is mentioned in Balinese literature as the place from where Maharishi Markandeya took Hinduism to Bali in the fifth century CE.

Hinduism in general does not encourage converting. This largely explains why there has never been any missionary activities in Hinduism. It is the belief of Hinduism that each person chooses their own path to reach god. You are never encouraged to stray from the path that you have chosen. Each religion is just a path to god. Converting to another religion takes you to an entirely new path, which in Hinduism is seen as unnecessary.

Shuddhi Movement

Started by Arya Samaj in early 20th century to bring back to Hinduism people converted to Islam and Christianity. Dayananda claimed to be rejecting all non-Vedic beliefs altogether. Hence the Arya Samaj unequivocally condemned idolatry, animal sacrifices, ancestor worship, pilgrimages, priestcraft, offerings made in temples, the caste system, untouchability and child marriages, on the grounds that all these lacked Vedic sanction. It aimed to be a universal church based on the authority of the Vedas. Dayananda stated that he wanted to make the whole world Aryanae. That is, he wanted to develop *missionary* Hinduism based on the universality of the Vedas.

To this end the Arya Samaj set up schools and missionary organisations, extending its activities outside India. It now has branches around the world. It has a disproportional amount of adherents among people of Indian ancestry in Suriname and the Netherlands, in comparison with India.

Hinduism is a way of life, an Indian tradition that encompasses several religious beliefs, cultural practices and ideologies. The exact date of Hinduism's origin is not known, though estimates vary from 3200 BC to 2500 BC. It is the world's oldest major religion. It is also the third largest religion with a following of approximately a 1.2 billion people. The Indian subcontinent is home to 98% of this populace. The Himalayan kingdom of Nepal is the only nation which has Hinduism for its state religion. The term Hindu itself derives from the name of the Sindhu river.

Hinduism comes under a branch of religions known as the Dharmic religions. The Dharmic religions are less prone to dogma and offer generic universal truths. Such universal truths serve as general guidelines for their follower's philosophies and actions. They remain open to interpretation, adaptation and enrichment at any date and in any age. This core makes Hinduism flexible in accommodating even contradictory opinions seamlessly within its fabric. Hinduism provides several paths to the common goal of divine bliss. The choice of a particular path is left to the ability, discretion and temperament of the follower.

Experience of the divine supreme knowledge, known as moksha, is the core concept of Hinduism. Hinduism teaches its followers the ability to differentiate between the pure actions of virtue and the wrongful actions of evil. The concept of karma lays forth free-willed human actions and how such actions can lead both to moksha and to the cycles of birth and death.

The soul is ever thirsty for this divine knowledge and it accumulates knowledge through all human experiences.

Virtuous actions take the soul closer to the divine supreme, Brahman. Realization and experience of the divine bliss makes all the soul's desires redundant, including the desire for another worldly-experience-giving cycle of birth. Evil hinders recognition of the Brahman and misleads the Atman (soul) to seek knowledge through experiences in various forms of worldly life. All human actions leave their imprint on the soul. They affect and even decide the form and circumstances of life sought by the soul in its next cycle of birth.

3

Important Symbolism and Themes in Hinduism

Hinduism, a religious tradition of Indian origin, comprising the beliefs and practices of Hindus. The word *Hindu* is derived from the river Sindhu, or Indus. *Hindu* was primarily a geographical term that referred to India or to a region of India (near the Sindhu) as long ago as the 6th century BC. The word *Hinduism* is an English word of more recent origin. *Hinduism* entered the English language in the early 19th century to describe the beliefs and practices of those residents of India who had not converted to Islam or Christianity and did not practice Judaism or Zoroastrianism.

In the case of most religions, beliefs and practices come first, and those who subscribe to them are acknowledged as followers. In the case of the Hindu tradition, however, the acknowledgment of Hindus came first, and their beliefs and practices constitute the contents of the religion.

Hindus themselves prefer to use the Sanskrit term *sanatana dharma* for their religious tradition. *Sanatana dharma* is often translated into English as "eternal tradition" or "eternal religion" but the translation of *dharma* as "tradition" or "religion" gives an extremely limited, even mistaken, sense of the word. *Dharma* has many meanings in Sanskrit, the sacred language of Hindu scripture, including "moral order," "duty," and "right action."

The Hindu tradition encourages Hindus to seek spiritual and moral truth wherever it might be found, while acknowledging that no creed can contain such truth in its fullness and that each individual must realize this truth through his or her own systematic effort. Our experience, our reason, and our dialogue with others—especially with enlightened individuals—provide various means of testing our understanding of spiritual and moral truth. And Hindu scripture, based on the insights of Hindu sages and seers, serves primarily as a guidebook. But ultimately truth comes to us through direct consciousness of the divine or the ultimate reality. In other religions this ultimate reality is known as God. Hindus refer to it by many names, but the most common name is Brahman.

In many religions truth is delivered or revealed from a divine source and enters the world through a single agent: for example, Abraham in Judaism, Jesus in Christianity, and Muhammad in Islam. These truths are then recorded in scriptures that serve as a source of knowledge of divine wisdom: the Hebrew Bible, the New Testament, and the Qur'an. In the Hindu tradition, by contrast, there is no single revelation or *orthodoxy* (established doctrine) by which people may achieve knowledge of the divine or lead a life backed by religious law. The Hindu tradition acknowledges that there are many paths by which people may seek and experience religious understanding and direction. It also claims that every individual has the potential to achieve enlightenment.

The Hindu community today is found primarily in India and neighbouring Nepal and in Bali in the Indonesian archipelago. Substantial Hindu communities are present in Sri Lanka and Bangladesh, Mauritius, Fiji, the West Indies, East Africa, and South Africa. Scattered Hindu communities are found in most parts of the Western world. Hindus today number nearly 900 million, including about 20 million who live outside India, making them the third largest religious community in the world, after Christians and Muslims.

Since ancient times, Hindu thought has transcended geographical boundaries and influenced religious and philosophical ideas throughout the world. Persian, ancient Greek, and ancient Roman thought may well have been influenced by Hinduism. Three other religions that originated in India are closely related to Hinduism: Buddhism, Jainism, and Sikhism. In the 19th century German philosopher Arthur Schopenhauer read both Hindu and Buddhist scriptures and based much of his thinking on them.

In the United States, 19th-century writers such as Ralph Waldo Emerson and Henry David Thoreau drew on Hinduism and its scriptures in developing their philosophy of transcendentalism. More recently, civil-rights leader Martin Luther King, Jr., studied the teachings of Hindu leader Mohandas Gandhi on nonviolent protest. In the sphere of popular culture, rock musician George Harrison embraced Hinduism during the 1960s, and some members of the United States counterculture explored Hinduism and Buddhism, as did the Beat poets (Beat Generation). Millions of Westerners today practice meditation or yoga to achieve relief from stress or physical fitness, indicating Western receptiveness to Hindu practices.

WHAT IS HINDUISM?

An encyclopedia article should have a definition at the outset, but this requirement presents unique difficulties in the case of Hinduism. This difficulty arises from Hinduism's universal world-view and its willingness to accept and celebrate diverse philosophies, deities, symbols, and practices. A religion that emphasizes similarities and shared characteristics rather than differences has a difficult time setting itself apart—unless this very quality is considered its defining feature.

This is not to say that there are no beliefs and practices that may be identified as Hindu, but rather that the Hindu tradition has concerned itself largely with the human situation rather than the Hindu situation. Instead of basing its identity on separating Hindu from non-Hindu or believer from nonbeliever, Hinduism has sought to recognize principles and practices that would lead any individual to become a better human being and understand and live in harmony with dharma.

The distinction of dharma from the Western sense of religion is crucial to understanding Hindu religious identity. To the extent that *Hinduism* carries with it the Western meaning of being a religion the words distort Indian reality. In the West a religion is understood to be conclusive—that is, it is the one and only true religion.

Second, a religion is generally exclusionary—that is, those who do not follow it are excluded from salvation. Finally, a religion is separative—that is, to belong to it, one must not belong to another. Dharma, however, does not necessarily imply any of these.

AHIMSA AND VEGANISM

A note of the element of ahimsa in Hinduism is vital to understanding the society that has arisen around some of its principles. The term first appears in the Upanishads. A large section of Hindus embraced vegetarianism in a bid to respect higher forms of life, restricting their diet to plants and vegetables. About 30% of today's Hindu population, especially in orthodox communities in South India, in certain northerly states like Gujarat, and in many Brahmin enclaves around the subcontinent, is vegetarian. While vegetarianism is not dogma, it is recommended as a sattwic (purifying) lifestyle in Yoga.

SACRED STATUS OF COW

Some of the Hindus who do eat meat even avoid the use of leather products. This is most likely because the largely pastoral Vedic people and subsequent generations of Hindus throughout the centuries relied so heavily on the cow for all sorts of dairy products, tilling of fields and fuel for fertilizer that its status as a willing 'caretaker' of humanity grew to identifying it as an almost maternal figure (so the term gau mata).

Thus, while scriptural injunctions against eating beef arose long after the Vedas had been written, the cow still holds an honoured place in Hindu society. It is said that Krishna is both Govinda (herder of cows) and Gopala (protector of cows), and Shiva's attendant is Nandi, the bull.

HINDU SYMBOLISM

Among the most revered symbols in Hinduism, two are quintessentially a part of its culture and representative of its general ethos:

Aum is the standard sign of Hinduism, and is prefixed and sometimes suffixed to all Hindu mantras and prayers. It contains an enormous and diverse amount of symbolism; Hindus consider its sound and vibration to be the divine representation of existence, encompassing all of manifold nature into the One eternal truth. The swastika (PS) is an Arya, or noble symbol. It stands for satya, truth, and stability within the power of Brahma or, alternatively, of Surya, the sun. Its rotation in four directions has been used to represent many ideas, but primarily describes the four directions and their harmonious whole. It has been used in Hinduism since the early Vedic culture and is still widespread in the Indian subcontinent.

FORMS OF WORSHIP: MURTIS AND MANTRAS

Contrary to popular belief, practiced Hinduism is neither polytheistic nor exclusive monotheistic. Contemporary Hinduism, at is practiced today, more strongly adheres to a Smarta model, which is a form of inclusive monotheism. The various gods and avatars that are worshipped by Hindus are understood as different forms of One truth, sometimes seen as beyond a mere God and as a formless Divine Ground (Brahman), akin but not limited to monism, or as one monotheistic principle like Vishnu or Shiva as the exclusive monotheistic faiths of Vaishnavism and Shaivism adhere to.

Whether believing in the One source as formless (nirguna Brahman, without attributes) or as a personal God (saguna Brahman, with attributes), Hindus understand that the one truth may be seen as different to different people. Hinduism encourages devotees to describe and develop a personal relationship with their chosen deity (ishta devata) in the form of a God or Goddess.

Worship of lesser deities is often done through the aid of pictures or icons (murti) which are said not to be God themselves but conduits for the devotee's consciousness, markers for the human soul that signify the ineffable and illimitable nature of the love and grandeur of God. They are symbols of the greater principle, representing and are never presumed to be the concept or entity itself. Thus, Hindu image worship is a form of iconolatry, in which the symbols are venerated as putative sigils of divinity.

Mantra

Reciting mantras is a fundamental practice in Hinduism. Much of mantra yoga, as it is called, is done through japa (repetition). Mantras are said, through their meaning, sound, and chanting style, to help meditational focus for the sadhaka (practitioner). They can also be used to aid in expression of love for the deity, another facet of Bhakti yoga akin to the understanding of the murti. They often give courage in exigent times and serve to help 'invoke' one's inner spiritual strength.

The most revered mantra in Hinduism is the famed Gayatri Mantra (see Sanskrit for pronunciation):

Transliteration: OM bhur bhuva sva |

tat savitur varenyam |

bhargo devasya dhimahi |

dhiyo yo na pra-codayat |

Translation: "May we attain that excellent glory of Savitar the God/so May he stimulate our prayers."

It is considered one of the most universal of all Hindu mantras, invoking the universal Brahman as the principle of knowledge and the illumination of the primordial Sun. Many Hindus to this day, in a tradition that has continued unbroken for at least 3,000 years, perform morning ablutions at the bank of a sacred river. Known as a universal mantra, it is revered as being the most condensed form of Divine Knowledge (Veda). Its presiding principle, Ma (Mother) Gayatri, is also known as Veda Mata (Mother of the Vedas) and is strongly associated with the Goddess of Learning and Illumination, Saraswati.

The chief aim of the Vedic religion is to achieve moksha, or liberation, through constant dedication to Satya (Truth) and eventual realisation of the atman (Universal Soul), held to be achievable by all, whether through meditation or pure love. The great rishis (Hindu sages) have termed the samsaric (one who lives in samsara, *i.e.* the temporal or earthly plane) who succeeds in living an honest, loving and dharmic life a jivanmukta (living free soul). Hinduism's fundamental truth is best expressed in the Upanishadic dictum, Tat Twam Asi (Thou Art That), and the ultimate aspiration as follows:

OM Asato ma sad gamaya, tamaso ma jyotir gamaya, mrityor ma aamritaam gamaya

"OM Lead me from ignorance to truth, from darkness to light, from death to immortality."

Hindu Sacred Texts: The overwhelming majority of Hindu sacred texts are composed in the Sanskrit language. The texts are divided into two categories: Shruti-that which is heard (*i.e.*, revelation) and Smriti-that which is remembered (*i.e.* tradition, not revelation).

Shruti

The Vedas are considered as shruti (inspired) by all Hindus. While the overwhelming majority of Hindus may never read the Vedas, the reverence for the more abstract notion of eternal knowledge (Veda means knowledge) is etched deep into the hearts of all those who follow Veda Dharma. The four Vedas (the Rig, Yajur, Sama and Atharva Vedas) were preserved by various shakhas or schools. Depending on the school, various commentaries and instructions are associated with each Veda. The oldest of these are the Brahmanas. The Shrautasutras and Grhyasutras form a younger stratum dealing with domestic ritual. The Aranyakas and the Upanishads were originally esoteric, mystical teachings related in secrecy.

While the Vedas and their early commentaries on one hand centre on ritual and sacrifice, the late Vedantic (End of Vedas) texts emphasize mystic insight and express abhorrence for ritual practiced at the expense of spiritual insight, claiming to streamline the excessive litany of praise to Vedic gods and to capture the essence of the Rig Vedic dictum "Truth Is One." They set Hindu philosophy apart with its embrace of a single transcendent and yet immanent force that is native to each man's soul, an identification of micro-and macrocosm as One. It can be said that while early Hinduism is most reliant on the four Vedas, Classical Hinduism, from the Yoga and Vedanta to Tantra and Bhakti streams, was moulded around the Upanishads.

Bhagwad Gita

The Bhagwad Gita occupies a special position in the hearts of most Hindus as a keystone yoga Upanishad whose eternal words perhaps are the most representative of all Hindu thought. The text documents a conversation between Arjuna, a warrior, and Lord Krishna immediately prior to the major battle described in the epic Mahabharata. While technically it is considered Smriti, it has singularly achieved nearly unquestioned status as Shruti, or revealed, and is thus the most definitive single Hindu text.

Smriti

The post-Vedic Hindu scriptures form the latter category, the most notable of which are the Mahabharata and the Ramayana, major epics considered scripture by most followers. Other texts considered important by today's Hindus include the Yoga Sutras, a key meditative yoga text of Shri Patanjali. There are also a number of revered Hindu Tantras and Sutras that command the respect of various Hindu sects of different persuasion, some including the Mahanirvana Tantra, Tirumantiram and Shiva Sutras. Other important scriptures are the sectarian Hindu Agamas which are texts dedicated to Vishnu, Shiva and Devi.

THE DHARMIC TRADITION

Dharma is an all-important concept for Hindus. In addition to tradition and moral order, it also signifies the path of knowledge and correct action. Because of Hinduism's emphasis on living in accordance with dharma, anyone who is striving for spiritual knowledge and seeking the right course of ethical action is, in the broadest sense, a follower of sanatana dharma.

Buddhism, Jainism, and Sikhism share with Hinduism the concept of dharma along with other key concepts, and the four religions may be said to belong to the dharmic tradition. At one level *Hinduism* can refer to the beliefs or practices of followers of any of the dharmic traditions. The word Hinduism retains this sense in some usages in the Indian Constitution of 1950. In the field of religious studies, however, Hinduism is used in a narrower sense to distinguish it from the other religions of Indian origin.

A Hindu is thus identified by a dual exclusion. A Hindu is someone who does not subscribe to a religion of non-Indian origin, and who does not claim to belong exclusively to another religion of Indian origin—Buddhism, Jainism, or Sikhism. This effort at definition produces a rather artificial distinction between Hinduism and other dharmic traditions, which stems from an attempt to limit a system that sees itself as universal to an identity that is strictly religious. In many ways, labelling the other dharmic traditions as non-Hindu has a basis that derives more from politics than from philosophy. Indeed, greater differences of belief and practices lie within the broad family labelled as Hinduism than distinguish Hinduism from other dharmic systems.

Indian historian Irfan Habib makes this point when he quotes an early Persian source that Hindus are those who have been debating with each other within a common framework for centuries. If they recognize another as somebody whom they can either support or oppose intelligibly, then both are Hindus. Despite the fact that Jains reject many Hindu beliefs, Jains and Hindus can still debate and thus Jains are Hindus. But such discourse does not take place between Hindus and Muslims because they do not share any basic terms.

Sanatana Dharma

Evidence from inscriptions indicates that Hindus had begun to use the word *dharma* for their religion by the 7th century. After other religions of Indian origin also began to use this term, Hindus then adopted the expression *sanatana dharma* to distinguish their dharma from others. The word *sanatana,* meaning immemorial as well as eternal, emphasized the unbroken continuity of the Hindu tradition in contrast to the other dharmas. The Buddhist, Jaina, and Sikh dharmas possess distinct starting points, whereas Hinduism has no historical founder.

The Hindu tradition might be said to begin in the 4th century BC when the growth and separation of Buddhism and Jainism provided it with a distinctive sense of identity as sanatana dharma. Some scholars prefer to date its beginnings to about 1500 BC, the period when its earliest sacred texts originated, although recent evidence suggests these texts may be even older. Certain beliefs and practices that can clearly be identified as Hindu—such as the worship of sacred trees and the mother goddess—go back to a culture known as Harappan, which flourished around 3000 BC. Other Hindu practices are even older. For example, belief in the religious significance of the new and full moon can be traced to the distant proto-Australoid period, before 3000 BC. It is with good reason that Hinduism perceives itself as sanatana dharma or a cumulative tradition. Its origins are shrouded in the mist of antiquity, and it has continued without a break.

A COMPREHENSIVE AND UNIVERSAL TRADITION

The Hindu tradition aims at comprehensiveness so far as religious beliefs and practices are concerned. First, it wishes to make the riches of Hinduism available to the Hindu and to any genuine seeker of truth and knowledge. But it does not limit Hindus to their tradition. Instead, it encourages them to explore all avenues that would lead to a realization of the divine, and it provides a system with many paths for such realization.

Second, in the manner of science, Hinduism is constantly experimenting with and assimilating new ideas. Also like science, it is far less concerned with the origin or history of ideas than with their truth as demonstrated through direct experience. Hinduism's openness to new ideas, teachers, and practices, and its desire for universality rather than exclusivity, set it apart from religions that distinguish their followers by their belief in particular historical events, people, or revelations.

Two events in the life of Mohandas Gandhi exemplify aspects of the Hindu tradition. First, Gandhi entitled his autobiography *The Story of My Experiments with Truth* (1929). In doing so, he was practicing the Hindu willingness to experiment continually as a means of discovering truth and to record the results of such experiments. Although Gandhi was seeking spiritual truth, he approached it in the spirit of science. Second, when asked, "What is your religion?" in 1936, Gandhi answered, "My religion is Hinduism, which for me is the Religion of humanity and includes the best of all religions known to me." Saintly figures such as Gandhi have periodically renewed Hinduism throughout its history and kept it abreast of the times. Because Hinduism has no central orthodoxy, and no belief in the need for one, renewal of its tradition has invariably come from sages in every age who base their knowledge on experience of the divine.

Hindu Teachings: *What Do Hindus Believe?:* Because defining Hinduism is so difficult and because we have called it the sum of the belief and practices of Hindus, it is best to approach Hinduism through its teachings.

Within Hinduism there are various schools of thought, which Hindu scholars have systematized in different ways. All of these schools have enriched Hinduism with their individual emphases: *Nyaya* on rigorous logic, *Vaiseshika* on atoms and the structure of matter, *Sankhya* on numbers and categories, Yoga on meditation techniques, *Mimamsa* on the analysis of sacred texts, and *Vedanta* on the nature and experience of spirituality. Their teachings are usually summarized in texts called sutras or aphorisms. These sutras can be memorized easily and recited as a means of gaining spiritual focus.

BRAHMAN: THE ULTIMATE REALITY

Various schools have contributed to Hindu thought, each school with a different emphasis. The school known as Vedanta has been the standard form of intellectual Hinduism. According to Vedanta, the highest aim of existence is the realization of the identity or union of the individual's innermost self (*atman*) with the ultimate reality. Although Vedanta states that this ultimate reality is beyond name, the word *Brahman* is used to refer to it.

Whether this ultimate reality is itself ultimately without distinguishing attributes (*nirguna*) or with personal attributes (*saguna*) has been a subject of extensive debate among Hindu scholars. To be ultimate Brahman must *transcend* (exist above and beyond) all limiting attributes, such as name, gender, form, and features. But how can the human mind, with its limitations, conceive of this transcendent reality? Human comprehension requires a more personal reality, with attributes.

Saguna Brahman is also called Ishvara, a name best translated as "Lord." A quotation attributed to 8th-century Hindu scholar Shankara illustrates the subtlety of these ideas: "Ishvara, forgive these three sins of mine: that although you are everywhere I have gone on a pilgrimage, although you are beyond the mind I have tried to think of you; and although you are ineffable [indescribable] I offer this hymn in praise of you."

Brahma, Vishnu, and Shiva: Aspects of Brahman

Saguna Brahman—that is, Brahman with attributes—generally takes the form of one of three main Hindu deities: Brahma, Vishnu, or Shiva. These personified forms of Brahman correspond to three stages in the cycle of the universe. Brahma corresponds to the creative spirit from which the universe arises. Vishnu corresponds to the force of order that sustains the universe. Shiva corresponds to the force that brings a cycle to an end—destruction acting as a prelude to transformation, leaving pure consciousness from which the universe is reborn after destruction. Other forms of Ishvara widely worshipped by Hindus are Shakti, the female aspect of divinity, and Ganesha, the elephant-headed deity associated with the removal of obstacles.

Brahman also may choose to take birth in a knowable form, or *avatar* (incarnation), to uphold dharma and restore balance to the world. Krishna, a well-known avatar of Vishnu, appears at times to save the world. Rama, another well-known avatar of Vishnu, is the subject of the Hindu epic Ramayana (Way of Rama). Whether nirguna or saguna, Brahman represents the ultimate reality (*sat*), ultimate consciousness (*sit*), and ultimate bliss (*ananda*).

Vishnu has ten major avatars, which are described in Hindu texts called the Puranas. These incarnations and their Hindu names are: fish (*matsya*), tortoise (*kurma*), boar (*varaha*), man lion (*narasimha*), dwarf (*vamana*), axe-wielding human (Parashurama), ideal person (Rama of the Ramayana), all-attractive perfect person (Krishna), the enlightened (Buddha), and a future incarnation (Kalki).

The majority of Hindus choose a personal deity, a saguna form of Brahman with whom they can feel a direct personal connection. Devotion to this deity can take a number of forms, including prayer, ceremonial worship, chanting of the deity's name, and pilgrimage to sites sacred to the deity.

Brahmanda: The Universe

The relationship of the universe, which Hindus call brahmanda, to the ultimate reality poses a deep philosophical problem: Whereas Brahman represents a permanent reality, the universe is constantly changing. The universe is also eternal, but it is eternally changing, whereas Brahman is eternal in another sense in that it is beyond change. According to Vedanta, Brahman alone is real. Such reality as the universe possesses is derived from Brahman, just as the light of the Moon really belongs to the Sun.

All of creation arises from Brahman, according to Hindu teaching. Brahman is both the efficient cause of the universe (creator) as well as the material cause (substance of which the universe is created). For this reason, all of creation is divine and deserving of our respect.

Time in the Hindu universe moves in endlessly recurring cycles, much like the motion of a wheel. The duration of the various phases of the universe's existence are calculated in units of mind-boggling astronomical duration organized around such terms as *yugas, mahayugas, manvantaras,* and *kalpas*.

Atman: The Innermost Self

We as individuals are also a part of this changing universe. Our bodies are constantly undergoing change, while our minds, formed of thoughts and feelings, are also in a state of flux. According to Vedanta, however, our self consists of more than mind and body.

At its core lies the unchanging *atman,* our innermost, transcendental self, as opposed to the material self (our body, thoughts, and feelings) that is part of the universe. The atman is our true self. But we lose sight of it because of our passionate involvement with our material self and its search for happiness in this universe. The universe can never provide perfect and permanent happiness, however, because it, like our material self, is in a state of constant flux. We attain true happiness only through an awareness of our atman and the discovery of its true relationship with Brahman.

By achieving awareness of our atman and its unity with Brahman, we attain not only happiness, but also *moksha,* or liberation. But liberation from what? At one level, the liberation is from unhappiness, but the answer provided by Vedanta Hinduism goes deeper: Moksha is liberation from a chain of lives.

Samsara: The Chain of Lives

We normally think of ourselves as coming into being when we are born of our parents and as perishing when we die. According to Hinduism, however, this current life is merely one link in a chain of lives that extends far into the past and projects far into the future. The point of origin of this chain cannot be determined. The process of our involvement in the universe—the chain of births and deaths—is called samsara.

Samsara is caused by a lack of knowledge of our true self and our resultant desire for fulfilment outside ourselves. We continue to embody ourselves, or be reborn, in this infinite and eternal universe as a result of these unfulfilled desires. The chain of births lets us resume the pursuit. The law that governs samsara is called karma. Each birth and death we undergo is determined by the balance sheet of our karma—that is, in accordance with the actions performed and the dispositions acquired in the past.

KARMA: ACTION AND ITS CONSEQUENCES

Karma is a crucial Hindu concept. According to the doctrine of karma, our present condition in life is the consequence of the actions of our previous lives. The choices we have made in the past directly affect our condition in this life, and the choices we make today and thereafter will have consequences for our future lives in samsara. An understanding of this interconnection, according to Hindu teachings, can lead an individual toward right choices, deeds, thoughts, and desires, without the need for an external set of commandments.

The principle of karma provides the basic framework for Hindu ethics. The word *karma* is sometimes translated into English as "destiny," but karma does not imply the absence of free will or freedom of action that destiny does. Under the doctrine of karma, the ability to make choices remains with the individual. We are subject to the "law" of karma just as our physical movements on earth are subject to the law of gravitation. But just as the law of gravitation does not take away our freedom to move about, the doctrine of karma does not leave us unfree to act. It merely describes the moral law under which we function, just as the law of gravitation is a physical law governing our being.

When we cause pain or injury, we add to the karmic debt we carry into our future lives. When we give to others in a genuine way, we lighten our karmic load. In the Bhagwad-Gita, an important Hindu text, Krishna states that the best way to be free of debt is by selfless action, or by dedicating every action as an offering to Krishna himself. In addition, human beings can purify themselves of karmic debt through different *yogas* (disciplines), *kriyas* (purification processes), and *bhakti* (devotions).

Purusharthas: Goals of Human Life

Hinduism takes a comprehensive view of our human condition and has classified all the things we seek in the world and beyond into four broad categories: *kama*, *artha, dharma,* and *moksha*. Kama includes the pleasure of the senses, both *aesthetic* (refined artistic) pleasures and sensual and sexual pleasure. Artha includes the pursuit of material well-being, wealth, and power. Dharma includes our striving for righteousness and virtue. Moksha describes our desire for liberation from the chain of lives.

The first three goals pertain to the world we know, whereas moksha involves freedom from the world and from desires for kama, artha, and dharma. Attaining moksha is an extraordinary goal, which only some people specifically seek. In preparing for it, the prior pursuit of dharma can be a great help. Dharma, in the sense of duty or desire to do right, occupies a central role in regulating artha and kama and promoting moksha. On account of dharma's centrality, the goals of human life are often listed in the following order: dharma, artha, kama and moksha.

Hinduism accepts all four purusharthas as valid goals of human endeavour. It does not look down upon kama or artha, as indicated by the *Kamasutra*, a work on sexuality from about the 4th century AD, and by the *Arthashastra.* The latter text by Kautilya, a minister to a king of the 4th century BC, discusses how a king should wield political and economic power.

However, the ultimate aim of human life is moksha, liberation from sorrow and desire and realization of the union with the Ultimate Reality. In our future lives we may not always enter the world in human form. Thus, Hindus consider that birth as a human being is a unique and valuable opportunity for seeking moksha, an opportunity that should not be wasted. To guide us along the way, the system of Vedanta and the yogas provide a good road map for the journey.

Jiva: The Individual

Our personality has a strong influence on the goal we seek. According to one Hindu scheme a human being consists of not one but three bodies. There is the gross physical body; a subtle body of thought and feelings; and an even subtler body, known as the causal body, where our primal ignorance of our true nature is located, along with the knowledge of that ignorance. The physical body disintegrates after our death; only the subtle and causal bodies travel from one life to the next.

Another Hindu system envisions the human being as consisting of five layers or sheaths, called koshas, that cover up the true self or atman. Beginning with the outermost, these layers are constituted by food or the physical body (*annamaya*), energy (*pranamaya*), mind (*manomaya*), consciousness (*vijnanamaya*), and bliss (*anandamaya*). Identification with one or more of these koshas—for example, imagining, "I am my physical body"—limits people and prevents knowledge of their true nature.

Other Hindu concepts of personality employ other schemes. One popular concept visualizes a person's dormant energy residing at the bottom of the spine like a coiled serpent (*kundalini*). Upon awakening, it confers liberation when it reaches the head after piercing nodal points, called chakras, along the spine. Hinduism offers spiritual and physical exercises for awakening and liberating all these aspects of the personality.

Yogas: Paths to Brahman

How do we proceed if we wish to rise toward Brahman? Hindu thought takes the personality of the seeker as the starting point. It divides human personalities into types dominated by physicality, activity, emotionality, or intellectuality. The composition of our personality intuitively predisposes us to a type of *yoga*—that is, a path we might follow to achieve union with Brahman. Although many people associate the word *yoga* with a physical discipline, in its original Hindu meaning *yoga* refers to any technique that unites the seeker with the ultimate reality.

While physical fitness buffs may seek such a union by practicing *hatha yoga*, people with different personality traits have other choices. For the action-oriented person there is *karma yoga,* the yoga of action, which calls for a life of selfless deeds and actions appropriate to the person's station in life. For the person of feeling, *bhakti yoga,* the yoga of devotion, calls for unconditional love for a personal divinity. For the person of thought, *jnana yoga,* the yoga of knowledge, calls for spiritual and physical discipline intended to bring direct insight into ultimate reality. The yogas do not represent tightly sealed compartments, merely convenient classifications. A well-balanced personality might well employ all four. These yogas are sometimes called margas (paths), suggesting that the same destination can be approached by more than one route, and indeed by more than one mode of travel.

Varna: Social Organization

The individual stands in relationship not only to Brahman but also to the society in which he or she lives. Two Hindu concepts—*varna* and *ashrama*—address this social dimension of human existence.

Every society distinguishes among occupations on the basis of power, wealth, education, or other factors. Hindu thought has long recognized four major occupational groupings. In the first group are priests, teachers, scholars, and others who represent knowledge and spirituality. People in this group are called brahmanas, or Brahmans. Those in the second group, called ksatriyas, are represented by kings, warriors, government bureaucrats, and others who represent power. Those in the third group, called vaishyas, are represented by farmers, traders, merchants, and other skilled workers. Those in the fourth group, called shudras, are represented by unskilled workers. A group sometimes known as untouchables has at times constituted a subcategory within the shudra class, sometimes referred to as a fifth group.

Hindu thinkers visualized these groups as constituting the four limbs of society conceived as a body. This hierarchical system, with Brahmans as the first category and shudras as the last, is known as the varna system. The system also indicates the different roles and responsibilities of each group within society and the relationship of the groups within a harmonious whole. The varna system was never intended as a permanent assignment of hereditary roles, and it once possessed considerable flexibility even though people tended to inherit the family profession, as in many other traditional societies.

The process of establishing the varna system was completed by the 4th century BC. By that time Hindu social organization accommodated thousands of subgroups called jatis, which were based upon marriage and other associations as well as on occupational specialization in crafts. Hindu law books from the 4th century BC onward bear witness to the blending of the varna and jati systems. In this process each jati became loosely linked with a varna. Yet the standing of jatis altered with changes in wealth, education, and political power. Over time, especially during the long period of Islamic rule, the groupings hardened into what became known as the caste system. The British census in the late 19th century helped formalize this system by mapping each jati to a specific varna.

Ashrama: Stages of Life

Much as the varna system provides the organizing principle of Hindu society, the *ashrama* system provides the organizing principle of an individual's life. According to the ashrama system, human life is divided into four stages, each succeeding the other. Ashrama provides a road map for the journey through these stages and provides a clear sense of purpose for each stage, including old age. Hindus consider the last stage of life highly meaningful. Ashrama also addresses the four goals that constitute a fulfilling life: dharma, artha, kama, and moksha.

The first stage is the life of a celibate student, a time when an individual acquires the values of dharma—that is, preparation and training for leading a proper life. It is followed by that of the householder, during which the individual seeks artha and kama by marrying, working, and raising a family as an active member of society. During this second stage, Hindu householders are expected to carry out their responsibilities in accordance with dharma and free themselves of debts owed to the gods, the sages, and their ancestors.

After the years of enjoyment and responsibility, the third stage of life begins. Around age 50, when the children are grown, the individual gradually begins to give up acquisitions and worldly ties and to take up spiritual contemplation in preparation for the next stage. The fourth and final stage involves renunciation of the world to seek liberation in sublime isolation. Renunciation allows the individual to be free of external responsibilities and to concentrate on an inner search. The life of the *sanyasi* (renunciant) focuses on achieving realization of the innermost self (atman) and union with the divine (moksha).

The ashrama system recognizes the division between active participation in life (*pravrtti*) and ascetic withdrawal from life (*nivrtti*). Although this division has applied to all Hindus, regardless of gender or caste, men of the three higher varnas (Brahmans, ksatriyas, and vaishyas) have been more likely to enact it through the ashrama system. Some Hindus choose to devote their entire lives to the quest for moksha. They become renunciants and are free from the obligations of varna and ashrama. Such people are called sannyasis. A sanyasi who joins a monastic order takes the title swami.

In addition to the duties belonging to each stage of life, Hinduism also emphasizes duties belonging to all human beings, especially cultivation of truth and nonviolence. Many Hindus choose not to eat meat because of their cultivation of nonviolence.

Hindu Rituals—What Do Hindus Do?: Hindus consider all of creation worthy of worship, and thus religious activity in Hinduism takes many forms. Rituals may be performed by the individual, the family, the village, the community or region; at home or in a temple; and frequently or infrequently. The prevalence and persistence of Hindu ritual may well provide the stabilizing factor in a tradition that is so flexible in doctrine. Ritual might even be considered the glue that holds Hindus and Hinduism together.

Many rites and observances that Hindus practice daily have come down from ancient times. Others grew up around the lives and teachings of Hindu saints and sages. While details of rituals may differ from region to region and jati to jati, their meaning and central practices have remained consistent over vast distances of time and space.

Virtually all rituals in Hinduism possess multiple meanings, including symbolic interpretations. Even the way Hindus regularly greet each other may be regarded as symbolically bowing to the divine. The Hindu greeting involves pressing the palms of the hands together, which symbolizes the meeting of two people; placing the hands over the heart where Brahman dwells, indicating that one meets the self in the other; bowing the head in recognition of this meeting; and saying *namaste,* a Sanskrit word that means "I bow to you" and signifies "I bow to the divine in you." Bindi, the red dot that many Hindu women wear on the forehead, is an auspicious mark and symbol of good fortune. Once worn only by married women, bindi can be seen today on girls and women of all ages. Its location, over a chakra (energy point), is intended to help focus concentration during meditation.

Categories of Ritual

The school of Hindu philosophy called Mimamsa, which is specially concerned with ritual, divides all religious activities in Hinduism into three types: (1) actions that are performed daily, called nitya; (2) actions performed on specific occasions, called naimittika; and (3) actions performed voluntarily according to personal desire, called kamya.

Hindus fulfil all three religious activities—nitya, naimittika, and kamya—through three types of ritual. These rituals are *yajna,* (involving a sacrificial fire); *puja* (devotional offerings, usually flowers); and *dhyana* (meditation). Yajnas are performed on major occasions, such as marriage and housewarming, when sacred substances are offered into the sacrificial fire. Puja may be performed publicly or privately. Public puja, usually performed in a temple, consists of anointing a statue of a deity and offering flowers, incense, and carefully prepared food to the deity. Chanting and devotional singing follow, accompanied by the waving of a small, camphor-burning lamp that illuminates the image of the deity. Most ceremonies have clearly marked opportunities for dhyana, or meditation.

Household Worship

Hindu religious activities also can be divided into those that take place at home and those that take place in public. Many rituals are performed at home, either by individual family members or by the head of the household. Some of these household rituals involve a deity or a sacred fire; other rituals commemorate important passages in life.

PUJA: DEVOTION

Many Hindus worship daily the deity they have personally chosen. This personal deity is known as the *ishta-devata.* Household puja usually consists of worshipping the *ishta-devata* with prayer and offerings of food, accompanied by chanting and the waving of a lamp or light. The offering of food acknowledges that all food has a divine source. After the offering, the food is ready to be shared by the worshippers. Household puja generally takes place in front of an image or statue of the *ishta-devata*, which may be set up as a domestic shrine. Hindus who are more deeply involved in ritual may also tend a domestic fire.

Puja possesses a markedly personal character and is more often performed privately by individuals and families than publicly at temples. The private nature of puja may arise from the extremely personal relationship that Hinduism nurtures with the divinity, as parent, friend, or other supportive person. It also could have evolved from Hindu historical experience under foreign occupation, during which expression of Hindu identity in public was frowned upon and even dangerous.

Samskaras: Sacraments to Mark Passages

Sacraments called *samskaras* punctuate the life cycle of the individual and have greater religious significance than puja. A standard list cites 16 samskaras, but in other sources samskaras range in number from a maximum of about 40 to a minimum of 2, marriage and death. The number varies with varna and gender.

The samskaras cluster in the early phases of life, including the prenatal phase. Four samskaras occur between birth and the beginning of studies at about age five. At birth a simple ceremony welcomes and blesses the newborn. The naming of the child, a significant event, occurs shortly after birth. Then come the taking of the first solid food and the first ritual shaving of the head. When the child is ready to study the Vedas (sacred Hindu scriptures), the major *samskara* of *upanayana* occurs.

In the course of it, the child receives a sacred thread and chants a mantra whispered into the child's ear: "Let us meditate on the glorious splendour of enlivening Sun-god. May he inspire our minds." In early times, a Hindu boy traditionally moved to the home of a *guru* (teacher) to study the Vedas after the upanayana samskara. After completing study of the Vedas, the student shaved the hair and was ready for marriage.

A Hindu wedding consists of ceremonies performed over several days, culminating in the joining of the bride and groom. As part of the marriage samskara, a knot is tied to join the bride's and the groom's garments, after which they walk around a sacred fire seven times. The sacred fire serves as a witness to the vows exchanged between the bride and the bridegroom. They then take seven steps together, symbolizing friendship and emphasizing the idea of companionship in marriage. To strengthen the union, the bride and groom place their right hands on each other's heart; the groom then recites a prayer from the Vedas, "I give you my heart. May our minds be as one." At the end of this ritual the pair become man and wife. Additional rites before and after the main Hindu marriage ritual vary from region to region.

The sacrament of death calls for *cremation* (burning of the dead body), at the end of which the ashes are collected and deposited, usually by the side of or in a river. For ten days after cremation, family members offer rice balls to the person who has departed. This offering provides a good example of the persistence of ritual in Hindu tradition: The rice symbolizes growth and is meant to provide the person with a body in which to dwell in the world of the ancestors.

The alternative, while waiting for the next birth, is the less pleasant prospect of wandering in the world of ghosts. These actions are required only of the Hindu householder and do not apply to the renunciate.

Other Domestic Rituals

Some Hindu rituals are performed to obtain a specific reward, according to instructions in the Vedas. Such rewards include securing a suitable life partner, conceiving a child, or attaining wealth, as well as warding off negative outcomes.

Communal Worship

Household religious activities involve the family or an individual member of the family. Other Hindu religious activities involve a larger community. A cluster of families may have a shrine where they worship periodically. Beyond the family and the cluster of families lies the village. At the village level, worship of the favoured deity of the village dominates. From the village level, worship moves to public rituals, which may be performed at temples and other sacred sites or at sacred times.

TEMPLE WORSHIP

Rituals performed at temples, like household rituals, may be described as those that take place daily, *nitya*; those performed on specific occasions, *naimitikka;* and those performed voluntarily, *kamya*. Hindu temples are dedicated to a deity or several deities who are believed to preside over the temple. Hindus visit temples to worship the temple deity or to worship another deity of their choosing by means of these three types of rituals. As at household shrines, they worship sculptures or painted images of the presiding deity and make offerings.

Basic rituals performed daily at most Hindu temples include rousing the deity from sleep at dawn, making the deity available for worship and offerings by visitors at midday, and putting the deity to bed at dusk. At some temples, the additional rituals of bathing and feeding the deity take place between dawn and midday. These rituals express the personal nature of Hindu love of and devotion to their deities.

Naimittika at temples is an occasion for carrying about the image of the temple deity. For example, a festival at the temple of Jagannath in the town of Puri celebrates the god Jagannath's annual visit to his birthplace, the temple site, in his chariot. More than 4,000 celebrants pull the god's wooden chariot, which stands about 14 m (45 ft.) high. The English word *juggernaut* comes from Jagannath. Public processions and festivals at the temples of Rama and Krishna mark the birthdays of these avatars of Vishnu. *Kamya puja* is typically performed at temples to gain a specific end. A visitor to a temple might request the performance of puja, or daily prayers, at the temple and make a donation for that purpose.

Sacred Sites

Hindus consider the entire Earth, as well as the Indian land mass known as mother India (*Bharata Mata*), to be sacred. This view once found expression in such practices as visiting the four corners of India as represented by the pilgrimage sites of Badrinath to the north, Puri to the east, Rameshvaram to the south, and Dwarka to the west. Hindus make pilgrimages to sacred sites in the hope of cleansing themselves of sins and lessening their karmic debt.

Certain parts of India are held in special veneration. For example, Hindu tradition regards seven cities as holy: Ayodhya (the birthplace of Rama); Mathura (where Krishna grew up); Haridwar (where the Ganges River widens onto a plain); Kasi (sacred to Shiva); Kanci (associated with the Hindu philosopher Shankara); Avanti or Ujjain (site of the temple of Mahakala); and Puri (associated with the later life of Krishna).

Other sacred Hindu locations involve rivers and events in Hindu epics. Particular regions also have their own sacred locations. Certain sites in India are sacred because of their association with the Great Goddess, Devi, who takes many forms. In the form of Devi Sati, according to legend, her dismembered body parts fell on 51 locations that became sacred to worshippers of Shakti (the female aspect of the divine). The Jvala Mukhi Temple near Jullundur, for example, is said to represent her tongue. Worshippers visit the Kamakshya Temple in Assam to partake of her cosmic energy.

Sacred Times

Religious festivals dot the Hindu calendar. A number of them commemorate events in the great Sanskrit epic Ramayana (Way of Rama) or in the life of Krishna. The timing of these festivals is related to the movements of the Sun and the Moon.

An important festival known as the Dusshera marks the victory of Prince Rama over the demon king Ravana in a struggle between good and evil that is related in the Ramayana. Dusshera takes place in September or October and is followed by Diwali (also known as Deepavali), the festival of lights. Diwali commemorates events that restored truth and light in early times: the victorious return of Rama with his bride Sita to Ayodhya in the north and the victory of Krishna over the monster Narakasura in the south. The festival of Holi celebrates the arrival of spring in February or March. During this festival people spray each other with coloured powders and coloured water, forget the cares of winter, and rejoice in the onset of spring. A popular family festival, Raksabandhana, occurs in July or August and renews the bonds of affection between brothers and sisters. Sisters tie lucky threads around the wrists of brothers and are rewarded with gifts. Other important festivals are Shivaratri, the night sacred to Shiva when worshippers recite prayers to be freed of sins, and Ganesha-Chaturthi, dedicated to the elephant god Ganesha, when worshippers recite prayers to remove obstacles in their lives. Shivaratri falls in the winter months, and Ganesha-Cahturthi in August or September. Among the major regional festivals are the Dolayatra, a spring festival in the eastern state of Orissa; Pongal, a winter festival in southern India; and Onam, a harvest festival in the southwestern state of Kerala.

SATSANGA: FELLOWSHIP

A popular form of participation in religious life is the *Satsanga*, which literally means keeping company with *sat* (truth and goodness). The Satsanga may consist of Hindus who gather for discussions of Hindu scripture or of a circle of devotees who have formed around a saintly figure. A saint ("sant" in Sanskrit) in Hinduism in someone who has realized the truth and attained recognition from the community for doing so. Other forms of worship that occur at satsangas are chanting or singing, especially devotional songs called bhajans. On religious occasions the chanting the *Om* sound is considered particularly holy.

Om: Sacred Symbol and Sacred Sound

The sacred syllable *Om* or *aum* functions at many levels. Hindus chant it as a means of meditating on the ultimate reality and connecting with the innermost self (atman) and Brahman. At one level, om possesses a vibrational aspect apart from its conceptual significance. If pronounced correctly, its vibrations resonate through the body and penetrate the atman. At another level, the three sounds that constitute the syllable—*a, u,* and *m*—have been associated with the states of waking, dreaming, and deep sleep, states to which all life can be reduced.

Thus, by repeating the syllable the chanter passes through all three states. Other associations of the three sounds are with the three states of the cosmos—manifestation, maintenance, and dissolution—and with the three aspects of Ishvara who preside over these cosmic states: Brahma, Vishnu, and Shiva. Om thus functions at a practical level as a mantra and at a cosmic level as signifying the trinity.

Guru: Teacher

Spiritual authority in Hinduism flows from enlightened sages called gurus. The guru is someone who has attained realization and acts as a guide for other human beings. He or she guides the individual seeker of truth and self-realization to the appropriate deity, practice, or yoga within Hinduism. The disciple's goal is to transcend the need for a guru through direct experience of the divine and self-awareness. Having a guide is considered critical for traversing the complexities of spiritual practice and self-discovery. The guru thus constitutes an important centre of spiritual activity in Hinduism. Numerous Hindu hymns express adoration for the guru.

Sacred Literature—What Do Hindus Read?: Although Hindu tradition maintains that the ultimate reality lies beyond all scriptures, it is equally convinced that the scriptures help people orient their minds and lives towards Brahman. This attitude has given rise to a body of sacred literature so vast that by one calculation it would take 70 lifetimes of devoted study to read all of it.

The Vedas

The four Vedas constitute the most important body of sacred Hindu literature, at least in theory. Other sacred literature, especially the Hindu epics, may be more popular with readers, but the Vedas, written in the ancient Sanskrit language, are the oldest and most respected scriptures. They are separately titled the Rig-Veda, Yajur-Veda, Sama-Veda, and Atharva-Veda, and collectively referred to as the Veda.

Each of the Vedas can be divided into four types of texts, which are roughly chronological in order: *mantra* or *samhita*, *brahmana*, *aranyaka*, and *upanishad*. The mantra or samhita portion largely consists of hymns addressed to the various deities. The brahmana texts gather the authoritative utterances of Brahmans (those with knowledge of Brahman, the ultimate reality) and describe the rituals, chiefly sacrificial offerings, in which the hymns are employed. The third section consists of aranyakas, or forest texts, presumably composed by sages who sought seclusion in the forests. The last section consists of the Upanishads, philosophical texts that have an air of mystery and secrecy about them.

Scholars have suggested that the four types of texts represent four different stages in the spiritual evolution of the Aryans, the peoples of the Vedas. During the earliest stage in their religious life, the Aryans may have recited simple hymns of praise for the divinities they felt dwelt around them. In the next stage ritual evolved out of the early worship and became increasingly elaborate, until people were driven to ask what it was all about. Sages then retired to the forests to reflect on the meaning of sacrifice and the person who makes the sacrifice. This reflection opened the floodgates of philosophical speculation found in the Upanishads.

Hindus traditionally have viewed the four types of texts as dating from the same period but serving different purposes. The first three texts deal with the realm of action and are concerned with dharma, artha, and kama, whereas the last text concerns knowledge of the self and moksha. In this view, following dharma while experiencing the ups and downs of life produces a devout and mature mind that is then able to fully grasp what the Upanishads have to say.

The Upanishads are also called Vedanta (meaning "end of the Vedas") because they represent the final essence of the Vedas. The Vedanta marks the culmination as well as the conclusion of the Vedas, although the Vedic canon was never formally closed.

SHRUTI AND SMRITI: ETERNAL TRUTH AND TRADITION

Hindu scriptures can be classified into two types: *shruti* and *smriti*. Shruti, meaning "heard," may be thought of as revelation or eternal truth, whereas smriti, meaning "remembered," is comparable to tradition. By distinguishing that which is eternally true from that which holds true for a specific time and culture, the categories of shruti and smriti enable Hindus to reform outdated practices while remaining faithful to Hinduism's essence. Where there is a conflict between the two, shruti takes precedence over smriti. The Vedas constitute shruti, whereas there are many different smriti texts.

The Vedas correspond, among the Hindus, to the Bible among Christians and the Qur'an among Muslims. However, unlike the revealed texts of Christianity and Islam, whose source is considered to be God speaking through the son or the prophet, the Vedas have no author. According to Vedanta, shruti is revelation without a revealer. Because in Hinduism the universe is without beginning or end, the Vedas appear along with creation at the beginning of each cycle of time. Then Brahma, who presides over the remanifestation of the universe, recites the Vedas and sages hear them anew. These divinely heard scriptures are then transmitted orally from master to disciple.

The Vedas as also called *shruti* because they are divinely "heard" by the sages at the beginning of a cycle; and also because they are transmitted orally from master to disciple thus once again justifying the meaning of *shruti* as audition.

The word *smriti* is applied to a vast category of literature in Hinduism. Unlike shruti, Sanskrit scripture without an author, smriti is considered to have an author and may even be written in one of the regional languages of India.

One category of smriti consists of more than 20 law books that lay down in detail the rules to follow in life, especially the rules that pertain to *varna* (social order) and *ashrama* (stages of life). Another category includes texts called Puranas, which deal with the lives of the gods and celestial beings. There are 18 Puranas, and they can be classified according to which of the three gods of the Hindu trinity they focus on—Brahma, Vishnu, or Shiva. The most famous of these is the Bhagavata Purana, which deals with the life of Krishna, an avatar of Vishnu, in the pastoral surroundings of Vrndavana. A third category of smriti consists of two texts of legendary history: the Ramayana and the Mahabharata. These are the two well-known epics of Hinduism. Scholars believe the Ramayana assumed its present form between 300 BC and AD 200, while the Mahabharata evolved over a period extending from about 400 BC to about AD 400.

RELIGION AND THE EPICS

Ramayana

The Ramayana of Valmiki consists of about 24,000 verses and describes the life of Prince Rama, an incarnation of Vishnu. The author, Valmiki, according to later tradition, belonged to the shudra varna and made his living by robbing travellers. After an encounter with the sage Narada, Valmiki turned his life around and became a poet and scholar. Classical Hinduism recognizes him as a brahman and as India's first poet. Rama and his wife Sita embody virtue and righteousness, and their lives demonstrate dharma in various spheres of activity. Their life stories contain lessons for Hindus on ideal behaviour in various roles, such as son, brother, wife, king, and married couple. Rama's reign ushers in a golden age, and the expression *Rama-rajya* (rule of Rama) describes the best of times in which the divine presence rules on Earth.

Mahabharata

The Mahabharata, an epic story of 100,000 verses, is attributed to a sage named Vyasa and considered to be the longest poem in the world. It traces the descendants of two sets of cousins, the Kauravas and the Pandavas, whose disputes eventually lead to the Mahabharata war. Krishna, an avatar of Vishnu, is central to the story. Like the Ramayana, the Mahabharata addresses many questions related to dharma and the actions of individuals and society. These discourses have provided inspiration for Hindus in many areas of life.

Bhagwad-Gita

One part of the Mahabharata, the Bhagwad-Gita, functions virtually as a text on its own in Hinduism. On the eve of the Mahabharata war, the hero Arjuna suddenly develops a disinclination to fight. Arjuna's decision leads to a prolonged dialogue with Krishna during which Krishna tries to resolve Arjuna's moral and metaphysical dilemmas in 700 verses. The way in which Krishna seeks to guide Arjuna has endeared the text to the Hindus as a guide to their faith.

In the Bhagwad-Gita Hinduism comes closest to possessing a universal scripture. Since the Gupta period (AD 320 to 550; *see* Gupta Dynasty) it has inspired a stream of commentaries, summaries, and translations, all of which attest to its wide popularity. The process shows no signs of letting up. The Bhagwad-Gita's doctrine of *svadharma* (understanding one's own role and responsibility) implies a cosmic mirroring of the essential nature of reality (Brahman) in the reality of the individual's essential nature (atman). This implication has proved spiritually intriguing for practitioner, believer, and scholar alike.

The Mahabharata and the Bhagwad-Gita carry meaning on multiple levels. In one interpretation, the Pandavas and Kauravas represent the forces of good and evil that exist within each person, and the contest between them represents the perpetual battle between these tendencies. The Bhagwad-Gita describes the techniques and paths by which the individual can attain realization of the Ultimate Reality with Krishna as the guide. As part of the Mahabharata, the Bhagwad-Gita technically falls in the category of smriti rather than shruti. However, it virtual enjoys the status of shruti by representing the words of the divinity, incarnated as Krishna and addressed to human beings through Arjuna.

Tantric Literature

Tantra represents another vast body of Hindu literature. After centuries of neglect, it has gradually begun to receive fuller recognition. The word *tantra* has two meanings. In one sense it refers to sacred literature which appeared from the 5th century onward and focused not only on Vishnu and Shiva, but also on the cults of earlier deities: Ganapati (another name for the elephant-headed god, Ganesha), Kumara (a son of Brahma), Surya (sun) and Shakti (the goddess). The second sense restricts *tantra* to texts that deal with the worship of Shakti. After the Gupta age ended in the 6th century the Tantric tradition heavily influenced Hinduism, Buddhism, and Jainism. If elite or intellectual Hinduism is Vedic in nature, then mainstream Hinduism is Tantric in orientation. Some accounts consider both traditions equally revelatory. Tantric literature largely eliminates caste distinctions in terms of religious practices. It also holds women in high regard. It thus provides a useful corrective to the negative stereotypes of Hinduism as *patriarchal* (male-controlled). Although smriti literature can be described as male oriented, Tantric literature is female oriented.

Consider these statements from Tantric literature. The *Gautamiya Tantra* clearly states that tantra is open to women and members of all castes. The *Mahanirvana Tantra* requires a man to fast for a day for talking rudely to a woman. The *Kubjikamata Tantra* states that all houses of women should be worshipped as holy shrines. In the *Shakta* model of Hinduism, which focuses worship on the Great Goddess, all women are regarded as gurus and may initiate others by reading out the mantra from an authoritative text. Men have no authority to do so. In addition, the Devi (goddess) is worshipped in her own right, rather than in relation to a male god.

Hindu gods are regularly displayed with their female counterparts. When they are invoked together, the female partner is named first, as in Sita-Rama and Radha-Krishna. In the case of Shiva and Shakti the relationship gets so close that they are represented as inhabiting a single body in the *Ardhanrishvara* (Lord-who-is-half-female) form. Tantra at times involves the balancing of these two aspects—Shiva (representing consciousness) and Shakti (representing energy)—in a manner reminiscent of *yin and yang* in Daoism.

Literature in Regional Languages

Most Hindus first encounter Hinduism through their regional languages, despite the special significance of Sanskrit. Almost every regional language in India has produced its own version of the Ramayana and the Mahabharata, sharing in the religious admiration given to the original versions.

Deservedly famous translations of the Ramayana include one in the Tamil language by the 9th-century Hindu scholar Kamban and one in Hindi and by the 16th-century poet and saint Tulsidas. A wave of literature in Tamil appeared in the 7th to 9th centuries as the result of a surge of devotion of Vishnu and Shiva. Most of the influential works of modern Hinduism were originally composed in English. Masters who have realized Brahman continually renew the Hindu tradition and express themselves in a language appropriate to their time and place.

The utilization of these various bodies of literature provides insight into how Hinduism tries to sanctify what it touches. Thus the title of Veda came to be conferred on any worthwhile body of knowledge, including writings on architecture, on music, and even on military science. Highly esteemed sacred texts that came after the Vedas have come to be described as the fifth Veda.

History of Hinduism

Hinduism does not attach the same religious significance to historical events that Judaism, Christianity, and Islam do. Some have compared Hinduism's indifference to the history of a religious idea or practice to a scientist's indifference to the history of science. What is of value to both is the idea or practice as such.

The history of Hinduism thus becomes a history of its quest to incorporate the various developments it has encountered or generated, rather than a history of conquest of or triumph over these historical developments. The contrast is apparent in the Biblical injunction to believe in one God who is the only God and the Vedic perception that "Truth is one, sages call it variously."

Considerable controversy remains over Hinduism's historical origins. At one time scholars believed that the arrival of the Aryan people in India about 1500 BC represented a critical moment in the history of Hinduism. The Aryans replaced the earlier Harappan culture in the Indus valley, and they are the people described in the Vedas, the earliest sacred literature of Hinduism. Although linguistic evidence tends to support the notion of an Aryan migration, most scholars now believe this view awaits confirmation by archaeology, especially because it has been challenged by the discovery of extensive sites in northwestern and western India. So far there is no clear-cut answer to the key question: Did Hinduism as described in the Vedas originate in India or did it arise as a result of migrations from outside? What is clear is that the Hinduism of the Vedas goes back at least to 1200 BC in India and perhaps much earlier.

Vedic Hinduism

The beginnings of Vedic Hinduism, no later than 1200 BC, trace back to the Rig-Veda, which contains hymns of praise to various deities called devas. *Agni* (deva of fire) and *Indra* (king of devas and deva of the atmosphere, storms, rain, and battle) were prominent, judging by the number of hymns addressed to them. Fire was the deity of the domestic hearth as well as of public ritual. The Rig-Veda calls the deity "smoke-bannered" as it carries the offering made into it toward the gods. Indra was a martial leader in the Rig-Veda who carried his followers to victory in battle and also battled drought as a rain-god. An entire book of the Rig-Veda is devoted to soma, a plant whose juice produced ecstatic experiences. It is already clear in the Rig-Veda that all these devas were aspects of one underlying reality.

By the 4th century BC Vedic Hinduism had appeared in virtually all of India and had assimilated and absorbed various local religious beliefs and practices. The resulting mixture is what we refer to comprehensively as Vedic Hinduism.

Classical Hinduism

The period from the 3rd century BC to the late 7th century AD is known as classical Hinduism. Even as Vedic Hinduism flourished throughout India, various aspects of its world-view had come under challenge by the 6th century BC. This challenge came from Upanishadic thinkers and from the rise of new sects including the Jains and the Buddhists. The Upanishadic thinkers considered themselves in the line of descent from

Vedic seers, while the followers of Buddhism and Jainism tended to question Vedic authority, although they retained many concepts from the Vedas. All were concerned about release from eternal rebirth and generally agreed that release was obtained not by sacrifice but by meditation and contemplation.

Buddhism and Jainism gradually gained strength in India during the centuries just before and just after the beginning of the first millennium. Buddhism benefited in the 3rd century BC from the patronage extended to it by King Ashoka, who ruled almost all of India. Jainism similarly benefited from royal patrons. By the start of the Gupta period, which lasted from about AD 320 to 550, Hinduism resurged, having integrated a variety of Buddhist and Jain beliefs and practices. These included the doctrine of *ahimsa* (nonviolence) and an emphasis on vegetarianism. The Gupta period is celebrated as a glorious epoch of classical Hindu culture.

During this classical Gupta period, Hindu thought and its systematization flourished. By then many *shastras* (classical works) of Hindu philosophy had been compiled. These shastras include the *Arthashastra* (principles of statecraft), *Nayashastra* (aesthetics of performing arts), poetry and dramatic works by writers such as Kalidasa and Bhavabhuti, grammars by Panini and Patanjali, works on human sexuality such as the *Kamasutra,* and the medical compendia of Charak and Susruta. In addition, the major epics—the Ramayana and Mahabharata—received their present form. Also during this period, rules were developed for representations of the deities and for building structures to house these statues and images.

Medieval Hinduism

As a vigorous and multifaceted Hinduism unfolded in India during the 7th century, a new religion made its appearance in Arabia: Islam. Within a century, Islam's dominions extended from Spain to Sindh (now part of Pakistan). By the 10th and 11th centuries the followers of Islam consolidated their hold on northwestern India. By 1200 Islamic rule was established in the city of Delhi in northern India, and it then spread in two waves over nearly the whole of India. The first wave of expansion occurred under the Delhi Sultanate, which ruled from 1206 to

1526. During the second wave, under the Mughal Empire (1526-1858), Islamic rule achieved its maximum extension.

This encounter between Hinduism and Islam lasted more than 800 years. During most of this time, Islam had the upper hand politically, a fact that had enormous consequences for Hinduism and that presented challenges for both Hinduism and Islam which continue to this day. Islam's military victories outside India were followed by the conversion of the masses to Islam, with the possible exceptions of Spain and the Balkans. In India, however, Islam succeeded in converting barely a quarter of the population to Islam by 1900. Although Hinduism had successfully incorporated all previous invaders and political conquerors within the Hindu religious system—from the Persians in 6th century BC to the Huns in the 6th century AD—its powers of assimilation failed in the face of Islam.

One response of Hinduism to the presence of Islam was political. It included the emergence of the Hindu Vijayanagar kingdom, which held power in southern India from about 1336 to 1565, and the Hindu Maratha state in western India during the 17th and 18th centuries. The rise of Sikhism and the Sikh Empire (1767-1846) in the Punjab can also be considered part of this response. Willing to use violence in self-defense, Sikhs took a militant stance toward the conquerors.

The Islamic presence evoked a paradoxical Hindu religious response that blended hostile rejection and active emulation. Mainstream Hinduism retreated into a defensive position under the protective cover of *orthodoxy* (conformity to rule), judging by the number of Hindu religious codes produced during this period. At the theological level, however, Hinduism witnessed the rise and flowering of the *bhakti* (devotion) movement.

This movement of ecstatic devotion to Vishnu or Shiva had gained a firm foothold in the south by the 9th century, and it swept over the rest of the country by the 17th century. Devotion to the divine (*bhakti*), rather than knowledge of the divine (*jnana*), became the dominant form of Hinduism, perhaps reflecting the historical circumstances. Bhakti poetry expressed love for the divine, often in the forms of Krishna and Rama. Among the mystical bhakti poets were Chaitanya, Tulsidas,

Mirabai, and Kabir. The bhakti movement also provided a point of contact with a mystical movement in Islam known as Sufism. Sufis were religious figures known for their piety and love of God. As they carried out their work in India, the two traditions of Hinduism and Islam came together in their love of God. This coming together, however, never crossed over from communion to union, but the rise of Sikhism points to a possible crossover. Sikhism rejects image worship and ritualism in keeping with Islam, while retaining many aspects of the Hindu world-view.

Modern Hinduism

Following the decline of the Mughal Empire during the late 17th century, the British gradually succeeded in establishing themselves as the paramount power in India during the next century. The process began with a British victory in the Battle of Plassey in 1757, followed by the defeat of the Marathas in 1818. British victory over the Sikhs in 1846 completed the process. By this time the British had made two decisions of far-reaching importance for the future of Hinduism: to allow Christian missionaries to operate within the British dominions, in 1813; and to introduce English as the language of public instruction, in 1835.

These decisions forced Hinduism to confront Christianity and Western modernity. At the same time, the Western world was exposed to Hindu scriptures translated into European languages.

Movements for Reform

One response to the encounter with Europe was reform. The Bengali scholar Ram Mohan Roy set the tone for reform in the early 19th century. Roy campaigned against medieval or regional Hindu practices that were objectionable in the modern world. He advocated allowing widows to remarry and abolition of the relatively rare practice of *sati* (self-immolation of a wife after her husband's death; *see* suttee). In 1828 Mohan Roy founded the Brahmo Samaj (Society of Brahma) to spread his ideas. Another movement kept India from moving too far toward imitation of the modern Christian West. The movement was named after Ramakrishna, a Hindu spiritual leader who served as a priest at the Dakshineshwar Temple in the city of Kolkata (Calcutta). His reputation as a mystic drew many to him, including Swami Vivekananda, who founded the Ramakrishna movement after Ramakrishna's death in 1886.

Vivekananda, a representative Hindu product of India's new English-language education system, became a devotee of Ramakrishna and renounced the world after the priest's death. His message was a return to the timeless wisdom of the Vedas. As an unknown swami, he turned up uninvited at the Parliament of World Religions in Chicago in 1893 to present Ramakrishna's teachings. He won instant celebrity and was hailed as a hero in India for his vigorous advocacy of Hinduism. In 1895 he founded the Vedanta Society in New York City to promote Hindu ideas.

Vivekananda primarily used English in his work of reforming Hinduism and stressing the inclusive aspects of Hindu spirituality over ritual and rules. Another reform-minded leader of the 19th century, Dayananda Saraswati, used Hindi in responding to the challenges of Christianity and modernity. Saraswati founded the Arya Samaj, a movement also dedicated to modernizing Hindu practices and asserting the universality of the Hindu tradition. These movements helped revitalize Hinduism.

Another issue that engaged Hindu reformers was the plight of the lowest social class, the panchama jatis who are also known as untouchables. Local movements, such as one led by Sri Narayana Guru in Kerala, were most successful at reform. Narayana, who was born in 1856, believed that education and greater self-esteem, rather than confrontation and blame, would elevate the untouchables. He established temples where all castes could pray together.

4

Popular Systems of Hindu Religious Thought

Hindu religious thought embodies a variety of ideas, principles and practices, giving rise to various religious schools (*sampradayas*). Each school venerates the Supreme Deity, which represents a particular aspect of the Ultimate Reality (*Brahman*). Each school has temples, *guru* lineages, religious leaders, pilgrimage centres, monastic communities and sacred literature.

Some of these schools hold such divergent views that each appears to be a complete religion in itself. Yet, they all believe in the central doctrines of Hindu religion, such as *karma, dharma*, reincarnation, divinity of the *atman*, sacraments, deity worship, *guru-shishya* (teacher-disciple) tradition and the scriptural authority of the Vedas. None of these schools is in any way superior or inferior to the others. They simply represent different ways of approach to the same goal and are meant for various classes of people having different tastes, aptitudes, temperaments, and exhibiting various levels of spiritual development.

VEDANTA

The science of Vedanta is enshrined in the original spiritual texts of India. It is founded on the authority of the Upanishads, the *Bhagwad Gita* and the *Brahmasutram* of Badrayana Vyasa. Vedanta brings out the mystical, ethical and metaphysical aspects of philosophy. The abiding knowledge of Vedanta rests in the vision of the One Reality, a vision that transcends race, class, creed, gender and nationality. Vedanta is the one principle of truth encompassing all religions. There are three different philosophies on this concept. *Advaita* (non-duality) implies that there is an identity of Brahman and *Jiva atman* while *Dvaita* (duality) differs from *Advaita* and maintains an ultimate diversity between Brahman and *Jiva atman*. *Vishistadvaita* (qualified non-duality) maintains a crucial differentiation as well as a fundamental identity.

Advaita is the oldest extant school of Vedanta founded by Adi Shankaracharya. Advaita asserts that the real, essential identity of the *jiva*, the individual self, is nothing other than *Brahman* itself. It asserts that Brahman, the 'impersonal' God and the universal soul, is the Absolute Truth. Brahman has multiple roles to play: the creator, the maintainer, and the destroyer all in one. The teaching follows from the statements of the Upanishads (*Mahavakyas*) like *tat tvam asi* and *aham brahmasmi*. It is in this cardinal doctrine that *Advaita* differs from all other schools of Vedanta.

The *Vishishtadvaita* philosophy was expounded by Sri Ramanuja. According to this desirable qualities *viz.*, *satyam, jnanam* and *anandam*. The main exponent of the *Dvaita* philosophy was Sri Madhava (Purnaprajna). It says that the supreme goal of life is service of god.

Other systems which are not quite popular as the above mentioned philosophies include *Dvaitadvaita* (dual-non-dual doctrine), *Suddhadvaita* (pure non-dualism) and *Acinntyaa bhedabheda* (oneness and difference) were expounded by Nimbarka, Vallabha and Vidyabhusana respectively. All the above philosophers have written commentaries on the *Prasthana-traya* (triple canon) of the *Vedanta*, which are the *Upanishads*, *Brahma sutra* and the *Bhagwad Gita*.

The Hindu religious systems have been classified by Adi Shankaracharya into six major paths, called *Shad-maths*. These are *Shaivism*, *Vaishnavism*, *Shaktism*, *Ganapathyam*, *Kaumaram*, and *Sauram* or *Jyotiam*.

SHAIVISM

The followers of Shaivism venerate the Ultimate Reality as Lord Shiva. This tradition has been traced back by scholars to the Indus Valley Civilization. The archeologists have discovered the so-called proto-*Pasupathy* seals of this civilization, which depict Shiva as Lord *Pasupathy*, seated in a yogic pose. There are many schools of Shaivism, of which the six major systems are *Shaiva Siddhanta*, *Pashupata Shaivism*, Kashmir *Shaivism*, *Vira Shaivism*, *Siddha Siddhanta* and *Shiva Advaita*. These systems differ somewhat in their doctrines pertaining to the relationship between Shiva, the *Atman* and the world.

Most Hindus worship Lord Shiva as a member of the Hindu Trinity. However, the followers of Shaivism, called S*haivas* or *Shaivites*, worship Him as the Ultimate Reality. The predominant philosophy of Shaivism is monistic-theism. According to this doctrine, Lord Shiva is both personal and impersonal. In the personal aspect, Shiva creates, controls and pervades all that exists. In this aspect, Shiva is what other religions call God. Shaivism declares that there is nothing outside Shiva and, thus, recognizes the oneness of *Pati-pau-pasa* (God-*Atman*-World). In the impersonal aspect, Shiva transcends all existence and in the liberated state the *Atman* is one with Shiva.

The main objects of Shiva worship are *shivalinga* and images of Shiva. The *linga* symbolizes both the creative and destructive power of the Lord and great sanctity is attached to it by the devotees. The *banalingas* are very sacred objects of worship to the followers of Shaivism. These are the elliptical stones of a special kind found in the bed of the river Narmada, one of the seven sacred rivers in India. Fresh flowers, pure water, young sprouts of *Kusha* (a holy grass) and *durva* (called bent or panic grass), fruit, *bilva* leaves and sun-dried rice are used in the ritual part of the Shiva worship.

According to tradition, offering leaves of the *bilva* tree (wood-apple) is considered very auspicious for the worship of Lord Shiva. *Mahashivaratri* (the great night of Shiva) is an annual festival that falls on the fourteenth day of the dark fortnight of *Phalguna* (February-March), and is dedicated to the worship of Lord Shiva. In mythology, Shiva is the husband of Parvati, the daughter of the Himalayas. They have two sons,

Ganesha and Karttikeya and a daughter Jyoti. Their residence is the snow-clad mountain Kailash. The mythology depicts Shiva both as God of terror as well as benevolence. His five powers are revealment (offering grace to the devotees), concealment (obscuring by His power of *maya*), creation, preservation and dissolution. The major scriptures of Shaivism are Vedas, Shaiva Agamas and Shaiva Puranas.

VAISHNAVISM

Vaishnavism venerates the Ultimate Reality as Lord Vishnu. This tradition began during the Vedic period when its earliest schools *Pancharatra* and *Bhagavata* became popular around 300 BC. Modern day Vaishnavism includes five popular schools founded by Ramanuja, Madhva, Nimbarka, Vallabha and Chaitanya. Most Hindus worship Lord Vishnu as a member of the Hindu Trinity. However, the followers of Vaishnavism, called *Vaishnavas* or *Vaishnavites*, worship Lord Vishnu as the Ultimate Reality.

Although the philosophy of Vaishnavism includes dualism of Madhva, qualified dualism of Ramanuja, and nearly monistic views of Vallabha, the predominant philosophy of Vaishnavism is dualism. According to this doctrine, there are two categories of the Ultimate Reality. Lord Vishnu as personal God is the Absolute Reality, and the *Atmans* (individuals souls) are the relative realities, eternally distinct from each other and Lord Vishnu, but dependent on Him. The doctrine of incarnation (*avatara*) is fundamental to all Hindus, especially to Vaishnavas. Lord Vishnu assumed each *avatara* for a particular end and as the situation demanded. The number of *avataras* of Lord Vishnu is generally accepted to be ten, with Rama and Krishna being the two most popular among Hindus.

Vaishnavism stresses on complete surrender (*prapatti*) to Lord Vishnu and His incarnations and advocates devotion (*bhakti*) as the highest spiritual discipline. The objects of worship are the images of Lord Vishnu and His incarnations, and *salagramas*, small stones of different colours (predominantly black) recovered from the bed of the river Gandaki, one of the tributaries of the Ganges river in India. Fresh flowers, water, fruits and leaves of the *tulasi* plant are used in the ritual part of the worship of Lord Vishnu and His incarnations. One of the unique features of the Vaishnava worship is *kirtana*, which consists of choral singing of the names and deeds of Lord Vishnu and His incarnations, accompanied by drums and cymbals and synchronized with rhythmic bodily movements. The major scriptures of Vaishnavism are Vedas, Agamas, Puranas, Ramayana, Mahabharata and Bhagwad Gita.

SHAKTISM

Shakti means "creative energy," and *Shaktism* means "Doctrine of the Creative Energy." Shaktism venerates the Ultimate Reality as the Divine Mother-*Shakti* or *Devi*-of the universe.

Archeologists have recovered thousands of female statuettes at the Mehrgarh village in India, which indicate that Shakti worship existed in India as far back as 5500 BC. There are references to the female deities in the Rig Veda, including a popular Hymn to the Divine Mother, which holds special sanctity to Hindus in general and *Shaktas* (the followers of Shaktism) in particular. Shaktism visualises the Ultimate Reality as having two aspects, transcendent and immanent. Shiva is the transcendent aspect, the supreme cosmic consciousness, and Shakti is the supreme creative energy. Shiva and Shakti are God and God's creative energy, which are inseparably connected. Metaphorically, Shiva and Shakti is an inseparable divine couple, representing the male and female principles in creation.

Shaktism greatly resembles Shaivism, but Shiva is considered solely transcendent and is not worshipped. Like Shaivism, the goal of Shaktism is to unite with Shiva. Such unity is possible only with the grace of the Divine Mother, who unfolds as *iccha shakti* (the power of desire, will and love), *kriya shakti* (the power of action), and *jnana shakti* (the power of knowledge and wisdom). Within Shaktism, Shiva is the unmanifest Absolute and Shakti is the Divine Mother of the manifest creation. The Divine Mother is worshipped in both the fierce and benign forms. The fierce forms of Goddess include Kali, Durga, Chandi, Chamundi, Bhadrakali and Bhairavi. The benign forms of Goddess include Uma, Gauri, Ambika, Parvati, Maheshvari, Lalita, Lakshmi, Saraswata and Annapurna. The major scriptures of Shaktism are *Vedas*, *Shakta agamas* and *Puranas*.

Ganapathyam

Ganesha, the elephant-headed deity, represents that aspect of the Ultimate Reality which removes obstacles. Hindus, therefore, invoke Lord Ganesha at the beginning of all undertakings, whether religious, spiritual or worldly, for Lord Ganesha removes obstacles and brings success to the enterprise. Ganesha is also called *Vighneshvara*, meaning "the Lord presiding over the obstacles." In the Rig Veda, Ganesha is the name of *Brihapati*, the Lord of prayer (the Holy Word). In mythology Ganesha is the first son of the divine couple Shiva and Parvati.

Ganapatyas, followers of Ganapathyam, venerate Lord Ganesha exclusively as the form of the Ultimate Reality (*Brahman*) that is accessible to the mind, senses and (through devotional practices) the heart. Ganapatyas regard Moraya Gosavi (1651 AD), the famous devotee of Ganesha, as their spiritual progenitor. Tradition holds that Moraya experienced a series of visions of Ganesha at a shrine at Moragaon, near Pune. An annual ten-day festival, *Ganesha Chaturthi*, is held in August-September to celebrate the birth of Ganesha. The major scriptures of this tradition are Vedas, Skanda Purana, and Mudgala Purana.

Kaumaram

The followers of this tradition venerate Lord Karttikeya, also called by other names such as Murugan, Kumara, Skanda, Subramanya and Shanmukhanatha, as their *Ishta Devata* (personal-God). Lord Karttikeya represents the power of the Ultimate Reality (Brahman) that destroys ignorance, bestows divine knowledge, upholds dharma (righteousness), removes worries and strengthens human will. In popular pictures and images, Karttikeya is shown holding a spear, which symbolizes his divine power to destroy ignorance and unrighteousness. On the day of Vaikasi Vishakham in May-June, elaborate *pujas* and special ceremonies (*abhishekam*) are conducted in homes and temples in the honour of Lord Karttikeya. His protection and grace are specially invoked on the day of *Skanda Shashthi*, which falls on the sixth day after the new moon in October-November. In January-February, another holy festival (*Tai Pusam*) is celebrated in his honour. Special *pujas* are performed in honour of Lord Karttikeya every month on *Krittika nakshatra* and *Shashthi*, the sixth day after the new moon.

Sauram

The power of the sun to dispel darkness, illuminate the world and nourish mankind is recognized by Hindus as an aspect of the infinite power of the Ultimate Reality (Brahman). The worship of this triple power of the Divine, symbolized by the Vedic deity Surya, the Sun-god, is called Sauram. Surya is worshipped by Hindus as an object of meditation during many physical exercises. Devout Hindus recite sacred verses selected from the epic and Puranic literature daily early in the morning before commencing the day's work. The best known of the hymns to the sun is one from Ramayana that was imparted to Rama during his battle with Ravana.

Hindus in general worship the sun every year on the seventh day after the new moon in the month that corresponds to January-February. Sacred mantras are recited for the special worship of the sun, especially on Sundays, birthdays and at other special functions. Prostrations are made to the sun after each tenth mantra until one hundred and thirty-two prostrations have been completed. These prostrations are called *Surya-Namaskara*.

The following most sacred Rigvedic prayer, named after its meter, is called *Gayatri*, meaning "the saviour of the singer." It is considered to be the mantra of all mantras, the most potent mantra, repeated as many times as possible by Hindus daily in *puja* and personal chanting to venerate the sun as the Creator (*Savitar*). The mystic power of this mantra is so high that it is called *Vedamatri*, meaning "Mother of the Vedas." *Gayatri Mantra* is imparted to a young boy for initiation into Vedic tradition.

Yamas & Niyamas—The Moral and Ethical Ideals of Hindus

Ethics can be described as the-science of morality, and morality as the living of a virtuous life. Hindus place greater emphasis on the attitude of the mind rather than on postulation of the elaborate theories of what is right and what is wrong. Accordingly, the Hindu vision of morality and ethics is characterized by the following considerations: *Ahimsa* (non-injury), *Satya* (truthfulness), *Asteya* (non-stealing), *Brahmacharya* (controlling sex), *Kshama* (forgiveness), *Dhriti* (firmness), *Daya* (compassion), *Arjava* (honesty), *Mitahara* (Refrain from consuming meat), *Shaucha* (purity), *Hri* (remorse), *Santosha* (contentment), *Dana* (tithing), *Astikya* (faith), *Pujana* (worship), *Shravana* (hearing of scriptures), *Mati* (cognition), *Vrata* (sacred vows), *Japa* (chanting) and *Tapas* (austerity).

5

The Hindu Mythology

Mythology is a part of every religion. Mythology is concretised philosophy. Mythology is the science which investigates myths or fables or legends founded on remote events, especially those made in the early period of a peoples existence. Mythology inspires the readers through precepts and laudable examples and goads them to attain perfection or the highest ideal.

The abstract teachings and high subtle ideas are made highly interesting and impressive to the masses through the garb of stories, parables, legends, allegories and narratives. The sublime and abstract philosophical ideas and ideals of Hinduism are taken straight to the heart of the masses through impressive stories.

MYTHOLOGY AND HISTORY

All religions have their own mythology. Mythology is slightly mixed up with a little history. It is difficult to make a fine distinction between history and mythology. If a Christian stands up and says:-My prophet did such and such a marvellous thing,- others will say:-This is only a myth. Our prophets did still more marvellous things which are really historical.-It is not easy to differentiate the two into watertight compartments.

The doctrine of Avatara of the Hindus is a myth for the people of other religions. To worship a cow is superstition for the followers of other religions. The beautiful image or idol of Lord Krishna, which captivates the hearts of the sincere devotees and inspires them to enter into Bhava Samadhi, is horrible to look at for some other religionists. A Christian, a Jew and all others have their own various superstitions and myths. But these myths are really historical for each of them, severally. Mythology has no reference to anything-unreal-, but presents truths as clothed in conceptual categories.

PHILOSOPHY, MYTHOLOGY AND RITUAL

In every religion there are three parts, *viz.*, philosophy, mythology and ritual. Philosophy is the essence of religion. It sets forth its basic principles or fundamental doctrines or tenets, the goal and the means of attaining it. Mythology explains and illustrates philosophy by means of legendary lives of great men or of supernatural beings. Ritual gives a still more concrete form to philosophy so that everyone may understand it. Ritual consists of forms, ceremonies, etc.

Puranas contain various myths. The cosmogonic myths of the Puranas are very interesting. A certain portion of Hindu mythology is even now presented to the public in the form of dramas during days of Hindu festivals. Thus the minds of the people are saturated with sublime ideas and ideals and lifted to great spiritual heights.

Study of Mythology and its Advantages

There are great truths behind the ancient mythology of Hinduism. You cannot ignore a thing simply because it has a garb of mythology. Do not argue. Shut up your mouth. Keep your intellect at a respectable distance when you study mythology. Intellect is a hindrance. It will delude you. Give up arrogance and vanity. Cultivate love for imagery. Sit like a child and open your heart freely. You will comprehend the great truths revealed by mythology. You will penetrate into the hearts of the Rishis and sages who wrote the mythology. You will really enjoy mythology now.

You study geography through maps. There is no real country or town in a map, but it helps you to know a great deal about the different countries. Similar is the case with myths. You can grasp the subtle philosophical truths through myths.

By studying mythology, you will get several object lessons for moulding your character and leading an ideal divine life.

The lives of Sri Rama, Sri Krishna, Bhishma, Nala, Harischandra, Lakshmana, Bharata, Hanuman, Yudhishthira, Arjuna, Sita, Savitri, Damayanti, Radha, etc., are sources of great spiritual inspiration for moulding your life, conduct and character. When you are in a dilemma as to what to do in puzzling situations and when there is conflict of duties, you will get the exact solutions through study of mythology.

Thus, mythology has its own benefits and advantages. It stamps on the minds the subtle and abstract teachings of the Vedas through instructive stories and illuminating discourses and paves the way for men to lead a divine life and attain perfection, freedom and immortality.

HINDU SYMBOLS

Outward symbols are necessary and beneficial. When viewed from the right angle of vision, you will find that they play a very important part in your material as well as spiritual life. Though they may look very simple and unimportant, they are very scientific and effective.

Tilaka—A Mark of Auspiciousness

Tilaka is a mark of auspiciousness. It is put on the forehead with sandal paste, sacred ashes or Kumkuma. The devotees of Shiva apply sacred ashes (Bhasma) on the forehead, the devotees of Vishnu apply sandal paste (Chandana), and the worshippers of Devi or Shakti apply Kumkuma, a red turmeric powder.

The scriptures say:-A forehead without a Tilaka, a woman without a husband, a Mantra the meaning of which is not known while doing Japa, the head that does not bend before holy personages, a heart without mercy, a house without a well, a village without a temple, a country without a river, a society without a leader, wealth that is not given away in charity, a preceptor without a disciple, a country without justice, a king without an able minister, a woman not obedient to her husband, a well without water, a flower without smell, a soul devoid of holiness, a field without rains, an intellect without clearness, a disciple who does not consider his preceptor as a form of God, a body devoid of health, a custom (Achara) without purity, austerity devoid of fellow-feeling, speech in which truth is not the basis, a country without good people, work without wages, Sannyasa without renunciation, legs which have not performed pilgrimages, a determination unaided by Viveka or discrimination, a knife which is blunt, a cow which does not give milk, a spear without a point-all these are worthy of condemnation. They exist for names sake only.-From this you can imagine the importance of Tilaka or the sacred mark.

Tilaka is applied at the Ajna Chakra, the space between the two eyebrows. It has a very cooling effect. Application of sandal paste has great medicinal value, apart from the spiritual influence. Application of sandal paste will nullify the heating effect when you concentrate and meditate at the Bhrumadhya. Tilaka indicates the point at which the spiritual eye opens. Lord Shiva has a third eye at the Bhrumadhya. When He opens the third eye, the three worlds are destroyed.

So also, when the third eve of the Jiva is opened, the three kinds of afflictions-Adhyatmika, Adhidaivika and Adhibhautika-are burnt to ashes. The three Karmas-Sanchita, Prarabdha and Agami-and also all the sins committed in the countless previous births, are burnt. When you apply the Tilaka, you mentally imagine:-I am the one non-dual Brahman free from all duality. May my eye of intuition open soon?-You should remember this every time you apply a Tilaka.

There are various methods of applying Tilaka. Shaivas apply three horizontal lines with the sacred ashes. The Vaishnavas apply three vertical lines (Tripundra) on the forehead. When they apply Tilaka, they say:-O Lord, protect me from the evil effects of the Trigunatmika Maya which has Sattva, Rajas and Tamas as its binding cords.-Some Vaishnavas apply only one vertical line. Only the method of application differs, but the significance is the same in both the Vaishnavas and the Shaivas.

The Tuft—Its Utility and Significance

Brahmins (Brahmanas) as well as the other castes grow Choti or Sikha, a tuft of hair. This tuff of hair was not so small in olden days, as seen in the present day. It covered the whole brain. They allowed the hair to grow. They never cut the tuft.

It protects the brain from any sudden stroke and keeps it cool. The heat of the sun does not affect the head directly. Lack of this tuff has necessitated the use of umbrellas, etc.

The tuft is most scientific as well as religious. Any religious act should be performed after tying the tuft. Only the funeral and death anniversaries are performed with tuft untied or with dishevelled hair. It is very inauspicious to remain with dishevelled hair.

It is done only in times of great sorrow or calamity. Draupadi took an oath in the assembly of the Kurus when she was molested by Dussasana that she would remain with dishevelled hair until the enemies were properly revenged. Kaikeyi remained with dishevelled hair in her apartment with the object of getting two boons from Dasaratha which were detrimental to the interests of Rama, the favourite of Dasaratha. Auspicious acts are never undertaken with tuft untied. Nowadays, very few people wear tuft, and even women are neglecting this vital point in their feverish anxiety to copy the West. The tuft of hair has a salutary effect on the essential parts of the brain and the central nervous system.

Significance of the Sacred Thread

Yajnopavita or the sacred thread is worn by the Brahmins, Kshatriyas and the Vaishyas. Wearing the sacred thread is a very holy and sacred ceremony amongst the Hindus. Brahmin boys between the ages of five and eight are invested with the sacred thread on a very auspicious day. By this ceremony, they become fit for the repetition of Gayatri. A Brahmin becomes a true Brahmin only after this ceremony. It is said:-*Janmana Jayate Sudrah Karmana Jayate Dvijah*-By birth one is a Sudra; by Karma (*i.e.*, the investiture with the sacred thread) he becomes a Dvija or Brahmin. Upanayana or thread ceremony is the second birth; hence, the Brahmins are called Dvijas (Dvija means-born twice).

The sacred thread or Yajnopavita consists of three threads. It denotes that one should be a Brahmachari in thought, word and deed. Each thread represents a Veda, *viz.*, the Rik, Yajus and Sama. It represents also Brahma, Vishnu and Shiva. The knot in the middle represents the formless Brahman, the Supreme Principle. The three threads represent also Sattva, Rajas and Tamas of the Trigunatmika Maya, and the knot represents the Isvara who controls Maya. Those who worship God at the three Sandhyas and repeat the Gayatri holding the Brahma knot of the sacred thread, derive immense strength and power.

In days of yore, a Brahmana meditating upon the Gayatri holding the Brahma knot, had the power to bless and curse others. The educated intelligentsia of the present day are quite ignorant of the power of the sacred thread and the performance of Sandhya. That is the reason why they have ignored it. The sacred thread is a great power for the Brahmin who leads a regulated life devoted to the worship of God. Kshatriyas and Vaishyas, too, acquire power, fame and wealth by the power of the sacred thread.

A householder wears, at the time of marriage, an additional sacred thread. A Brahmachari has only one. The additional thread at the time of marriage is intended for the well-being of the partner. The sacred thread should be on the body always. The custom of washing it after removing it from the body or sending it to the washerman, is a wrong procedure. Some people are ashamed to wear the thread when they go to the office and they leave it at home. How ignorant they are!

Yajnopavita, the Choti, caste-mark, etc., are the external symbols to show that one is a Hindu. Purity, self-restraint, non-violence, patience, love for ones fellow-beings-these are the internal marks of a Hindu.

ACHAMANA AND PROKSHANA

Achamana is sipping water three times, repeating the Names of the Lord. Prokshana is sprinkling water over ones body for the sake of purity, when a bath is not possible. This is for internal as well as external purity. While sipping water, the following Mantras are repeated:-*Achyutaya Namah*-prostrations to the immutable Lord; *Anantaya Namah*-prostrations to the unlimited Lord; *Govindaya Namah*-prostrations to the Lord who is known by the Name of Govinda.-

Then the various Names of the Lord-Keshava, Narayana, Madhava, Govinda, Vishnu, Madhusudana, Trivikrama, Vamana, Sridhara, Rishikesh, Padmanabha and Damodara-are repeated, touching the various parts Of the body, *viz.*, the eyes, the ears, the face, the navel, the head, etc. One becomes pure by doing Achamana after he answers calls of nature, after walking in the streets, just before taking food and after food, and after a bath.

This reminds you of the Lord now and then. Every act, every ritual, every symbol has a deep philosophical importance. They help you in changing the mental substance from Rajas and Tamas to Sattva. They give you an opportunity to think of God frequently.

Offering Food to God, Guests and the Pancha-Pranas

Before sitting for food, the place is purified, a seat is put and in a leaf the articles of food are served. Before taking the food, a little water is sprinkled making a line all round the leaf repeating some Vedic Mantras. This repetition purifies the food. Then a little water is sipped. According to science as well as medicine, a little water, if drunk before the food is taken, is highly beneficial.

Then the food is offered to the five Pranas and Brahman seated in the heart, by repeating *Om Pranaya Svaha, Apanaya Svaha, Vyanaya Svaha, Udanaya Svaha, Samanaya Svaha,* and lastly, *Brahmane Svaha*. Just mark the importance of this offering. The person who takes the food offers it to the deities who dwell in the body in the form of Prana, Apana, etc. He does not eat for himself. The physical body is not the eater. It is the Pancha Prana that takes the food. Thus, taking food also can be converted into an act of Yoga or sacrifice.

One should daily offer to the Lord the food that he has prepared, before he partakes of it. He should say:-*Tvadiyam Vastu Govinda Tubhyameva Samarpaye*-I offer to Thee, O Govinda, this (food) which belongs to Thee only.-The custom of the Hindus is that they should feed the guest who comes to their house before they take food. The guest is a representative of the Lord. The Srutis say:-*Athhi Devo Bhava.*-

Bells, Lights, Dhupa, Camphor and Sandal Paste

Bells are rung in temples while doing Puja, to shut out the external sounds and to make the mind inward and concentrated.

Lights are waved before the Deity. This denotes that the Lord is Jyotis-Svarupa. He is all-light. The devotee says: O Lord! Thou art the self-effulgent Light of the universe. Thou art the light in the sun, moon and fire. Remove the darkness in me by bestowing your divine light. May my intellect be illumined?-This is the significance of waving lights.

Dhupa or scented incense sticks are burnt before the Deity. The smoke spreads the whole room. It acts as a disinfectant. Burning of Dhupa denotes that the Lord is all-pervading and that He fills the whole universe by His living presence. It is to remind this fact that Dhupa is burnt. The devotee prays:- O Lord! Let the Vasanas and Samskaras dormant in me vanish like the smoke of this Dhupa and become ashes. Let me become stainless.

Burning of camphor denotes that the individual ego melts like the camphor and the Jivatman becomes one with the supreme Light of lights.

The sandal paste reminds the devotee that he should, in his difficulties, be as patient as the sandal. Sandal emanates sweet odour when it is rubbed on a hard surface and made into a paste. So also the devotee should not murmur when difficulties arise, but on the other hand, remain cheerful and happy and emanate sweetness and gentleness like the sandal. He should not hate even his enemy.

This is another precept we learn from this. Though the sandalwood is crushed and made into a paste, it silently wears out emanating only very sweet odour. One should not wish evil even to his enemy.

PRASADA—ITS SACREDNESS AND GLORY

Prasada is that which gives peace. Prasada is the sacred food offering of the Lord. During Kirtana, worship, Puja, Havan and Arati, the devotee offers sweet rice, fruits, jaggery, milk, coconut, plantain and such other articles to the Lord, according to his ability. After offering them to the Lord, they are shared between the members of the house or the Bhaktas in a temple.

Water, flowers, rice, etc., are offered to the Lord in worship. This denotes that the Lord is pleased with even the smallest offering. What is wanted is the heart of the devotee. The Lord says in the Gita:-*Patram Pushpam Phalam Toyam Yo Me Bhaktya Prayacchati; Tadaham Bhaktyupahritamasnami Prayatatmanah*-Whoever offers a leaf, a flower, a fruit or even water, with devotion, that I accept, offered as it is with a loving heart.-It is not necessary that one should offer gold, silver and costly dress to the Lord. The devotee offers these according to his ability and position in life, thereby denoting that the whole wealth of the world belongs to the Lord. A rich man offers costly things to the Lord. He feeds the poor and serves the sick, seeing the Lord in his fellow-beings.

Puja is done with Bael leaves, flowers, Tulasi, Vibhuti and these are given as Prasada from the Lord. Vibhuti is the Prasada of Lord Shiva. It is to be applied on the forehead. A small portion can be taken in. Kumkuma is the Prasada of Sri Devi or Shakti. It is to be applied at the space between the eyebrows (Ajna or Bhrumadhya). Tulasi is the Prasada of Lord Vishnu, Rama or Krishna. It is to be taken in. They are charged with mysterious powers by the chanting of Mantras during Puja and Havan. The mental Bhava of the devotee offering Bhog to the Lord has a very great effect. If an ardent devotee of the Lord offers anything to the Lord, that Prasada, if taken, would bring very great change even in the minds of atheists. The Grace of the Lord descends through Prasada. Go through the life of Narada. You will realise the greatness of the sacred leavings of the Lord as well as those of advanced Sadhakas and saints.

Namadeva offered rice, etc., to Panduranga Vitthala and He ate the food and shared it with Namadeva as well. If the food is offered with an yearning heart, sometimes, the Lord takes that food assuming a physical form. In other cases, the Lord enjoys the subtle essence of the food offered, and the food remains as it is in the shape of Prasada. While feeding Mahatmas and the poor people, that which is left behind is taken as Prasada.

When a sacrifice is performed, the participants share the Prasada which bestows the blessings of the gods. When Dasaratha performed Putrakameshti (a sacrifice performed wishing for son), he got a vessel full of sweetened rice which he gave to his queens, by taking which they became pregnant. Prasada is the most sacred object for a devotee. One should consider himself lucky to take the Prasada, and there is no restriction of any kind in taking Prasada. Time and place, and the condition in which one is placed-all these do not affect him in any way. Prasada is all-purifying.

The benefits of Prasada and Charanamrita are beyond description. They have the power to change entirely the outlook of a mans life. Prasada and Charanamrita have the power to cure diseases and even bring back to life dead persons. There had been ever so many instances in the past in this holy land of ours which bear witness to the potency and efficacy of Prasada. Prasada destroys all pains and sins. It is an antidote for misery, pain and anxiety. Faith is the important factor in testing the accuracy of this statement. For faithless persons, it brings very little effect.

Those who are brought up in modern education and culture have forgotten all about the glory of Prasada. Many English-educated persons do not attach any importance to Prasada when they get it from Mahatmas. This is a serious mistake. Prasada is a great purifier. As they are brought up in the western style of living, they have imbibed the spirit of westerners and forgotten the spirit of the true children of Indian Rishis of yore. Live for a week in Vrindavana or Ayodhya or Varanasi or Pandharpur. You will realise the glory and the miraculous effects of Prasada.

Many incurable diseases are cured. Many sincere devotional aspirants get wonderful spiritual experiences from mere Prasada alone. Prasada is a panacea. Prasada is a spiritual elixir. Prasada is the Grace of the Lord. Prasada is a cure-all and an ideal pick-me-up. Prasada is an embodiment of Shakti. Prasada is Divinity in manifestation. Prasada energises, vivifies, invigorates and infuses devotion. It should be taken with great faith.

THE JAPA MALA

Significance of the Number of Beads: Generally, the rosary or Mala used for Japa contains 108 beads. A man breathes 21, 600 times every day. If one does 200 Malas of Japa, it becomes 21, 600; thereby, he does one Japa for every breath. If he does 200 Malas of Japa every day, that amounts to remembrance of God throughout the day. Malas may contain beads which form divisions of 108 also, so that the same calculation can be maintained. The Meru (the central bead in the Mala) denotes that you have done your Japa 108 times. This also denotes that every time you come to the Meru bead, you have gone one step further on the spiritual path and crossed over one obstacle. A portion of your ignorance is removed. A rosary or Mala is a whip to goad you to do Japa. Mohammedans also have a rosary (Tasbi) in their hands when they repeat their prayers. They roll the beads and repeat the name of Allah. Christians have their paternoster.

The Raksha Stotra: Before sitting for Japa and meditation, the Raksha Stotra is generally repeated. It means:-May the Lord protect me, staying in every part of my body.-Each part is separately named and a particular Name of the Lord is repeated for the protection of that part. Anganyasa and Karanyasa also have the same effect. They drive away the evil effects of evil spirits, if any. The obstacles that stand in the way of concentration and meditation are removed. Evil thoughts will not enter the mind. This is a prayer to remove obstacles in Japa and meditation.

THE OCHRE CLOTH AND THE SHAVEN HEAD

Symbols of Renunciation: The ochre colour (Gerua) of the dress of a Sannyasin indicates that he is as pure as fire itself. He shines like the burnt gold, free from all impurities of desires and Vasanas. It denotes purity. It stands for purity. For an aspirant who has taken to the path of Nivritti Marga, it is a help. He will swerve and shrink from evil actions. This cloth will remind him that he is not entitled to worldly enjoyments. Gradually his nature will be moulded. This coloured cloth serves as an external symptom to show that one is a Sannyasin.

A Sannyasin shaves his head completely. This removes from him all beauty. He will not have to take care about dressing his hair with scented oils, etc. This shows that he has renounced all external beauties and that he dwells in the Self which is Beauty of beauties. This Mundana (shaving of head) indicates that he is no more of the world. He should not desire any sensual object.

It is only an external symbol of the mental state of complete dispassion and turning away from the pleasures of the world. He removes his Choti also at the time of Sannyasa to indicate that he is no more bound by the various Nitya and Naimittika Karmas and that they have been burnt in the fire of Vairagya. Further, this shaving of the head is suitable for a wandering life.

The existence of long hairs will prevent him from taking bath whenever he likes. Shaving will relieve him of much worry, and the time he would have otherwise spent in drying, combing and dressing his hair he may spend in prayers and meditation.

The Vedas and the Upanishads state that the ultimate truth in its pure and naked form, very unceremoniously. The Itihasas, Puranas and Agamas give this truth a homely, personal and symbolic touch through narration of history, legend and mythology.

Do not neglect outward symbols. Make a research study of our Vedic customs and injunctions. You will find wonderful and precious gems in every one of them. Their utility and efficacy will be revealed in following them.

May you all tread the path of Dharma and attain Kaivalya Moksha in this very birth.

Infertility, Artificial Insemination & Surrogate Mother in Hindu Mythology

Having children has always been important since time immemorial, and the continuity of the family unit has been of major significance in Hindu culture. Infertility is a social stigma even today, and Indian mythology is full of stories about what couples have done in the past to overcome their problem of infertility. Ancient tales hold the key to the unconscious desires of a people. They help us appreciate the fears and insecurities of people who visit state-of-the-art infertility clinics.

Debt to Ancestors: The following story of sage Agastya from the great Hindu epic Mahabharata (written 2000 years ago) tells us why Hindus, in particular, and Indians, in general, are so obsessed with children. Besides social factors like 'someone to take care of me in my old age', it directs our attention to a profound religious demand for a child, especially a male one.

The sage Agastya wanted moksha-, liberation from the endless cycle of rebirths. So he broke all social bonds, went to the forest, meditated and performed austerities. He believed that by refusing to succumb to any desire, by refusing to yield to the illusory pleasures of the material world, his soul would break free from the prison that was his body. He spent years mortifying himself. Liberation eluded him. Then, one night, he had a vision: he saw his ancestors hanging head down over a gaping hole.

They were crying, "We are trapped in the land of the dead. And there is no hope of escape." "What can I do to help?" asked Agastya. They replied, "Father children, so that we can be reborn. Help us return to the land of the living so that we too can work towards our moksha.

Or else, you will land up in the hell known as Put and suffer there for all eternity. Repay the debt you owe your ancestors." Thus admonished, Agastya returned to his village, got married, fathered children, and only after they had become independent did he return to the forest.

Hindus believe that all men come into this world burdened by a debt – the pitr-runa (pitr = ancestor; runa = debt). The only way to repay this debt is to father a male offspring. During funerary rites, known as shraadha, Hindu males are reminded of this debt. In the Dharmashastras, Hindu law books written between 500-1000 AD, it is said that those who fail to repay this debt end up in the Hell known as Put where they suffer for all eternity. Since the birth of a child, preferably male child, liberates a man from his debt, the Sanskrit word for son is putra (deliverer from Put). The daughter or putri is also a deliverer from Put, but to a lesser extent.

Dharma and Karma

Two words that play a crucial role in the understanding the Hindu (as well as Buddhist and Jain) attitude towards life are dharma and karma.

Dharma is essentially duty that must be performed for the sake of social as well as cosmic stability. Failure to do so leads to social anarchy and cosmic chaos. Duty is traditionally defined by one's inherited caste (teacher, protector, provider, servant) and by one's stage in life (student, householder, senior citizen, hermit). Producing a child is one's biological duty applicable all human beings. Those who wanted to renounce the world were only allowed to do so after they had fulfilled all worldly duties.

Men who could not fulfil their biological obligations because of a physical problem (impotence) or a mental quirk (homosexuality) were termed rather derogatorily kliba or napunsaka, sexually dysfunctional non-man. In the Manu Smriti, an ancient Hindu law book, such men were debarred from sacred rituals and from inheritance.

Only by producing children, were a man and woman considered biologically fulfilled. It must be remembered, that only after marriage was a man in Hindu society given the right to enjoy worldly pleasures and possess worldly wealth. A king could not be king unless he was married. And an impotent man or a man who could not father a child was not allowed to be king. Hence, in the Mahabharata, when the king Pandu learns that he will die the moment he has sex with his wife, he renounces his crown – his inability to father a child debars him from kingship.

Karma means both action and fate. Hindus (as well as Buddhists and Jains) believe that every action leads to a series of reactions. All creatures are obliged to experience the repercussions of their (conscious and unconscious) actions, either in this life or the next. Thus, every event is the result of past actions. If one is barren, it is because of events that occurred in the past, either in this life or in the one before. A folk story based on the Mahabharata illustrates this point. At the end of a great war, queen Gandhari is informed that all her hundred children are dead. She weeps and seeks a reason for this unfair situation, to which a sage replies, "In your last life, you sat on a stone under which there were a hundred turtle eggs. The eggs were crushed. So the mother-turtle cursed you that you too would experience the loss of hundred children."

A situation in governed by karma, but one's reaction to is governed by free will. Astrology helps understand what karma has in store for us. The result of karma can be either endured or it can be modified by certain occult rituals, by the power of holy men or by the grace of god. This is the reason why childless men in India visit temples, go on pilgrimages, seek the intervention of holy men or perform elaborate rituals.

White Seed and Red Seed: Why a male offspring is more important to a Hindu (besides social factors) can be traced to certain beliefs. In the Mahabharata, it is said that the soul of a man lies locked in the semen. Semen is the medium through which ancestors slip into the land of the living. The soul in semen is embodied in the womb.

According to ancient Hindu seers known as rishis, within the womb is the red seed known as rajas (the counterpart of the white male seed known as shukra). The rajas wraps the soul in flesh and blood. The shukra, besides being a medium for the soul, is also the source of bones. Thus all living creatures come into being because of the father's white seed and the mother's red seed. The former generates consciousness and transforms into the skeleton while the latter creates the flesh.

There is an interesting story in this regard from the Padma Purana. A king had two wives but no children. He asked some sages to make a potion that would make his wives pregnant. He died before the potion was ready. The two widowed queens did not want to waste the magic potion. So the elder queen drank it while the younger queen made love to her 'like a man'. In due course, the elder queen gave birth to a child, but it was only a lump of flesh. The sages said, "Since no white seed was part of the conception, the child had no bones and no consciousness." They appeased the gods and the child was 'repaired'.

Power of the White Seed: Indian men are known for their obsession with virility. Virility here refers to many things, physical strength, mental agility, sexual energy as well ability to father a male child. So when an Indian says, "I have less strength (takat kum hai)," he could refer to malaise or lethargy or impotence or inability to father a male child. Here again is an ancient belief that physical strength is reflected in semen strength.

The ancient seers believed that food consumed is transformed in the body into sap (plasma), then flesh, then blood, then bone, then marrow and finally seed (Hence the traditional Indian belief that out of a thousand drops of blood comes one drop of semen). The seed can produce a new life or if retained can transform into a magical substance called ojas that gives a man superhuman strength and occult powers. It also helps man escape from the cycle of rebirths.

In women, the red seed is shed every month. Hence, women are considered to be the weaker sex–they cannot attain 'spiritual' status because they have no access to ojas.

Men on the other hand can retain their white seed and become 'holy'. This is the reason given to explain the presence of greater number of holy men than holy women in India. This is also the reason why powerful warrior gods like Hanuman and Ayyappa are associated with both virility and celibacy.

In the Mahabharata, it is said that a male child is born when the white seed is stronger than the red seed. Thus a virile man (one whose semen is strong) fathers only male children. When the red seed is strong, the child is female. When both white and red seed are equal the child is neither this nor that (this was the traditional explanation for transexuality and homosexuality).

This belief perhaps explains why, despite modern genetic data on X and Y chromosomes, it is the woman in India who is 'blamed' for the feminization of the fetus and why she is given special diets to make the fetus male. This also explains why men feel angry and ashamed when they father daughters. The sex of the child is linked to their virility, or lack of it.

The Fertile Period: According to the Dharmashastras, though sex for pleasure was permitted, greater importance was given to sex for procreation. Men who had to father male offsprings were advised not to waste semen. They were advised to have intercourse only when the woman was in 'season'. This period was known as ritu and it roughly corresponds to the fertile period, the days in the menstrual cycle when a woman is most likely to conceive. Women were advised to make themselves beautiful and present themselves to their husbands after their periods.

If a woman who was in her fertile period approached a man for sex, he was obliged to have sex with her, the reason being – a fertile period should not be wasted. Every time a fertile period was lost, an ancestor lost his opportunity to be reborn. When a woman menstruated, she was held responsible for the opportunity last. She was equated with 'death' and hence considered polluted. She was asked to isolate herself during her periods, just as men who cremate the dead are isolated from the rest of the community.

A man who turned down a woman who approached him during her fertile period was described as a eunuch and held in disdain. In the Mahabharata, there are tales of women who approached men who were not their husbands during their fertile period because their husbands were unavailable. This was legally sanctioned. The sage Aruni was horrified when his guru's wife approached him for sex. She explained, "Your guru has gone on a pilgrimage. Asking you do fulfil his biological obligations is a lesser sin than wasting this fertile period."

The time when men and women had sex affected the nature of the child conceived. In the Bhagavata Purana is the story of Diti who approached her husband, the sage Kashyapa, for sex in the evening, a time reserved for prayers to ward of malevolent spirits. As a result, she conceived children who were demons. When a man approached a woman, before intercourse, he was expected to invoke the gods, especially Vishnu, the god who sustains natural order, and Tvastr or

Vishvakarma, the god who makes things. Only through their blessings, was it believed that a child could be conceived. This was known as the garbhadhana sanskara, or the rite of conception.

The Sterile Man: When a man could not produce a child on his wife, he was given the benefit of the doubt and allowed to marry again, and again. If despite this, he failed to father a child, it was concluded (but never explicitly stated) that he was sterile. In such circumstances, the Dharmashastras suggested that another man be invited to cohabit with the wives. This practice was known as niyoga or levirate.

In the Mahabharata, when king Vichitravirya (vichitra = odd; virya = virility) dies, his mother invited the sage Vyasa to produced children on his widowed daughters-in-law. Children thus produced were called children of Vichitravirya (the legal father), not the children of Vyasa (the biological or surrogate father).

It is alleged that this practice of niyoga is followed (rather clandestinely) even today, whereby sterile men make their wives cohabit with relatives or with holy men. Though religiously sanctioned, this practice is socially frowned upon and hence no one talks about it openly.

In the Kathasaritsagar, a collection of stories written in the 11th century AD, there is the story of a king who makes an offering of rice balls to his ancestors. As he about to throw the offering in the river, three hands reach up–one of a farmer, one of a priest and one of a warrior. The oracles revealed, "The farmer is the man who married your mother, the priest is the man who made your mother pregnant and the warrior is the man who took care of you." The king is advised to give the rice ball to the farmer because scriptures describe him as the true father. Thus was the practice of surrogate fatherhood established.

Artificial Insemination: There are tales that suggest that the ancients were familiar with the 'idea' of artificial insemination. For example, we learn of 'magic potions' being created by sages for queens of childless kings that makes the women pregnant. What were these magic substances? Could they be 'fertility drugs' or could they be metaphors for 'donated semen'?

One story states that the god Shiva once spurted semen when he saw Vishnu in the form of the celestial enchantress Mohini. Sages collected this semen and gave it to the wind-god Vayu who poured it into the 'ear' (a common mythical metaphor for the womb) of Anjani, a monkey, who gave birth to Hanuman, the monkey-god. Devoid of the mythical aura, one might say that the tale refers to the practice of artificial insemination: semen is transferred to the womb without sexual intercourse).

The Surrogate Mother: In the Bhagvata Purana, there is a story that suggests the practice of surrogate motherhood. Kans, the wicked king of Mathura, had imprisoned his sister Devaki and her husband Vasudeva because oracles had informed him that her child would be his killer. Every time she delivered a child, he smashed its head on the floor. He killed six children. When the seventh child was conceived, the gods intervened. They summoned the goddess Yogamaya and had her transfer the fetus from the womb of Devaki to the womb of Rohini (Vasudeva's other wife who lived with her sister Yashoda across the river Yamuna, in the village of cowherds at Gokul). Thus the child conceived in one womb was incubated in and delivered through another womb.

Serpent Power: In India today, when a couple does not have children, they often visit shrines and pray. Some visit holy men. Others offer cradles and dolls at shrines of mother-goddesses. Still others visit serpent shrines.

Serpents in many ancient cultures have been associated with fertility (don't forget that the serpent continues to be the symbol of medicine). There are many reasons for this. Probably because the serpent could slough its skin, it was believed to possess the power of rejuvenation. Probably because the serpent lived under the earth, it was believed to be the keeper of the secret that transforms seeds into plants. Farmers in India worship serpents in the hope they have a good harvest. Women worship serpents so that they are fertile and their husbands, virile.

In modern times, these practices may seem silly and superstitious. But for centuries they have offered hope to a people who believed that producing children was their biological duty. They offer the psychological support that today counsellors provide. While these support structures can turn into crutches, their place in culture demands the be understood rather than be summarily dismissed.

'Sevikas' Serve the Cause of Religion: As we stand on the threshold of the new millennium there is a realization that the modern world is becoming increasingly complex and chaotic. Incredible progress in the field of science and technology has made man's life very comfortable but has cost him dearly in terms of his peace of mind and sense of security.

The slow dissolution of traditional codes of social customs and beliefs, the steady breakdown of inherited sanctions of religion and law, the confusion in regard to social ethics is some of the most striking features of our age. This is making man turn towards religion in his search for solutions to his conflicts and dilemmas: for religion, world over, is considered an anchor and a means of support to mankind.

Since times immemorial woman has been fostering, preserving and perpetuating human values in the framework of religion at the family level. In the present context there is an added responsibility on woman to arrive at the essence of religion and propagate it effectively for the benefit of mankind. Thanks to the increased awareness and education of woman, she is able to discharge this responsibility.

1. *The Role of Woman in Religious Education:* Hinduism recognizes the mother as the first and foremost teacher. Hindu mythology is replete with stories of prenatal learning. It is rightly believed that the attitudes and values of the mother have a direct bearing on the personality of the child. There are examples where mothers have influenced the mindsets of their children who have gone on to become nation builders, social reformers and religious leaders. Great Indian leaders like Mahatma Gandhi, Swami Vivekananda, Shivaji, have all been groomed by their mothers through simple

stories, songs and lullabies subtly conveying the essence of religion to them.

Marriage and motherhood were treated as normal vocation for women all over the world until recently. In India, the role of the woman was largely confined to her own house and the upbringing of the children in a large household. There was no separate order to train woman teachers. Even now we find that women who have received modern education still adhere to household rituals religiously and identify the philosophy of life bound with these.

However, keeping with the present trends of the nuclear family and working mothers, many religious organizations are training woman in conducting religious discourses, organizing weekly workshops and religious training centres for children. These women are rightly called sevikas, for they serve the cause of religion.

2. *Dominant Values in Religious Education:* The underlying philosophy of each religion manifests itself in the value system of that religion. These values discipline the mind and a disciplined mind is the seat of happiness.

Hinduism deeply believes that material comforts do not lead to real happiness. Religious education in India is not dogmatic. It is a rational synthesis, which goes on gathering into itself new conceptions as philosophy progresses.

Hinduism believes that the fundamental truths are eternal and universal in nature. Therefore all religions have the same fundamental truths though approaches differ. Religious values form the bedrock of moral and ethical principles. Moral values are indispensable to maintain a good quality of life-set of dos and don'ts in the form of *yama* and *niyamas* are laid down in the Indian tradition. Yamas consists of concepts which discipline man like non-violence, honesty, self-control etc. Niyamas concentrate on the cultivation of virtues like purity, contentment, fortitude, devotion etc. The purpose of these is to eliminate the mental impurities such as greed, egotism, and cruelty. Ethical disciplines are prescribed depending on individual capacity and equipment. It is based on the premise that if individuals are virtuous social welfare would automatically follow.

3. *Is Religion Liberating or Restricting, Promoting or Frustrating?:* Whether religion liberates or frustrates an individual is a highly subjective question. The answer varies depending on the individual experiences and circumstances, attitude and approach. Religion should elevate an individual on to a higher plane of consciousness.

   As the Hindu term for religion, *dharma*, indicates it should provide sustenance and support. The ultimate aim of religion is to lead the individual on to the path of *Moksha* or salvation. Religion can be liberating when the emphasis is on the universal principles. When religious dogmas and creeds interfere with individual lifestyles, religion can be restricting.

   When the faith a person has in God generates a power, a soul force that gives him the courage to face the exigencies of life, religion is promoting. When religion imposes itself on man curtailing his freedom and thwarting his growth then it can be highly frustrating. If the supremacy of religion and of social tradition hampers the free pursuit of Philosophy, it leads to frustration.

   It is sad but true that in many religions there has been a misrepresentation of facts and a misinterpretation of ideas. Most of the social evils like poverty, ignorance and hatred are offshoots of misinterpreted religion. Many of the religious rituals and customs are outdated and outmoded so they have lost their significance and have become redundant. Every fresh epoch in the progress of thought has to be accompanied by a reform in logic. When it is not so, it has invariably led to suffering or revolt. Religion has to be a perennial spring of fresh thoughts and ideas and not a stagnant pool.

4. *Various Perspectives of Continuity of Tradition, Religious Ritual and Ceremony in Family Life and Society:* The practice of religious rituals and ceremony is what gives each family its unique identity and binds the members of the family. Traditions and customs of each family are a precious heritage that is passed on from generation to generation linking them emotionally, culturally and spiritually. Every religion can be understood to have three components-philosophy, mythology and rituals. Rituals are an accepted aspect of every religion which subtly project the philosophy of that religion. These rituals intend to discipline a person and help him adhere to positive values.

The Hindu way of life is ritualistic. His daily routine like bath, prayer and eating are not mere chores for a Hindu, they are sacred rituals with religious undertones. There are sixteen important rituals in the life of every Hindu from conception to burial. These rituals help in the smooth transition from one stage to another. The Hindu concept of rebirth and the rituals followed during funerals help him in taking away the agony and sorrow at death and make it appear as the next natural stage in life.

Most of the rituals, customs and festivals bring about a strong bonding in the community leading to social harmony. An individual learns to submit his personal interest for the common good. They also ensure the participation of the community in individual growth and development. The participation of woman (wife, mother) is obligatory in almost all Indian customs. She is a *sahadharmini*, an equal partner in the man's religious quest.

To ensure a harmonious existence in a religiously plural world Tolerance and Trust should be the hallmark of all religions. When one has faith in himself and the religion he practices then one learns to trust and to be tolerant. By virtue of the qualities of Tolerance and trust women have always been the custodians of the family traditions and rituals. By the very quality of their being women are the missionaries of the civilization they belong to. In the present global scenario women are expected to take on greater responsibilities and play a more assertive role.

Mantra is a syllable or string of syllables, from the Sanskrit language, first found in Hinduism. Mantras may or may not conform to grammatical rules. Their use varies with the school and philosophy associated with the mantra. They are primarily used as spiritual conduits, words and vibrations that instill one-pointedness in the devotee. Other purposes have included religious ceremonies to accumulating wealth, avoiding danger, or eliminating enemies. Mantras originated in India with Vedic Hinduism and were later adopted by Buddhists and Jains, now popular in various modern forms of spiritual practice which are based on practices of these Indian religions.

Mantra Generally

Mantras (Sanskrit) have some features in common with spells, in that they are a translation of the human will or desire into a form of action. As symbols, sounds are seen to effect what they symbolize. Vocal sounds are frequently thought of as having magical powers, or even of representing the words, or speech of God.

For the authors of the Hindu scriptures of the Upanishads, the syllable P 'Aum', itself constituting a mantra, represents Brahman, the Godhead, as well as the whole of creation. Merely pronouncing this syllable is to experience the divine in a very direct way.

Kukai suggests that all sounds are the voice of the Dharmakaya Buddha – *i.e.* as in Hindu Upanishads and Yoga thought, these sounds are manifestations of ultimate reality. We should not think that this is peculiar to Eastern culture, however. Words do have a mysterious power to affect us. Accepted scholarly etymology links the word with 'manas' meaning 'mind' and 'trana' for protection so that a mantra is something which protects the mind – however in practice we will see that mantra is considered to do far more than simply protect the mind.

For many cultures it is the written letters that have power– the Hebrew Kabbalah for instance. Letters can have an oracular function even. But in India special conditions applied that meant that writing was very definitely inferior to the spoken word. The Brahmins were the priestly caste of the Aryan peoples. It was they that preserved the holy writings–initially the Vedas, but later also the Upanishads.

For years, they were the only ones who knew the mantras or sacred formulas that had to be chanted at important occasions. However, with the advent of egalitarian Hindu schools of Yoga, Vedanta, Tantra and Bhakti, it is now the case that intra-family and community mantras are passed on freely as part of generally practiced Hindu religion. Such was the influence of the orthodox attitude of the elite nature of mantra knowledge, that even the Buddhists, who repudiated the whole idea of caste, and of the efficacy of the old rituals, called themselves the shravakas, that is 'the hearers'. A wise person in India was one who had "heard much". Mantras then are *sound symbols*. What they symbolize, and how they function depends on the context, and the mind of the person repeating them. Studies in sound symbolism suggest that vocal sounds have meaning whether we are aware of it or not.

And indeed that there can be multiple layers of symbolism associated with each sound. So even if we do not understand them, mantras are no simply meaningless mumbo jumbo–no vocal utterance is entirely without meaning. We can look at mantra is a range of different contexts to see what they can mean in those contexts: Om may mean something quite different to a Hindu and a Tibetan Buddhist.

Tantras eventually came to see the letters as well as the sounds as representatives of the divine, it was when Buddhism travelled to China from India, that a shift in emphasis towards writing came about. China lacked a ecclesiastic language like Sanskrit, and achieved its cultural unity by having a written language that was flexible in pronunciation but more precise in terms of the concepts that each character represented. In fact the Indians had several scripts which were all equally serviceable for writing Sanskrit. Hence, the Chinese prized written language more highly than did the Indian Buddhists, and the writing of mantras became a spiritual practice in its own right. So that whereas Brahmins had been very strict on correct pronunciation, the Chinese, and other Far-Eastern Buddhists were more concerned with correctly writing something down. The practice of writing mantras as a spiritual practice, became very refined in Japan, and the writing in the Siddham script in which the Sanskrit of many Buddhist Sutras where written, is only seen in Japan nowadays. However, mantra-repetition written in Sanskrit, with any number of scripts, is well-known to many Hindu sects in India as well.

Mantra in Hinduism

Mantras was originally conceived in the great Hindu scriptures, known as the Vedas. Within practically all Hindu scriptures, the writing is formed in painstakingly crafted two line 'shlokas' and most mantras follow this pattern, although mantras are often found in single line or even single word combinations.

The basic mantra is 'Aum', which in Hinduism is known as the 'pranava mantra,' the source of all mantras. The idea behind this is the Hindu philosophy of nama-rupa (name-form), which supposes that all ideas or entities in existence, within the phenomenological cosmos, have name and form. The basic name and form is the primordial vibration of Aum, as it is the first manifested nama-rupa of Brahman. Before existence and beyond existence, there is only One reality, Brahman, and the first manifestation of Brahman in existence is Aum.

For this very reason, Aum is considered to be the most fundamental and powerful mantra, and thus is prefixed and suffixed to all Hindu prayers. While some mantras may invoke individual Gods, the fundamental mantras, like 'Aum,' the 'Shanti Mantra,' the 'Gayatri Mantra' and others, all focus on the One reality.

In the Hindu Tantras the universe is sound. The supreme (para) brings forth existence through the Word (Shabda). Creation consists of vibrations at various frequencies and amplitudes giving rise to the phenomena of the world. The purest vibrations are the varna, the imperishable letters which are revealed to us, imperfectly as the audible sounds and visible forms. Varnas are the atoms of sound. A symbolic association was built up between letters and the elements, gods, signs of zodiac, parts of the body–letters became rich in these associations. For example in the Aitrareya-aranya-Upanishad we find:

> *"Mute consonants represent the earth, the sibilants the sky, the vowels heaven. The mute consonants represent fire, the sibilants air, the vowels the sun... The mute consonants represent the eye, the sibilants the ear, the vowels the mind"*

In effect each letter became a mantra and the language of the Vedas, Sanskrit, corresponds greatly to the nature of things. Thus Vedas come to represent reality itself. The syllable 'Om', represents the underlying unity of reality, which is Brahman

Japa

Japa was a concept of the Vedic sages that incorporates mantras as one of the main forms of worship, whose ultimate end is seen as moksha/liberation. Essentially, japa means repetition, and has become an established practice of all Hindu streams, from the various Yoga to Tantra. It involves repetition of a mantra over and over again, in cycles of auspicious numbers (in multiples of three), the most popular being 108. For this reason, Hindu malas (bead necklaces) developed, containing 108 beads and a head 'meru' bead. The devotee performing japa using his/her fingers counts each bead as he/she repeats the chosen mantra. Having reached 108 repetitions, if he/she wishes to continue another cycle of mantras, the devotee must turn the mala around without crossing the 'meru' bead and repeat. It is said that through japa the devotee attains one-pointedness, or extreme focus, on the chosen deity or principle idea of the mantra. The vibrations of the mantra are considered extremely important, and thus reverberations of the sound are supposed to awaken the prana or spiritual life force and even stimulate chakras according to many Hindu schools of thought.

Some Hindu Mantras

The most representative mantra of all the Hindu mantras is the famed 'Gayatri Mantra':

Om Bhur Buvah Svah, Tat Savitur Varenyam

Bhargo Devasya Dhimahi, Dhiyo Yo Nah Pracodayat

Gayatri Mantra is the most universal Hindu mantra and invokes the Brahman as the principle of knowledge and the illumination of the primordial Sun. Many Brahmins till today, in a tradition that has continued for at least 5,000 years, perform morning ablutions at the bank of a river and while holding the sacred thread given to them at adolescence, repeat the Gayatri Mantra.

Lead me from Ignorance to Truth

asato ma Sadhgamaya, tamaso ma jyothir-Gamaya

mrityor-ma amritham Gamaya, Om santi santi santih

"Aum Asato ma sad gamaya, tamaso ma jyotir gamaya, mrityor ma aamritaam gamaya"

"Aum Lead me from ignorance to truth, from darkness to light, from death to immortality."

Hare Krishna Mantra

A very famous mantra is that created by Shri Chaitanya Mahaprabhu, a great Vaishnava bhakta (loving devotee) of the Hindu Lord Vishnu in the 15th century. It is beloved by most Hindus as very powerful, Vaishnavs and Shaivaites alike:

"Hare Krishna Hare Krishna Krishna Krishna Hare Hare/Hare Rama Hare Rama Rama Rama Hare Hare"

When A.C. Bhaktivedanta brought his ISKCON (International Society for Krishna Consciousness) brand of Hindu Vaishnavism to the West, he framed the "Hare Krishna" mantra as the sole mantra for moksha/liberation and his sect is now commonly known in the West by the name 'Hare Krishnas.'

***Shanti Mantra*:** The Mantra of Peace:

Aum Saha Navavatu/Saha Nau Bhunaktu/Saha Viryam Karvavahe/Tejaswi Navadhi Tamastu/Ma Vidvishavahe/Aum Shanti Shanti Shantihi/Hari Hi Aum

(Om, May the Lord protect us, May the Lord allow us to enjoy, May we work together. May our studies be thorough and faithful, May we never misunderstand each other, Om, Peace, Peace, Peace!)

Universal Prayer

Sarvesaam Svastir Bhavatu/Sarvesam Santir Bhavatu/ Sarvesam Purnam Bhavatu/Sarvesam mangalam Bhavatu (May good befall all, May there be peace for all, May all be fit for perfection, and May all experience that which is auspicious.)

Sarve Bhavantu Sukhinaha/Sarve Santu niramayaha/Sarve Badrani Pasyantu/ma Kascidh-dhuhkha Bhaga-Bhavet (Om, May all be happy. May all be healthy, May we all experience what is good and let no one suffer, Om, Peace, Peace, Peace!)

Thou Are That

Tat Twam Asi

To list most of the main Hindu mantras would take reams of paper. Indeed, simple two-lined shlokas from holy Hindu texts like the Vedas, Upanishads, Bhagwad Gita, Yoga Sutra, even the Mahabharata and Ramayana, are considered powerful and finely honed enough to be repeated to great effect.

A very common mantra is formed by taking a deity's name and saluting it with in such a manner: 'Aum namah' or 'Aum Jai (Hail!)' or several such permutations. Common examples are 'Aum namah Shivaya' (Aum to Lord Shiva), 'Om Jai Jagadish Hare' (Salutations to the Universal God Vishnu), 'Aum Shri Ganeshaya Namah' (Aum to Shree Ganesha) and 'Jai Ma Kali.' Needless to say, there are more mantras of this sort than names of the Hindu deities. Another example of Hindu mantras is seen in the Surya Namaskara, whose practice is found recorded as far back as in the Hindu scripture of the Ramayana. As each of the twelve postures is performed, a salutatory mantra is recited to the Lord Surya, the Sun.

The Hindu Bija Mantra

In Hinduism the concept of mantra as mystical sounds was carried to its logical conclusion in 'seed' (Sanskrit *bija*) mantras that have no precise meaning but instead are thought to carry within their sounds connections to various spiritual principles and currents. For example, worship of the Mother Goddess Kali, in mantra form, is famously reduced to the powerful Bija mantras of the Shakti tradition of Hinduism:

"Aum Kreeng Kreeng Kreeng Hoong Hoong Hreeng Hreeng Dakshina Kalike |

Kreeng Kreeng Kreeng Hoong Hoong Hreeng Hreeng Swaha | |"

Of course, the most revered of all Bija mantras is Om/Aum.

The Bija mantra is part of the Hindu monist theory that while reality manifests itself as many/multiple, it is ultimately one.

Hindu Scriptures

Hindu scripture, which is known as "Shastra" is predominantly written in Sanskrit.

Classification of Hindu Scripture

Hindu scripture is divided into two categories: Sruti – that which is heard (*i.e.*, revelation) and Smriti – that which is remembered (*i.e.*, tradition, not revelation).

The Sruti scriptures are of divine origin, whose truths were directly revealed to ancient rishis (sages) in their deep meditations. The Smriti scriptures are of human origin and were written to explain the Sruti writings and make them understandable and meaningful to the general population. Sruti scriptures include the four Vedas (Rig, Yajur, Sama and Atharva) and the Bhagwad Gita, and constitute the highest religious authority.

Smriti literature includes Itihasas (epics like Ramayana, Mahabharata), Puranas (mythological texts), Agamas (theological treatises) and Darshanas (philosophical texts). Hindu texts are typically seen to revolve around many levels of reading, namely the gross or physical, the subtle, and the supramental. This allows for many levels of understanding as well, implying that the truth of the texts can only be realized with the spiritual advancement of the reader.

Vedas

The Vedas are referred to as the Shruti. The Vedas are the oldest extant Hindu texts. The ideas expressed in the Vedas were traditionally handed down orally from father to son and from teacher to disciple. Therefore, these ideas had been in circulation for a long time before their codification and compilation, which are attributed to a Rishi named Veda Vyasa (literally, "the splitter of the Vedas,"). He was named that way as it was he who was accredited with forming the large mass of knowledge and hymns of the Vedas and 'splitting' them into comprehensible sections for the rest of humanity.

The Vedas have been divided in various ways. One simple way is to divide the Vedas into two sections according to their subject matter:

1. The Karma Kanda ("the action part"), deals with karma, rituals, and sacrifices the purpose of which is to attain material prosperity on earth and the benefits of heaven after death, and
2. The Jnana Kanda ("the knowledge part"), is concerned with the spiritual Knowledge that brings liberation from ignorance and realization of the Ultimate Truth. The Upanishads constitute a major portion of the Jnana Kanda.

The Vedas are four in number. The Rig-, Yajur-, Sama-and Atharva Vedas represent various shakhas, or branches, of knowledge.

Upanishads

The Upanishads ("Sittings Near) (a Teacher]") are part of the Hindu Shruti; these religious scriptures primarily discuss philosophy and "cosmic reality"; they also contain transcripts of various debates or discussions. They are commentaries on the Vedas and their branch of Hinduism is called Vedanta.

Bhagwad Gita

Many a Hindu has said that the most succinct and powerful abbreviation of the overwhelmingly diverse realm of Hindu thought is to be found in the Bhagwad Gita. Essentially, it is a microcosm of Vedic, Yogic, Vedantic and even Tantric thought of the Hindu fold. Bhagwad Gita (literally: Song of the God) is a part of the epic poem Mahabharata and is revered in Hinduism. It speaks not only to Vaishnavas but to all people, and it is accepted by the members of all Hindu streams as a seminal text. Indeed, the "tag line" of each chapter of the Bhagwad Gita refers to the book as the "Gita Upanishad" and as a "scripture of yoga," thereby establishing that in this text, Lord Krishna speaks the truths of yoga and the Upanishads for all.

What holds the devotee's mind foremost is Krishna's repeated injunction to abandon the mortal self to the infinite love of the Lord. He not only speaks to the mind and to the Hindu's innate sense of Dharma, but calls for overwhelming love. By loving God one also loves the immortal Self, finds harmony in oneself, and finds oneself at peace with the entire cosmos. The Gita speaks of cultivating the intellect, properly using the body, and always remaining equipoised in relation to the greater Self. The Bhagwad Gita truly presents itself as a liberation scripture universal in its message.

Itihasas

The Itihasas (itihasa is Sanskrit for "history" or "thus verily happened") are narrative traditions composed as supplementary Vedic literature to helps explain the rituals of the Vedas and the highly compressed philosophy of the Vedanta-sutras by using historical events of the universe and factual stories of many great sages, and so forth.

Mahabharata

Included in the Itihasas is the Mahabharata, written by Srila Vyasadeva. It is an historical epic about the great kingdom of Bharatavarsa, or the region of India. It contains 110,000 couplets making it the longest poem and greatest epic in world literature. It is divided into 18 sections called parvas, such as the Adi Parva, etc.

It is a treasure house of Indian lore and holds within it a code of life for ethical, social and spiritual relations. Throughout this great epic every sort of human situation is described and every kind of emotion is aroused. There is a saying that if it is not in the Mahabharata then it is not to be found.

Ramayana

The Ramayana consists of 24,000 verses, and first written during the time of Lord Ramachandra by the great poet Valmiki, which describes the life of Lord Ramachandra, an incarnation of God, and His wife Sita. This is also a most touching and exciting adventure which explains how Lord Ramachandra lived in the forest and fought against and killed the great demon Ravana and his armies in order to rescue His wife, Sita, who had been kidnapped.

Many other stories are included in this storehouse of wisdom that has been an inspiration for thousands of years to all people who have read it. In the incarnation of Lord Ramachandra, God appears as the perfect king and ruler, and inspires all His subjects with the greatest love for Him.

Written in high Sanskrit in the form of rhyming couplets, the Ramayana contains seven sections (kandas):

1. Bal Kanda-Rama's boyhood
2. Ayodhya Kanda-Rama's life in Ayodhya until his banishment
3. Aranya-Rama's life in the forest and his abduction by Ravana
4. Kishkinda-Rama's stay at Kishkinda, the capital of his monkey ally Sugriva
5. Sundara-Rama's journey to Sri Lanka
6. Yuddha (or Lanka)-Rama's battle with Ravana, the recovery of Sita and their return to Ayodhya
7. Uttara-Rama's life as king in Ayodhya, the birth of his two sons, Sita's test of innocence and return to her mother, and Rama's demise

Puranas

The Puranas are a vast literature of stories and allegory. There are 18 primary Puranas, 18 upa-puranas, and numerous minor Puranas. 18 are considered to be Mahapuranas, or Great Puranas, and thus authoritative references on the Gods and

Goddesses, religious rites and holy places (most of which are in the Indian subcontinent, known as Bharat). Six devoted to worship of Shiva, six to Vishnu, and six to Brahma. The primary Puranas describe these five subjects: sarga (creation), pratisarga (recreation), vamsa (history of the sages), manvantara (periods of Manu), and vamsanucarita (geneology of kings). The most important Puranas are:

- Vishnu Purana
- Bhagavata Purana (Krishna)
- Shiva Purana
- Markendeya Purana (to the Goddess)

Lord Vishnu is the predominating Deity of the following six Puranas:

- Bhagavata Purana has 18,000 verses, and is a jewel of the Vedas, providing all instruction on the science of self-realization.
- Vishnu Purana has 23,000 verses, including stories of various devotees, a description of varnasrama, the six angas of the Veda, a description of the age of Kali, a description of Sveta Varaha Kalpa, and Vishnu dharmotara.
- Naradiya Purana has 25,000 verses, and contains a synopsis of the complete philosophy. It describes Jagannath Puri, Dwarka, Badrinath, and other holy sites.
- Padma Purana has 55,000 verses, and contains the glory of Srimad-Bhagavatam, and stories of Rama, Jagannath, Matsya, Ekadasi, Bhrgu, and others.
- Garuda Purana has 19,000 verses, and discuss the subject of Bhagwad-gita, reincarnation, Vishnu-sahaasra-nama, and a description of Tarsya Kalpa.
- Varaha Purana has 24,000 verses, and describes the different vratas and Lord Vishnu's glories.

Lord Brahma is the predominating Deity of the following six Puranas:

- Brahmanda Purana has 12,000 verses, and describes the vedangas and the Adi Kalpa.

- Brahmavaivarta Purana has 18,000 verses, and describes the glories and pastimes of Sri Sri Radha-Krishna.
- Markandeya Purana has 9,000 verses, and tells the stories of Rama and Krishna.
- Bhavisya Purana has 14,500 verses, and describes the glories of devotional service to Sri Krishna, along with the prediction of Lord Chaitanya.
- Vamana Purana contains 10,000 verses, and tells the story of Lord Trivikrama.
- Brahma Purana has 10,000 verses, and describes the teachings of Lord Brahma to Daksa.

Lord Shiva is the predominating Deity of the following six Puranas:

- Matsya Purana has 14,000 verses, and describes the Vamana and Varaha Kalpas, and temple construction.
- Kurma Purana has 17,000 verses, and describes the conversation between Krishna and the Sun-god, Dhanvantari, and the Laksmi Kalpa.
- Linga Purana has 10,000 verses, and describes the glories of Lord Nrsmhadeva, the stories of Janardhana and Ambarisa, and the glories of Gayatri.
- Shiva Purana has 24,000 verses, divided into six samhitas. It was recited by Vedavyasa's disciple Romaharshana.
- Skanda Purana has 81,000 verses, and describes the slaughter of the demon Tarakdsura by Skanda (Subrahmanya). Skanda Purana is very similar to the Kumarasambhava of Kalidasa.
- Agni Purana has 15,400 verses, and describes Salagrama and the Isana Kalpa.

Agamas & Tantras

Scriptures of the three major theological traditions: Shaivism, Vaishnavism, and Shaktism.

Manuals of Philosophy

The Sutras

- Brahma Sutra: Vedanta philosophy of Sage Vyasa
- Mimamsa Sutra: Philosophy of rites and rituals of Sage Jaimini
- Nyaya Sutra: Logical analysis of Sage Gautama (not Buddha)
- Vaisheshika Sutra: Atomic school of philosophy of Sage Kanada
- Sankhya Sutras: Sankhya philosophy of Sage Kapila
- Yoga Sutras: Yoga philosophy of Sage Patanjali

Essence of Hindu Scriptures for Mankind

During their spiritual quest, the ancient rishis experienced sparks of divinity in all things and beings of the world. The vision of the Hindu scriptures is thus a vision of the unity of all existence, summarized as follows:

- There are many ways of conceiving the Supreme Reality (Brahman) and numerous ways of approaching It. To insist that one's own way is the only way is thus wrong and harmful.
- God is the source of goodness and truth. Man's goal in life is to seek union with Him. This union can be sought in many ways, all requiring sincerity of purpose, self-sacrifice and discipline.
- The highest religious experience is the one in which an individual transcends the intellect and realizes God immediately.
- The concept of "survival-of-the-fittest" is God's law for the animals. Harmlessness to all creatures is His law for humans.
- There is natural order (rita) inherent in the natural world. There must be moral order (dharma) inherent in human life. Everyone must be responsible for his (or her) actions and their consequences (karma). We cannot blame God for our ills.

- Individual responsibility and one's ethics are a foundation for individual happiness and social stability.
- The universe is a wheel-of sacrifice (yajna). At the beginning the Supreme Lord performed self-sacrifice to create the universe and set the wheel in motion. The water sacrifices to form clouds, the clouds sacrifice to make rains, the rains sacrifice to grow food, and the food sacrifices to feed humans. In turn, humans must sacrifice for the welfare of the Mother Earth and all its creatures.
- There is no intrinsic evil in Nature nor any evil force in the world to oppose God. Man commits evil only due to ignorance (maya).
- Love, freedom and peace are fruits of the tree of divine consciousness, which can be planted by worshipping God regularly and systematically through yoga, meditation, study of scriptures, by performing religious rites and ceremonies-as enjoined by scriptures-and selfless work.

Hindu Scriptures and Authoritative Texts

Hindu authoritative writings constitute an immense literature. Keep in mind that the vast family (of religions, beliefs, sects, traditions) that constitutes Hinduism, not all that is listed here is considered sacred (or is even known) by every Hindu.

The categories of literature mentioned here are those that have had the most effect on the last 3000 years of Hindu thought.

The writings of Hinduism fall into two sections: *Shruti* and *Smriti*.

Shruti is considered a closed canon, and cannot be added to. Smriti, which is based in Shruti, is considered an open canon, and can be added to—even to this day. The two most well-known texts of Hinduism are the *Rig Veda* and the *Bhagwad Gita*. The Rig Veda (Shruti) is not only the oldest text in Hinduism, it is one of the oldest texts of any Indo-European language. The Bhagwad-Gita (Smriti) is but one book of the epic *Mahabharata*.

- Shruti means *that which is heard*, and refers to the works of ancient, unknown poets and writers considered to be fully authoritative as Holy Scripture. Modern scholarship classifies Shruti in four main collections called *Vedas*. These are the *Rig Veda, Sama Veda, Yajur Veda,* and *Atharva Veda*.

Each Veda contains several kinds of writings or general components:

- *Samhitas*—collections of hymns, verses and sayings.
- *Brahmanas* (9 existing)—texts that explicate the homologies, the mystical, philosophical, anthropological and cosmological meanings of the Vedic sacrifice.
- *Aranyakas*—or Forest Books—texts featuring esoteric meditations about the meaning of the sacrifice and the structure of the cosmos.
- *Upanishads* (108 in total, of which 12-18 are considered of principal importance). A codified collection of texts said to reveal hidden eternal truths regarding the metaphysical connections between the ultimate and the human worlds.

SMRITI means *that which is remembered*, and refers to less ancient writings and oral traditions that are not considered as authoritative as Shruti. Among the various literary forms of Smriti are:

- *Puranas*—Ancient Narratives. Compendiums of Hindu mythology, history, philosophy, ritual and much else. Many discuss technical subjects such as architecture, ethics and medicine (human and veterinary). It is traditionally agreed that there are 18 major Puranas, however, it is not always agreed upon as to which these 18 are. The 29 listed here were composed between ca 200 CE-1700 CE
- *Epics*, of which there are two—the Mahabharata and the Ramayana.
    - o *Mahabharata—The Great War of the Bharata Tribe*, consists of 18 books, including the *Bhagwad-Gita*

or The Song of the Lord, which is the 6th book. This epic, composed over a time span of 600-800 years (ca. 300 BC.-300 CE), is ten times the size of the *Illiad* and the *Odyssey* combined.

- o *Ramayana—The Deeds of Rama*. This epic was composed over a 400 year time span (roughly ca. 200 BC.-200 CE).

- *Dharmashastras, Dharmasutras* (lawbooks). Texts of classical teachings pertaining to the proper conduct of virtually every aspect of human life including life-cycle rituals, correct livelihood, the order of society, statecraft and law.
- *Tantras*. Dating from about the 7th century CE, these writings deal with esoteric practices (sometimes quite unorthodox to the Hindu societal laws).
- *Darshana Literature*. Treatises of the various schools of Indian philosophy.

Mahabharata Epic: The Bhagwad-Gita (another translation) (another translation) The Bhagwad-Gita (Prabhupada) The Bhagwad-Gita (Arnold) The Bhagwad-Gita (Beck)

6

Sacred Places of Hindus

India is a vast country, peopled with diverse and ancient civilizations, and its religious geography is highly complex. To grasp the complexity of the situation, it is important to consider two aspects of Indian life: its characteristic of being an ethnic and cultural mosaic, and the ancient rural foundations of many of its religious and cultural patterns.

The process of racial and cultural mixture that began in India more than 5000 years ago has been continuous into historical times. Although isolated from the rest of Asia by oceans on three sides and impassable mountain ranges to the north, India has experienced a near-constant influx of differing cultural influences, coming mostly by way of the far northwest. India in the third millennium BC was inhabited in the tropical south by a people called the Dravidians, in the central and northeastern regions by aboriginal hill and forest tribes, and in the northwest by the highly advanced Indus Valley civilization known as the Harappan culture.

The religion of the city-building Harappan peoples seems to have been a fertility cult centred on the Great Mother, while the rural Dravidians and the various tribal cultures worshipped a wide variety of nature spirits, both benevolent and demonic. Around 1800 BC a nomadic people from the steppes of Central Asia entered northwest India. Known as the Aryans, they brought with them a sophisticated religion called Vedism, or Brahmanism, which worshipped such powerful gods as Indra, the god of rain; Agni, the god of fire; and Surya, the sun god. Continuing waves of Aryan invaders entered northwest India until about 600 BC. During this time the religion of Vedism developed an increasingly complex form with esoteric rituals and magical Sanskrit chants codified in the sacred texts known as the Vedas.

The religion identified as Hinduism did not appear until the centuries immediately preceding the Christian era.

Hinduism is the aggregation of innumerable religious cults, beliefs, customs and practices deriving from the Vedism of the Aryans, the Great Mother fertility cults of the Harappan peoples, and the animistic, shamanistic, and devotional practices of the widely varying, rural-dwelling indigenous cultures of south, central, and eastern India. Adding to and further enriching this mix were the concurrently developing religions of Buddhism and Jainism. Indian culture has thus developed a fascinating collection of religious beliefs and customs that range from simple animistic worship of nature spirits in a common rock or tree to the complex, highly codified Brahmanic rituals practiced at the great pilgrimage centres.

In India we find the oldest continually operating pilgrimage tradition in the entire world. The practice of pilgrimage in India is so deeply embedded in the cultural psyche and the number of pilgrimage sites is so large that the entire subcontinent may actually be regarded as one grand and continuous sacred space. Our earliest sources of information on the matter of sacred space come from the Rig Veda and the Atharva Veda. While the act of pilgrimage is not specifically discussed in these texts, mountain valleys and the confluences of rivers are spoken of with reverence, and the merits of travel to such places are mentioned.

Following the Vedic period the practice of pilgrimage seems to have become quite common, as is evident from sections of the great epic, the Mahabharata (350 BC), which mentions more than 300 sacred sites spanning the entire continent. It is highly probable that most of these sites had long been considered sacred by the aboriginal inhabitants of the region, but came to be listed in the Mahabharata only as these regions came under the influence of Aryanization. By the time of the writing of the Puranas (sacred texts of the 2nd to

15th centuries AD), the number of sacred sites listed had grown considerably, reflecting both the ongoing assimilation of pre-Aryan sacred places and the increased importance of pilgrimage as a customary religious practice.

Hindus call the sacred places to which they travel tirthas, and the action of going on a pilgrimage tirtha-yatra. The Vedic word tirtha means river ford, steps to a river, or place of pilgrimage. In Vedic times the word may have concerned only those sacred places associated with water, but by the time of the Mahabharata, tirtha had come to denote any holy place, be it a lake, mountain, forest, or cave. Tirthas are more than physical locations, however. Devout Hindus believe them to be spiritual fords, the meeting place of heaven and earth, the locations where one crosses over the river of samsara (the endless cycle of birth, death and rebirth) to reach the distant shore of liberation. Writing in Benares: City of Light, Diana Eck speaks of tirthas as being:

> *"primarily associated with the great acts and appearances of the gods and heroes of Indian myth and legend. As a threshold between heaven and earth, the tirtha is not only a place for the upward crossings of people's prayers and rites, it is also a place for the downward crossings of the gods. These divine descents are the well-known avataras of the Hindu tradition. Indeed, the words tirtha and avatara come from related verbal roots.one might say that the avataras descend, opening the doors of the tirthas so that men and women may ascend in their rites and prayers."*

Although tirthas are primarily those places where a god or goddess or some spirit has dwelled or is still dwelling, there is another reason certain places may be accorded sanctity in the Hindu tradition. Saintly individuals who lead exemplary lives imbue their environments with the holiness that accrues from their spiritual practices. Devotees who had visited the saints while they were alive often continued to seek inspiration in the same places after the saint had died. Over many centuries, folk tales about the lives of the saints attained legendary proportions, attracting pilgrims from great distances. If miracles were reported at the shrine, the saint's legends would spread across the entire country, attracting still more pilgrims.

In India all temples are considered sacred places and thus religious visitors to the temples may be described as pilgrims. For the purpose of our discussion, however, for a temple to be considered a true pilgrimage shrine it must have a long-term history of attracting pilgrims from a geographic area beyond its immediate region. Given this condition, the number of pilgrimage sites in India is still extremely large; one text, the Kalyana Tirthanka, describes 1,820 shrines of importance.

Based on years of research and pilgrimage in India, I have chosen a smaller number of shrines, approximately 150, as the primary pilgrimage sites. Those sites include the Four Dhams or Divine Abodes at the four compass points; the Seven Sacred Cities and their primary temples; the Jyotir, Svayambhu, and Pancha Bhutha Linga temples; the Shakti Pitha temples; the Kumbh Mela sites; major Vaishnava sites; the Nava Graha Sthalas (temples of the planets); the seven sacred rivers; the four Mutts of Sri Adi Shankaracharya (Badrinath/Joshimath, Puri, Sringeri, and Dwarka); and certain other shrines that do not fit into any of the categories listed here.

In discussing pilgrimage places in the Hindu tradition, it is important to say a few words about the number and diversity of deities in Hinduism and about the iconic and aniconic forms in which those deities are found. The personification of the mysterious forces of the universe into the anthropomorphic deities of the Hindu tradition involves both a convergence into certain supreme deities (the main three deities today are the gods Shiva and Vishnu and the goddess Shakti) and a splintering into a myriad of lesser deities. Certain writers call this polytheism, but the term is inaccurate in this case. No Hindu seriously believes in the multiplicity of gods but rather is aware that each of the many gods and goddesses are merely aspects of the One God (who is also the god of all other religions). The majority of Hindus ally their beliefs with one or the other of the three cults, worshipping Shiva, Vishnu, or Shakti as the highest principle. In doing so they do not deny the existence of the other two deities but regard them as complementary, though minor, expressions of the same divine power. Hinduism is thus, in its essence, monotheistic; a Hindu's worship of a particular personal deity is always done with the awareness that all deities are simply representations of one unconditioned, transcendental, supreme existence, known as Brahman. Each of the greater and lesser deities is understood as a sort of window or lens through which the whole of reality may be glimpsed.

The primary intention of a pilgrim's visit to a holy site is to receive the darshan of the deity resident in the temple's inner sanctum or open-air shrine. The word darshan, difficult to translate into English, generally means the pilgrim's having a sight and/or experience of the deity. Hindus believe that the deity is actually manifest in the image, statue, or icon of the temple. To receive the darshan of the deity is to have a spiritual communion with it. The image of the deity may either be an iconic, or representational, image that bears some resemblance to its mythic subject; or an aniconic form that merely symbolizes the deity.

In a large number of celebrated shrines in India no beautiful statues of the gods and goddesses are found, but only aniconic blocks of stone or stumps of wood. This tradition of aniconic images derives from the rural folk religions of ancient India and bears witness to the great antiquity of the sanctity of certain places.

The shrine in its initial phase may have been only a crude little hut covering a stone that both represented and contained some spirit of the natural world. As millennia passed and the small rural village grew slowly into a larger and larger town, both the myths concerning the stone and the shrine surrounding that stone were richly elaborated. It is therefore important when studying or visiting the monumental pilgrimage shrines of India to remember that they had their architectural genesis in the simple nature sanctuaries of the pre-Aryan rural folk.

The myths and legends of these sacred places have their roots in the ancient peoples' felt experience of the characteristics or qualities of the natural place. The various mythological personality characteristics of the deities in pilgrimage shrines may therefore be interpreted as metaphors for the way in which the spirit of the place has affected human beings.

This spirit of place is not just a fanciful story, it is an actuality, an energy, a presence that touches human beings and affects them profoundly. Why are certain places said to be the dwelling place of a feminine deity and others the dwelling place of a masculine deity? Is it not perhaps because some ancient rural people, deeply in touch with the earth as a living entity, sensed either a feminine or masculine presence at a place and spoke about it in anthropomorphic terms? These terms were then given representational form by the artistic rendering of a statue or image.

Looking deeper into this matter, let us then ask why there are not simply male and female deities but, more precisely, why there are different kinds of male and female deities? Conventional explanations refer to such things as the fanciful human imagination, the rich and varied proto-religious inputs into formative Hinduism, and prehistoric deification of charismatic human figures into legendary archetypes. While all these things did occur, they are not the only explanations.

The central premise of my theory is that the different personality characteristics of the deities derive from the various characteristics of the Earth spirit as it manifests at different geographical locations. To understand the quality or character or power of a place, we need only study the nature of the deity enshrined there. Encoded in the deity's mythological form is a clear message telling us how the sacred site will affect us.

The most recent Ice Age, which reached its greatest extent between 20,000 and 18,000 BC, lowered global sea level as much as 350-400 feet by capturing much of the earth's water in massive continent-sized glaciers. Geologists calculate that nearly 5 percent of the earth's surface (an area of ten million square miles, or 25 million square kilometres, or the combined areas of the United States and all of South America) was then covered by rising sea-levels since the end of the last Ice Age. Geologists, specializing in the new science of inundation mapping, are able to produce accurate models of ancient shorelines at specific dates.

Allahabad

According to Hindu mythology, the creator god Lord Brahma chose a piece of land at which the three sacred rivers-the Ganga, the Yamuna and the mythical Saraswati-would flow into a quiet confluence. That land, now known as Allahabad ("City of God"), is one of the most sacred pilgrimage destinations of India.

Today's Allahabad is on the site of the ancient holy city of Prayaga ("confluence of rivers"), one of four sites of the Kumbh Mela.

In 1575, the Mughal Emperor Akbar realized the area's strategic importance as a waterway and founded a lavish city there, which he named Allahabad. The monarch also built a impressive fort on the riverbanks, which still stands today.

Under British rule, Allahabad was the capital of the United Provinces till the 1920s. It was well-known as an educational centre, and in the first few decades of the 20th century, the Allahabad University had earned for itself the epithet of "Oxford of the East." It was also a major literary centre for Hindi, and numerous literatures were connected to it in some way or the other.

Allahabad was at the forefront of political activities during India's struggle for independence. Alfred Park in Allahabad was the site where, in 1931, noted revolutionary Chandrashekhar Azad killed himself when surrounded by the British police. After independence, the park was renamed as Chandrashekhar Azad Park. Modern Allahabad is an important city where history, culture and religion meet like the three sacred rivers. The sacred Sangam is the confluence of three of the holiest rivers in Hindu mythology-Ganga, Yamuna and the mythical Saraswati. It is believed that it is at the Sangam, that a few drops of the nectar 'Amrit Bindu' fell, making its waters truly magical. It is during the festivals of Kumbh Mela and the Ardh Kumbh that the Sangam truly comes alive, attracting the devout from all across the country.

Built by the Mughal Emperor Akbar in 1583 AD, the Allahabad Fort stands on the banks of the Yamuna, near the confluence site. In its prime, the fort was unrivalled for its design, construction and craftsmanship. This huge, majestic fort has three magnificent galleries, flanked by high towers.

Within the underground Patalpuri Temple, which is inside the fort, lies the Akshayavat, or immortal tree. The gigantic Ashoka Pillar, of polished sandstone, stands 10.6 m high, dating back to 232 BC. The pillar has several edicts, and a Persian inscription of Emperor Jahangir inscribed on it, commemorating his accession to the throne.

The Hanuman Temple is a unique temple at the Sangam. It is the only one in North India where the idol of Lord Hanuman is in a reclining posture. Situated near Saraswati Ghat, on the banks of the Yamuna, the Mankameshwar Temple is one of the famous Shiva temples of Allahabad.

Also in Allahabad is the All Saints Cathedral, one of the finest cathedrals in India. Designed more than a century ago by Sir William Emerson, the structure has exceptional stained glass windows.

"Mela" means "festival" in Hindi. The Magh Mela takes place every year in the month of Magh (January-February) of the Hindu calendar.

The Kumbh Mela takes place every 12 years and has more significance than the Magh Mela. These fairs take place on the banks of the holy river Ganga. In the Kumbh Mela of 2001, almost 75 million people visited the banks of Allahabad's rivers to take part in the festivals.

During the Melas, entire temporary townships are built at Allahabad, including functioning hospitals, fire stations, police stations, restaurants and other facilities.

Badrinath

Badrinath is one of the four sites in India's Char Dham pilgrimage. It is sacred as the seat of the god Vishnu in his aspect of Badrinarayan.

It is generally a two-day's journey from either Kedarnath or one of the main disembarkation points on the plains. The temple and its substantial surrounding village are accessible by road. By far the most important of the four Char Dham sites, Badrinath receives many more visitors than the other three sites.

As the route to Badrinath is for much of the way also the route to Hemkund Sahib, an important Sikh pilgrimage site, the road to Badrinath is especially crowded.

The temple of Badrinath is a striking building whose bright colours evoke the painted Buddhist *ghompas* of the region—some think the temple was originally controlled by Buddhists.

Bodhgaya

Bodhgaya (also written Bodh Gaya) is the site of the Buddha's enlightenment and the most important of four main Buddhist pilgrimage destinations. Known as Uruvela in the Buddha's time, the city of Bodhgaya is now a village of about 30,000 permanent residents in northeastern India.

The two major sacred sites in Bodhgaya are the Mahabodhi Temple and the Bodhi Tree, around which many other temples and monasteries of various Buddhist traditions (Japanese, Tibetan, Bhutanese and others) have been built.

Every year, millions of Buddhist pilgrims, mainly from Asian countries, flock to Bodhgaya to be inspired, dissipate negative karma and earn merit by visiting the holy site where the Buddha became the Buddha ("Enlightened One"). Throughout the day and night in the height of the pilgrimage season, monks in colourful robes can be seen meditating where the Buddha did, studying dharma texts, making offerings to the many statues and stupas on the site, and circumambulating (walking around) the sacred Mahabodhi Temple.

Bodhi Tree

This is a descendent of the tree under which Siddhartha Gautama attained enlightenment after 49 days of meditation and became the Buddha, the "Enlightened One."

Mahabodhi Temple

This sacred stupa marks the site of the Buddha's enlightenment and is the main destination for Buddhist pilgrims. The temple dates from the 2nd century AD but has been restored over the years.

Char Dham Pilgrimage

The Char Dham ("four abodes") is the most important pilgrimage circuit in the Indian Himalayas. Located in the Garhwal section of the state of Uttaranchal (formerly the northwestern section of Uttar Pradesh), the circuit consists of four sites: Yamunotri, Gangotri, Kedarnath and Badrinath. While each site in the circuit has an autonomous history and significance that predates and remains distinct from their status as a circuit, inclusion in the Char Dham has, over time, caused them be viewed together in popular imagination and actual pilgrimage practice.

The origins of the Char Dham are obscure. Originally, Char Dham was a name reserved for India's most famous pilgrimage circuit, four important temples—Puri, Rameshwaram, Dwarka, and Badrinath—grouped together by the great 8th century reformer and philosopher Shankaracharya (Adi Shankara), into the archetypal All-India pilgrimage circuit to the four cardinal points of the subcontinent.

At some point, Badrinath, the last visited and the most important of the four sites in the original Char Dham, also became the cornerstone site of a Himalayan pilgrimage circuit dubbed the Chota (little) Char Dham. Unlike the original Char Dham, the sites of the Chota Char Dham do not share a single sectarian affiliation. Instead, the three major sectarian movements in modern devotional Hinduism all have representation, with the Vaishnava site Badrinath joined by one Shaiva site (Kedarnath) and two Devi sites (Yamunotri and Gangotri).

As late as the mid-twentieth century, the "Chota" designation was still used consistently to delineate the Himalayan version of the Char Dham. This usage probably reflects the relative importance of the circuit for most of its history. Accessible until recent times only after a two-month trek that repeatedly exceeds 4000 meters, the Chota Char Dham was long dominated by wandering ascetics and religious professionals, along with a handful of devoted retires and wealthy patrons (who could afford an entourage). While the individual sites and the circuit as a whole were important to Hindus on the plains below, they were not a particularly visible aspect of yearly religious culture.

After the 1962 war between India and China, however, accessibility to the Chota Char Dham improved drastically, as India's short-lived efforts at Himalayan expansionism required massive infrastructure investments. As pilgrim buses began to arrive, the Chota appendix seems to have dropped away, though the prefix "Himalayan" (Hindi: *Himalaya ki Char Dham*) is sometimes still added to avoid confusion.

With infrastructure improvements, the importance of the Char Dham as both an actual destination and an object of the national Hindu religious imagination has increased significantly. Buoyed by the development of new forms of bourgeois "religious tourism" and by the rise of a conservative Hindu population compelled by sites that speak to the existence of an all-India Hindu culture, the Char Dham has become an important destination for pilgrims from throughout South Asia and the diaspora, particularly Marwaris, Gujaratis, Delhi-and U.P. sites, and of course citizens of Uttaranchal.

Today, the Char Dham sees upwards of 250,000 unique visitors in an average pilgrimage season, which lasts from approximately April 15 until Diwali (sometime in November). The season is heaviest in the two-month period before the monsoon.

Once the rains come (sometime in late July), travel is extremely dangerous: extensive road building has critically destabilized the rocks, and fatal landslides and bus/jeep accidents are a regular yearly occurrence, with mortality rates for a season often surpassing 200. Despite the danger, pilgrims do continue to visit the Char Dham in the monsoon period, as well as after the rains end. Although temperatures at the shrines in the early winter months (October and November) are inhospitable, it is said that the incredible mountain scenery that surrounds the sites is most vivid after the rains have had a chance to moisten the dust of the plains below.

Most pilgrims to the Char Dham embark from the famous temple town of Haridwar. Others leave from Haridwar's sister city, Rishikesh, or from Dehra Dun, the capital of Uttaranchal. From there, the tradition is to visit the sites in the following order:

1. Yamunotri
2. Gangotri
3. Kedarnath
4. Badrinath

Yamunotri, the source of the Yamuna River and the seat of the goddess Yamuna, is one of the four sites in India's Char Dham pilgrimage.

Yamunotri is a full day's journey from Rishikesh, Haridwar or Dehra Dun. The temple is only accessible by a 6 km walk from the town of Hanuman Chatti (horses and palanquins are available for rent).

The current temple is of recent origin, as past iterations have been destroyed by the weather and elements. Lodging at the temple itself is limited to a few small ashrams and guesthouses.

Ritual duties at Yamunotri such as the making and distribution of *prasad* (ritual offerings) and the supervision of *pujas* (ritual venerations) are performed by the Uniyal family of *pujaris* (priests).

Raw rice is cooked and made into prasad using the hot springs at Yamotri.

Gangotri, the source of the Ganga (Ganges) River and seat of the goddess Ganga, is one of the four sites in India's Char Dham pilgrimage.

Gangotri can be reached in one day's travel from Rishikesh, Haridwar or Dehra Dun, or in two days from Yamunotri. More popular and important than its sister site to the east, Gangotri is also accessible directly by car and bus, meaning that it sees many more pilgrims. A small village of guesthouses and restaurants serves the pilgrim community. Ritual duties are supervised by the Semwal family of pujaris. The *aarti* ceremony at the Gangotri is especially impressive, as is the temple, a stately affair that sits on the banks of the rushing Ganga (Ganges River).

Adventurous pilgrims can make an overnight 17 km trek to Gaumukh, the actual source of the Ganga.

Kedarnath, where a form of the god Shiva is venerated as one of the 12 *jyotirling* (linga of light), is one of the four sites in India's Char Dham pilgrimage. It is a two-day's journey from either Gangotri or one of the main disembarkation points on the plains.

Besides its affiliation with Shiva, Kedarnath is also believed to be the site of Shankaracaraya's samadhi (achievement of beatified afterlife).

The actual temple, an impressive stone edifice of unknown date, is accessible only after a steep 13 km walk (horses or palanquins are available for rent).

The most remote of the four Char Dham sites, Kedarnath is flanked by breathtaking snowcapped peaks.

No specific family of pujaris supervises rituals at Kedarnath, which focus around veneration of the stone lingam that rests in the inner sanctum of the temple.

Elephanta Caves

The Elephanta Caves are a complex of Shiva temple caves on Elephanta Island, an hourlong ferry ride from Mumbai (Bombay), India.

A visit to Elephanta Island, designated a UNESCO World Heritage Site in 1987, is a worthy destination in itself, and it also provides a view of the city's skyline from the water and a welcome escape from the chaos of Mumbai's streets.

The hourlong ferry ride provides a good introduction to Hinduism, as the guides on board describe the religious significance of what you're about to see. If you can, plan your trip so that you can see the sunset over the Mumbai skyline on your return journey. The origins and artists of the temple caves, thought to date from about the 7th century, remain obscure. We do know, however, that the island was originally called Gharapuri; the Portuguese renamed it Elephanta after they found a large stone elephant near their landing place. (The figure collapsed in 1814 and was subsequently moved to the far-off Victoria Gardens and reassembled.)

Shortly before the Elephanta temples were created, Bombay had experienced the golden age of the late Guptas, under whom the talents of artists had free range. Sanskrit had been finely polished, and under the court's liberal patronage, Kalidasa and other writers had helped incite a Hindu religious revival. Shaivism, the worship of Shiva, inspired the building of these temples. Elephanta Island is quiet and picturesque, with light-green foliage and monkeys scampering about. Try not to bring food to avoid harassment by the monkeys.

Entry to the caves is via the main northern entrance to a massive hall, supported by large pillars, where the enormous Mahesamurti statue is housed. At 6.3m (18 ft.), the remarkable sculpture depicts Shiva in his three-headed aspect: as Creator (facing right), Protector (the crowned face at the centre), and Destroyer (facing left, with serpents for hair).

Other sculptures near the doorways and on side panels celebrate Shiva's accomplishments. One shows Shiva bringing the Ganges River down to Earth, letting it trickle through his matted hair. He is also depicted as Yogisvara, lord of Yogis, seated on a lotus, and as Shiva Nataraja, the many-armed cosmic dancer. The beauty of this stonework lies in the grace, balance, and sense of peace conveyed in spite of the subject's multiple actions.

Left of the Mahesamurti is Shiva as both male and female, Ardhanarishvara, an aspect suggesting the unity of all opposites.

Many of Elephanta's priceless statues were damaged or destroyed by the Portuguese, who apparently used the Hindu gods for target practice. There have also been reports of vandalism and carelessness by modern visitors, so be sure to take extra care to show this ancient site the respect it deserves.

A spectacular dance festival is held at Elephanta Island every February, hosted by the Maharashtra Tourism Development Corporation (MTDC).

Ellora Caves

The Ellora Caves are a complex of Buddhist, Hindu and Jain cave temples and monasteries built between the 6th and 10th centuries AD in the ancient Indian village of Ellora, Maharashtra State.

The closest major town to Ellora is Aurangabad. The caves at Ellora were excavated out of the vertical face of the Charanandri hills and number 34 in all: 12 Buddhist caves, 17 Hindu caves and 5 Jain caves.

The coexistence of structures from three different religions demonstrate the prevalent religious tolerance of India. The Ellora Caves were designated a UNESCO World Heritage Site in 1983.

The Hindu Caves at Ellora

The Hindu caves represent a different style of creative vision and execution skill than the Buddhist caves. The Hindu temples were carved from top to bottom and required several generations of planning and coordination to take shape.

One of the caves is dedicated to Lord Shiva, the cosmic destroyer. Another cave, the Rameshvara, has figurines of river goddesses at the entrance.

The most notable Hindu cave represents Mount Kailash, the abode of Lord Shiva, and is called the Kailashnath or Kailash Temple. This is a stupendous piece of architecture with interesting spatial effects and varied sculpture. The construction was a feat of human genius–it entailed removal of 200,000 tons of rock, took 100 years to complete and covers an area double the size of Parthenon in Athens.

Kushinagar (Kusinara)

Kushinagar (also spelled Kusinagar or Kusinara) is the site of the Buddha Shakyamuni's death. It is located next to Kasia, a rural town in the state of Uttar Pradesh, 52 km from Gorakhpur, in northern India.

Kushinagar is one of the four major pilgrimage destinations said to have been authorized by the Buddha himself. The other three sites are: Lumbini (birth); Bodh Gaya (enlightenment); and Sarnath (first teaching).

Kushinagar was a celebrated centre of the Malla kingdom of ancient India. At this location, near the Hiranyavati River, Gautama Buddha attained Parinirvana (passed away), and was cremated.

Many of the ruined stupas and viharas at Kushinagar date back to 3rd century BC to the 5th century AD when prosperity was at its peak. The Mauryan emperor Ashoka is known to have contributed to significant construction at this site.

Prior to its rediscovery in the nineteenth century, there was a silence of more than half a millennium at Kasia. Due possibly to violent invasions, Kushinagar lost its vitality and eventually was neglected. The notable Buddha Temple, when rediscovered, was covered in a 40 foot high mound of bricks surrounded by a dense thorny forest.

Excavations began in the late 1800s and many important remnants of the main site such as the Matha Kuar and Ramabhar stupa were unveiled.

Today, Kushinagar is a much-frequented pilgrimage site, especially for Buddhists from Asian countries.

Temples have been constructed on the site by Chinese, Sri Lankan, Thai, and Japanese Buddhists alongside the ruins of ancient monasteries and stupas. Temples and sights at Kushinagar include:

- Indo-Japanese-Srilankan Temple
- Mahaparinirvana Temple
- Matha Kuar Shrine
- Meditation Park
- Museum
- Ramabhar Stupa
- Thai temple

Mumbai

Bombay, known officially and alternatively since 1995 as Mumbai, is the largest city in India and the capital of

Maharashtra state. Bombay was originally a conglomeration of 7 islands on the Konkan coastline which over time were joined to form the island city of Bombay.

The city has an estimated metropolitan population of 17 million (2005), making it the 6th largest metropolis in the world. Bombay is also one of India's largest port cities and looms large as the commercial capital of India. Bombay's nature as the most eclectic and cosmopolitan Indian city is symbolised in the presence of Bollywood within the city.

Hindus comprise 68% of Mumbai's population, Muslim 17%, Christian 4% and Buddhist 4%. The remaining are followers of Parsi, Jain, Sikh and Jewish religions and atheist ideology. In light of this diversity, Mumbai's sacred sites are rich and varied. Most are associated with Hinduism or Islam, and there are some Christian sites left from colonial times (Portuguese and British) as well.

Banganga Tank

The sacred waters of the Banganga Tank in Mumbai, India, are a vivid representation of the paradox of traditional life coexisting with unbridled modernization.

The temple complex of Banganga, overlooked by many tourists, is one of Mumbai's holiest sites and the oldest surviving structure in the city.

Near the edge of the Arabian Sea at the southern tip of Malabar Hill, several small crumbling stone-turreted temples and flower-garlanded shrines surround a rectangular pool of holy water in an area of looming modern-day skyscrapers and encroaching urbanization.

Ritual bathers who come to the Banganga Tank believe the mossy waters have healing powers and originated from a natural spring created by an arrow shot by Rama (the hero of the epic *Ramayana*), who rested here while on a mission to rescue his beloved Sita from the demon king's abode in Lanka.

The source of the spring is said to be an underground offshoot of the Ganges, and the waters are considered just as sacred as those of the great river itself. In the shadow of one of present-day Mumbai's most prosperous neighbourhoods, Banganga continues to function as a timeless devotional hub, its tolling bells and mantra-chanting pujaris drawing devotees to worship the divine.

Sarnath

Sarnath, located just 12 km from the Hindu holy city of Varanasi, is the site of the deer park where Gautama Buddha first taught the Dharma after his enlightenment. Sarnath is one of four holy Buddhist sites sanctioned by the Buddha himself for pilgrimage. The other three sites are: Lumbini (birth); Bodh Gaya (enlightenment); and Kushinagar (death).

Sarnath has also been called Mrigadava, meaning "deer park," and Isipatana, meaning the place where holy men (Pali: *isi*) fell to earth. The latter name is based in the legend that when the Buddha was born, devas came down to announce it to 500 holy men. The holy men all rose into the air and disappeared, and their relics fell to the ground.

The current name Sarnath, from Saranganath, means "Lord of the Deer" and relates to another old Buddhist story in which the Bodhisattva is a deer and offers his life to a king instead of the doe he is planning to kill. The king is so moved that he creates the park as a sanctuary for deer.

After his enlightenment in Bodhgaya, the Buddha went to Sarnath seeking his five former companions. He found them, taught them what he had learned, and they also became enlightened. This event is referred to as "the turning of the wheel of the Dharma" and also marks the founding of the Sangha, or the community of monks.

Buddha's first ever discourse delivered here at Sarnath is known in Pali as the *Dhammacakkhapavathana Sutta*. Other Suttas include the *Anattalakhana Sutta* and the *Saccavibhanga Sutta*. The Buddha's central teaching after his enlightenment centred around the Four Noble Truths (concerning the meaning of life) and the Noble Eightfold Path (concerning the right way to live).

The Buddha spent the next rainy season in Sarnath at the Mulagandhakuti vihara. The Sangha having grown to 60 in number, the Buddha sent them out to teach the Dharma to others.

Buddhism flourished in Sarnath in part because of the support of kings and wealthy merchants based in nearby Varanasi. By the 3rd century Sarnath had become an important centre for the arts, which reached its zenith during the Gupta period (4th-6th century AD). When Hsuan Tsang visited from China in the 7th century, he found 30 monasteries and 3000 monks living at Sarnath.

Sarnath became a major centre of the Sammatiya school of Buddhism, one of the Nikaya or Hinayana schools. The presence of images of Heruka and Tara indicate that Vajrayana Buddhism was also practiced here.

At the end of the 12th century, Sarnath was sacked by Turkish Muslims. The site was subsequently plundered for building materials and has remained in ruins until the present day. The site was entirely deserted until 1836, when the British began excavations and restoration.

All of the ancient buildings and structures at Sarnath were damaged or destroyed by the Turks. However, amongst the ruins the Dharmekh Stupa is impressive at 128 feet high, and 93 in diameter. This dates from around 200 BC and is the sport where the Buddha is said to have preached his first sermon. Only the foundations remain of the Dharmarajika Stupa, but it is notable as a rare pre-Ashokan stupa.

The decaying ruins of the Mulagandhakuti vihara mark the place where the Buddha spent his first rainy season in meditation. In the 7th century, a writer described it as 200 feet high and containing 100 niches containing a Buddha carving along each wall. A life-sized statue shows the Buddha turning the wheel of the law. To the east is the modern Mulagandhakuti Vihara with its beautiful wall paintings; behind it is the Deer Park, which is maintained as an open animal park and still attracts deer.

Remains of the Ashoka Pillar at Sarnath. *Photo by Prince Roy.* The Ashoka Pillar at Sarnath survived the Turkish invasion but was broken during excavations. The base still stands in its original spot and has some interesting carvings. The splendid lion capital that topped the pillar, which thankfully survived its 45-foot drop to the ground is on display at the Sarnath Archeological Museum. The museum also houses some of the greatest treasures of Indian Buddhist art, including almost 300 images.

There is also a Bodhi tree planted by Anagarika Dharmapala which was grown from a cutting of the Bodhi tree at Bodh Gaya. It is located next to a Sri Lankan monastery.

Six national temples have been built by various Asian communities at Sarnath since the site's restoration

Varanasi

Varanasi (also known as Benares, Benares, Kashi and Kasi) is a Hindu holy city on the banks of the Ganges River in the north Indian state of Uttar Pradesh.

The modern name Varanasi is derived from the twin tributaries of Ganga Varuna and Asi on whose shores the city stands. Just 12 km from Varanasi is Sarnath, an important Buddhist sacred site.

Varanasi has a unique culture, quite different from other places in the region, and it is one of the major cultural centres of northern India.

Varanasi is the site of the holy shrine of Lord Kasi Viswanatha (a form of Lord Shiva) and is one of the revered 12 Jyotirlingas of the Lord.

Along with its positional advantage of being on the banks of the sacred Ganges River, this has given Varanasi a place at the forefront of the Hindu religion. Varanasi is considered the most sacred place for all Hindus, irrespective of denomination.

Hindus have long believed that bathing in the Ganges or dying in the holy city of Varanasi circumvents reincarnation and hence provides a permanent place in the Swarg (Heaven). This belief that has encouraged the establishment of innumerable nearby geriatric homes and also the disposal of half-burnt corpses into the river. This latter practice continues to cause great damage to the river's ecology, but the ministry of water resources has finally taken up the restoration of the Ganga by banning cremation on the city's ghats (ghats are the banks of a holy river, stepped to facilitate bathing).

Vrindavan

Vrindavan, in the Mathura district of Uttar Pradesh, is on the site of the original forest of Vrindavana. It is about 15km away from Mathura city, near the Agra-Delhi highway.

Vrindavan has many ancient and modern temples and religious institutions based on the connections with Krishna's childhood. It is the most important Vaishnava place of pilgrimage.

The Madan Mohan Temple located near the Kali Ghat which was built by Kapur Ram Das of Multan. This is the oldest existent temple in Vrindavan today. The temple is closely associated with the saint Chaitanya Mahaprabhu. The original image of Lord Madan Gopal was shifted from the shrine to Karauli in Rajasthan for safe keeping during Aurangzeb's rule. Today, a replica of the image is worshipped at the temple.

The Banke-Bihari Temple built in 1864 is the most popular shrine at Vrindavan. The image of Banke-Bihari was discovered in Nidhi Vana by Swami Haridas, the great Krishna devotee, belonging to the Nimbarka sampradaya.

The famous Radha Vallabh Temple set up by the Radha-Vallabh sampradaya, has the crown of Radha-Rani placed next to the Shri Krishna image in the sanctum.

The Jaipur Temple which was built by Sawai Madhav Singh, the Maharaja of Jaipur in 1917, is a richly embellished and opulent temple. The fine hand-carved sandstone is of unparalleled workmanship. The temple is dedicated to Shri Radha Madhava.

The Shahji Temple, another popular temple at Vrindavan, was designed and built in 1876 by a wealthy jeweller, Shah Kundan Lal of Lucknow. The deities (images) at the temple are popularly known as the Chhote Radha Raman. Noted for its magnificent architecture and beautiful marble sculpture, the temple has twelve spiral columns each 15 feet high. The 'Basanti

Kamra'-the darbar hall is famed for its Belgian glass chandeliers and fine paintings.

The Rangaji Temple, built in 1851 is dedicated to Lord Ranganatha or Rangaji depicted as Lord Vishnu in his sheshashayi pose, resting on the coils of the sacred Sesha Nag. The temple built in the Dravidian style has a tall gopuram (gateway) of six storeys and a gold-plated Dhwaja stambha, 50 feet high. A water tank and a picturesque garden lie within the temple enclosure. The annual festival of Jal Vihar of the presiding deity is performed with great pomp and splendour at the tank. The temple is also famous for its 'Brahmotsdav' celebration in March-April, more popularly known as the 'Rath ka Mela'. The ten day long celebrations are marked by the pulling of the rath (the chariot car) by the devotees from the temple to the adjoining gardens. The Govinda Deo (Govindaji) Temple was once a magnificent seven storeyed structure built in the form of a Greek cross. It is said that the Emperor Akbar donated some of the red sandstone that had been brought for the Red Fort at Agra, for the construction of this temple. Built at the astronomical cost of one crore rupees in 1590 by his general Man Singh, the temple combines western, Hindu and Muslim architectural elements in its structure. It was destroyed by Mughal ruler Aurangzeb.

The Shri Krishna-Balram Temple built by the International Society for Shri Krishna Consciousness (ISKCON), is one of the most beautiful temples in Vrindavan today. The principal deities of this temple are Shri Krishna-Balram and Shri Radha-Shyama Sundar. Adjoining the temple is the samadhi of Shrila A.C. Bhaktivedanta Swami Prabhupada, the founder of ISKCON, built in pure white marble. The Seva Kunj is where Lord Krishna once performed the Raaslila with Radha-Rani and the gopis and Nidhi Van where the divine couple rested. The samadhi of Swami Haridas is situated here.

Other places of interest include the Sriji Temple, Jugal Kishore Temple, Kesi Ghat, Lal Babu Temple, Raj Ghat, Meera-Bai Temple, Imli Tal, Kaliya Ghat, Raman Reti, Varaha Ghat and Chira Ghat.

7

Hindu Art and Architecture

INTRODUCTION

The man who knows nothing of music, literature, or art is no better than a beast," ancient Hindu wisdom warned, "only without a beast's tail or teeth." The arts of Civilization's armour, her weapons and shield against all the pitfalls of life, lighting the darkest corner of the trail, helping us to cross its most dangerous passes. Indian wisdom has always extolled art as a key to the salvation of ultimate release sought by all good Hindus. There is a holistic quality about Indian art, a unity of many forms and artistic experiences. Like the microcosmic universe of a Hindu temple, they help us to climb from terrestrial trails and samsaric fears.

Art pervades every facet of Indian life, is found on every byway of Indian Civilization. Indian art in its purest form is Yoga, a disciplined style of worship and self-restraint that may also be thought of as India's oldest indigenous "science." Shiva, the "Great God" of yogic practice, visually represented as "King of Dance" (Nataraja), is the most remarkable single symbol of divine powers ever created by Indian artistic genius.

Indian artists have celebrated and immortalized the beauty of human bodies in bronze and stone for more than 5,000 years. We do not know the name of a single genius among the many who brought gods to life in the Ellora, Ajanta or Elephanta, Karli caves or those who created the Chola Natarajas as magnificent as any work by Benvenuto Cellini. The great Rodin was possibly the most sensitive and perceptive of the admirers of Indian art.

The transition from cave excavation and carving to the creation of Hindu temples is most dramatically and powerfully depicted at Ellora, where an entire mountain has literally been scooped out over several centuries by patient devoted artists and architectural geniuses, who envisioned and "extracted" Lord Shiva's Mount Kailash temple inside that enormous rock dome. Ellora's Kailasantha cave temple remains one of the true "wonders" of the world of art and a unique monument to Hindu devotion. Captain Philip Meadows Taylor (1808-1876) author, says: "the carving on some of the pillars, and of the lintels and architraves of the doors, is quite beyond description. No chased work in silver or gold could possibly be finer. But what tools this very hard, tough stone could have done wrought and polished as it is, is not at all intelligible at the present day."

Indian art is so intimately associated with Indian religion and philosophy that it is difficult to appreciate it fully unless one has some knowledge of the ideals that governed the Indian mind. In Indian art there is always a religious urge, a looking beyond. From the exuberant carvings of the Hindu temples to the luminous wall-paintings of Ajanta, to the intriguing art of cave sites and sophisticated temple-building traditions, the Indian subcontinent offers an amazing visual feast.

"Indian art is essentially religious. The conscious aim of Indian art is the intimation of Divinity. But the Infinite and Unconditioned cannot be expressed in finite terms; and art, unable to portray Divinity unconditioned, and unwilling to be limited by the limitation of humanity, is in India dedicated to the representation of Gods, who to finite man represent comprehensible aspects of an infinite whole. Shankaracharya prayed thus: "O Lord, pardon my three sins: I have in contemplation clothed in form Thyself that has no form; I have in praise described Thee who dost transcend all qualities; and in visiting shrines I have ignored Thine omnipresence."

From its Indo-Sumerian and Vedic-Mound beginnings to the various peaks reached during the Maurya, Sunga, Andhra, Kusana and Gupta periods, Indian art has been influential for centuries. The grave and sensuous and infinitely varied arts of India have long been admired around the world. India is vast (the size of Europe); the birthplace of great religions, including Hinduism, Buddhism, and Jainism; and the home of sophisticated civilizations dating back more than 4,000 years.

These factors combine to give India one of the longest and most complex art traditions of the world. Most important is the realization that "the consistent fabric of Indian life was never rent by the Western dichotomy between religious belief and worldly practice"—hence the easy coexistence in India of extreme religious asceticism and the overt eroticism that pervades temples like Khajuraho and Patan.

A grand sweep, from the ancient cities of the Indus valley, the development of Buddhist art (which by the 12th century had faded away in the land of its birth), the glorious paintings of Ajanta.

In India, anonymity of artists has not been accidental; it is a distinctive national trait. "The modern world, with its glorification of the personality of authors," observes Ananda K. Coomaraswamy, "produces work of genius and works of mediocrity, following the peculiarities of individual artists.

In India, the virtue or defect of any work is the virtue or defect of the race in that age. The names and peculiarities of individual artists, even if we could recover them, would not enlighten us: nothing depends upon (individual) genius or requires the knowledge of an individual psychology for its interpretation. To understand it at all, we must understand experience common to all men of the time and place in which a given work was produced."

This is true of the Vedas, as well as the marvellous Kailas excavations; equally true of Mohenjadaro, about five thousand years ago. This monumental anonymity is indeed writ large on the brow of our civilization.

"Like India herself Indian Art is of great antiquity and one cannot but marvel at the height reached by Indian artists during the Classical Age."

"Indian art has contributed a unique chapter in the history of human civilization", says E. B. Havell. Its continued vitality, its astonishing range-specially in the field of painting, sculpture, and architecture, no less than the lasting sense of beauty and power it conveys, has placed the artistic heritage among the major cultural legacies of the world.

The architecture that created the temples of Madurai, Tanjore, Khajuraho, Orissa, the rock-cut pagodas of Mahabalipuram, the sculpture that executed the Mathura image of Buddha, Trimurti of Elephanta, the famous Nataraja of Tanjore and the paintings which had its efflorescence in the haunting world of beauty in the caves of Ajanta and Ellora, and thousand others, have nothing to lose by comparison with the whole artistic wealth of Europe during its entire history.

"Art for a Hindu is life as it is interpreted by religion and philosophy. Art for art's sake is consequently unknown. Instead a symbolism was created to express various qualities of the superhuman soul and superhuman figures."

Shiva Vishnu-destructive and creative forces of God embodied in one being.

"Indian Art is a blossom of the tree of the Divine wisdom, full of suggestions from worlds invisible, striving to express the ineffable."

Annie Wood Besant (1847-1933) was an active socialist on the executive committee of the Fabian Society along with George Bernard Shaw. George Bernard Shaw regarded her the "greatest woman public speaker of her time." Was a prominent leader of India's freedom movement, member of the Indian National Congress, and of the Theosophical Society. She has said,

"Indian Art is a blossom of the tree of the Divine wisdom, full of suggestions from worlds invisible, striving to express the ineffable, and it can never be understood merely by the emotional and the intellectual; only in the light of the Spirit can its inner significance be glimpsed."

The extant remains of Indian art cover a period of more than two thousand years. During this time many schools of thought have flourished and decayed, invaders of many races have poured into India and contributed to the infinite variety of her intellectual resources; countless dynasties have ruled and passed away. But just as through all Indian schools of thought there runs like a golden thread the fundamental idealism of the Upanishads, the Vedanta, so in all Indian art there is a unity that underlies all its bewildering variety.

"Before Indian art, as before every phase of Indian civilization, we stand in humble wonder at its age and its continuity. From the time of Mohenjadaro to the present, through the vicissitudes of five thousand years, India has been creating its peculiar type of beauty in a hundred arts. The record is broken and incomplete, not because India ever rested, but because war and the idol-smashing ecstasies of Moslems destroyed uncounted masterpieces of building and statuary, and poverty neglected the preservation of others. Probably no other nation known to us has ever had so exuberant a variety of arts."

"We shall never be able to do justice to Indian art, for ignorance and fanaticism have destroyed its greatest achievements, and have half ruined the rest. At Elephanta the Portuguese certified their piety by smashing statuary and bas-reliefs in unrestrained barbarity; and almost everywhere in the north the Moslems brought to ground those triumphs of Indian architecture, of the 5th and 6th centuries, which tradition ranks as far superior to the later works that arouse our wonder and admiration today.

The Moslems decapitated statues, and tore them limb from limb; they appropriated for their mosques, and in great measure imitated, the graceful pillars of the Jain temples." Time and fanaticism joined in the destruction, for the orthodox Hindus abandoned and neglected temples that had been profaned by the touch of alien hands."

"We may guess at the lost grandeur of north Indian architecture by the powerful edifices that still survive in the south, where Moslem rule entered only in minor degree, and after some habituation to India had softened Mohammedan hatred of Hindu ways. Col. Ferguson had counted some thirty southern temples any one of which, in his estimate, must have cost as much as an English cathedral." Only a Hindu pietist rich in words could describe the lovely symmetry of the shrine at Ittagi, in Hydrabad, or the temple at Somnathpur in Mysore, in which gigantic masses of stone are carved with the delicacy of lace; or the Hoyshaleshwara Temple at Halebid Here, Ferguson adds, "the artistic combination of horizontal and vertical lines, and the play of outline and of light and shade, far surpass anything in Gothic art. The effects are just what the medieval architects were often aiming at, but which they never attained so perfectly as was done at Halebid."

If we marvel at the laborious piety that could carve eighteen hundred feet of frieze in the Halebid temple, and could portray in them two thousand elephants each different from all the rest, what shall we say of the patience and courage that could undertake to cut a complete temple out of the solid rock? But this was a common achievement of the Hindu artisans. At Mamallapuram, on the east coast near Chennai, they carved several rathas or pagodas, of which the fairest is the Dharma-raja-ratha, or monastery for the highest discipline.

At Ellora, a place of religious pilgrimage.. excavating out of the mountain rock great monolithic temples of which the supreme example is the Hindu shrine of Kailash-named after Shiva's mythological paradise in the Himalayas. Here the tireless builder cut a hundred feet down into the stone to isolate the block-250 by 160 feet-that was to be the temple; then they carved the walls into powerful pillars, statues and bas-reliefs; then they chiselled out of the interior, and lavished there the most amazing art: let the bold fresco of "The Lovers" serve as a specimen. Finally, their architectural passion still unspent, they carved a series of chapels and monasteries deep into the rock of three sides of the quarry.

Richard Lannoy (1928-) author of several books including, The Speaking Tree: A Study of Indian Culture and Society has pointed out that the caves of India are the most singular fact about Indian art, and he is right, for they serve to distinguish it from that of other civilizations. A prodigious amount or labour, spread over a period of about 1,300 years, was expended in this "art of mass", the excavations of rock sanctuaries and monasteries. These caves were hewn out of solid rock; in other words, they were "constructed" through the excavation of space. These sanctuaries were cut from nearly-perpendicular cliffs to a depth of a hundred feet: in all cases, this excavation was carried out by means of a chisel ¾ inches wide; the same chisel was also used to carve out elaborately decorated columns, galleries, and shrines. The two largest structures of the kind are staggering in their dimensions.

Alain Danielou a.k.a Shiv Sharan (1907-1994), son of French aristocracy, author of numerous books on philosophy, religion, history and arts of India. He was perhaps the first European to boldly proclaim his Hinduness. He had a wide effect upon Europe's understanding of Hinduism. He explained:

> *"The artist must prepare a geometrical design in accordance with the symbolic proportions required for the image he wants to represent. He must concentrate his vision and his thought on the magic diagram or yantras, till he perceives through the geometrical outlines the form he is to sculpture. This concentration of the artist is one of the highest and completest form of concentration."*

Dr. Ananda Kentish Coomaraswamy (1877-1947) Indian art historian, a remarkable critic, scholar and mystic, late curator at the Boston Museum, who dazzled the Western world with his message concerning the spiritual greatness of Indian art. A pioneer historian of Indian art and foremost interpreter of Indian culture to the West. He detected in India "a strong national genius since the beginning of her history." He found Indian art and culture "a joint creation of the Dravidian and Aryan genius." Of Buddhism, he wrote:' "the more profound our study, the more difficult it becomes to distinguish Buddhism from Brahmanism, or to say in what respects, if any, Buddhism is really unorthodox. The outstanding distinction lies in the fact that Buddhist doctrine is propounded by an apparently historical founder. Beyond this there are only broad distinctions of emphasis."

Indian art had accompanied Indian religion across straits and frontiers into Sri Lanka, Java, Cambodia, Siam, Burma, Tibet, Khotan, Turkestan, Mongolia, China, Korea, and Japan; "in Asia all roads lead to India." Angkor Vat a masterpiece equal to the finest architectural achievements of the Egyptians, the Greeks, or the cathedrals of Europe. An enormous moat, twelve miles in length, surrounds the temple; over the moat runs a paved bridge guarded by dissuasive Nagas in stone; then an ornate enclosing wall; then spacious galleries, whose relief's tell again the tales of the Mahabharata and Ramayana; then the stately edifice itself, rising upon a broad base, by level after level of a terraced pyramid, to the sanctuary of the god, two hundred feet high.

Here magnitude does not detract from beauty, but helps it to an imposing magnificence that startles the Western mind into some weak realization of the ancient grandeur once possessed by Oriental civilization.

"The Hindus do not regard the religious, aesthetic, and scientific standpoints as necessarily conflicting, and in all their finest work, whether musical, literary, or plastic, these points of view, nowadays so sharply distinguished, are inseparably united.

"All that India can offer proceeds from her philosophy, a state of mental concentration (yoga) on the part of the artist and the enactment of a certain amount of ritual being postulated as the source of the 'spirituality' of Indian art."

In the process of comparing both the European and Oriental traditional philosophy of art, a task, it would seem, which had convinced him of the perennial value of the traditional point of view since the works of art as in the case of the Indian subcontinent and its environs appeared to him to endure and increase in value down through the ages.

Rizwan Salim reviewer, and assistant editor, American Sentinel, has written eloquently about Hindu art:

> *"It is clear that India at the time when Muslim invaders turned towards it (8 to 11th century) was the earth's richest region for its wealth in precious and semi-precious stones, gold and silver; religion and culture; and its fine arts and letters. Tenth century Hindustan was also too far advanced than its contemporaries in the East and the West for its achievements in the realms of speculative philosophy and scientific theorizing, mathematics and*

knowledge of nature's workings. Hindus of the early medieval period were unquestionably superior in more things than the Chinese, the Persians (including the Sassanians), the Romans and the Byzantines of the immediate preceding centuries. The followers of Shiva and Vishnu on this subcontinent had created for themselves a society more mentally evolved-joyous and prosperous too-than had been realized by the Jews, Christians, and Muslim monotheists of the time. Medieval India, until the Islamic invaders destroyed it, was history's most richly imaginative culture and one of the five most advanced civilizations of all times."

Ancient Hindu temple architecture is the most awe-inspiring, ornate and spellbinding architectural style found anywhere in the world. No artists of any historical civilization have ever revealed the same genius as ancient Hindustan's artists and artisans.

Dr. Ernest Binfield Havell (1861-1934) principal to the Madras College of Art in the 1890s and left as principal of the Calcutta College of Art some 20 years later. His major ideas about Indian art theory are to be found in his two works, Indian Sculpture and Painting (1908) and, more important, The Ideals of Indian Art (1911). The Ideals of Indian Art was written with the express purpose of changing the prevailing European indifference to Indian art and bringing about a proper appreciation of its aesthetic qualities.

"Indian artistic expression begins from a starting-point far removed from that of the European. Only an infinitesimal number of Europeans, even of those who pass the best part of their lives in India, make any attempt to understand the philosophic, religious, mythological and historical ideas of which Indian art is the embodiment."

In other words, he was perceptive enough to see that it was vital to judge work of Indian art on the basis of standards of art criticism evolved within the Indian tradition instead of employing European standards which were extraneous to the tradition.

"'The opposition of Western materialism to the philosophy of the East always makes it difficult for the Europeans to approach Indian art with anything like unprejudiced minds. The whole of modern European academic art-teaching has been based upon the unphilosophical theory that beauty is a quality which is inherent in certain aspects of matter or form..."

Indian thought takes a much wider, a more profound and comprehensive view of art. The Indian artist has the whole creation and every aspect of it for his field; not merely a limited section of it, mapped out by academic professors. Beauty, says the Indian philosopher, is subjective, not objective. It is not inherent in form or matter; it belongs only to spirit, and can only be apprehended by spiritual vision."

He also pointed out the fallacy and absurdities of some Western historians to find some foreign influence on Indian art. He said:

> *"Indian art was inspired by Indian Nature, Indian philosophy and religious teaching, and no one."*

Havell thought Indian art was conceptual, aiming at the realization of 'something finer and subtle than ordinary physical beauty. The image that the Indian created came from inside his head; he had no need of a goose-pimpled model posing uncomfortably in his studio. His achievement was not that of capturing real life in art, but of giving birth to an abstract ideal. He said: "A figure with three heads, and four, six or eight arms, seems to a European a barbaric conception, though it is not less physiologically impossible than the wings growing from the human scapula in the European representation of angels. But it is altogether foolish to condemn such artistic allegories a priori because they do not conform to the canons of the classic art of Europe. All art is suggestion and convention, and if Indian artists can suggest divine attributes to Indian people with Indian culture, they have fulfilled the purpose of their art."

Just as angels are given wings, or saints halos, or just as the Holy Spirit was portrayed as a dove, so Shiva or Vishnu were given extra arms to hold the symbols of their various attributes, or extra heads for their different roles. Havell showed how consummately the Indian artist could handle movement. Taking the example of the famous Nataraja (dancing Shiva) bronzes of south India, he first explored its symbolism. No work of Indian art is without a wealth of allegory and symbol, ignorance of which was, and still is, a major stumbling block for most non-Indians. The Nataraja deals with the divine ecstasy of creation expressed in dance.

"Art will always be caviare to the vulgar, but those who would really learn and understand it should begin with Indian art, for true Indian art is pure art, stripped of the superfluities and vulgarities which delight the uneducated eye. Yet Indian art, being more subtle and recondite than the classical art of Europe, requires a higher degree of artistic understanding, and it rarely appeals to European dilettanti, who with a smattering of perspective, anatomy, and rules of proportion added to their classical scholarship, aspire to be art critics, amateur painters, sculptors or architects, and these unfortunately have the principal voice in art administration in Indian."

Comparing the European and Hindu art, Havell says:

"European art has, as it were its wings clipped: it knows only the beauty of earthly things. Indian art, soaring into the highest empyrean, is ever trying to bring down to earth something of the beauty of the things above."

Dr. James Fergusson architectural historian, has made the following observation regarding Hindu art:

"When Hindu sculpture first dawns upon us in the rails of Buddha Gaya and Bharhut, 220 to 250 BC it is thoroughly original, absolutely without, a trace of foreign influence, but quite capable of expressing in ideas, and of telling its story with a distinctness that never was surpassed, at least in India.For an honest, purpose-like, pre-Raphaelite kind of art, there is probably nothing much better to be found anywhere."

Baron John Emerich Edward Dalberg Acton (1834-1902) English historian, was greatly struck with the architecture of Dwarka, which he calls 'the wonderful city," and says:

"The natives of that country (India) have carried the art of construction and ornamenting excavated grottoes to a much higher degree of perfection than any other people."

According to Rene Grousset (1885-1952) French art Historian. Author of several books including Civilization of India and The Empire of the Steppes: A History of Central Asia.

He writes about the Indian influence in South East Asia:

"In the high plateau of eastern Iran, in the oases of Serindia, in the arid wastes of Tibet, Mongolia, and Manchuria, in the ancient civilized lands of China and Japan, in the lands of the primitive Mons and Khmers and other tribes of Indo-China, in the countries of the Malaya-Polynesians, in Indonesia and Malay, India left the indelible impress of her high culture, not only upon religion, but also upon art, and literature, in a word, all the higher things of spirit."

"There is an obstinate prejudice thanks to which India is constantly represented as having lived, as it were, hermetically sealed up in its age-old civilization, apart from the rest of Asia. Nothing could be more exaggerated. During the first eight centuries of our era, so far as religion and art are concerned, central Asia was a sort of Indian colony. It is often forgotten that in the early Middle Ages there existed a "Greater India," a vast Indian empire. A man coming from the Ganges or the Deccan to Southeast Asia felt as much at home there as in his own native land. In those days the Indian Ocean really deserved its name."

He gives a fine interpretation of the image of Nataraja:

"Whether he be surrounded or not by the flaming aureole of the Tiruvasi (Pabhamandala) – the circle of the world which he both fills and oversteps – the King of the Dance is all rhythm and exaltation. The tambourine which he sounds with one of his right hands draws all creatures into this rhythmic motion and they dance in his company. The conventionalized locks of flying hair and the blown scarfs tell of the speed of this universal movement, which

crystallizes matter and reduces it to powder in turn. One of his left hands holds the fire which animates and devours the worlds in this cosmic whirl. One of the God's feet is crushing a Titan, for "this dance is danced upon the bodies of the dead", yet one of the right hands is making a gesture of reassurance (abhayamudra), so true it is that, seen from the cosmic point of view...the very cruelty of this universal determinism is kindly, as the generative principle of the future. And, indeed, on more than one of our bronzes the King of the Dance wears a broad smile. He smiles at death and at life, at pain and at joy, alike, or rather,..his smile is death and life, both joy and pain...'

From this lofty point of view, in fact, all things fall into their place, finding their explanation and logical compulsion. Here art is the faithful interpreter of a philosophical concept. The plastic beauty of the rhythm is no more than the expression of an ideal rhythm. The very multiplicity of arms, puzzling as it may seem at first sight, is subject in turn to an inward law, each pair remaining a model of elegance in itself, so that the whole being of the Nataraja thrills with a magnificent harmony in his terrible joy.

And as though to stress the point that the dance of the divine actor is indeed a sport, (lila) – the sport of life and death, the sport of creation and destruction, at once infinite and purposeless – the first of the left hands hangs limply from the arm in the careless gesture of the gajahasta (hand as the elephant's trunk). And lastly, as we look at the back view of the statue, are not the steadiness of these shoulders which uphold world, and the majesty of this Jove-like torso, as it were a symbol of the stability and immutability of substance, while the gyration of the legs in its dizzy speed would seem to symbolize the vortex of phenomena."

He speaks of the Trimurti statue at Elephanta Caves: *"Universal art has succeeded in few materialization of the Divine as powerful and also as balanced. He believed that it is "the greatest representation of the pantheistic god created by the hands of man."*

He concludes with poetic enthusiasm: "Never have the overflowing sap of life, the pride of force superior to everything, the secret intoxication of the inner god of things been so serenely expressed."

In the words of Rene Grousset, "The three countenances of the one being are here harmonized without a trace of effort. There are few material representations of the divine principle at once as powerful and as well balanced as this in the art of the whole world. Nay, more, here we have undoubtedly the grandest representation of the pantheistic God ever made by the hand of man Indeed, never have the exuberant vigor of life, the tumult of universal joy expressing itself in ordered harmony, the pride of a power superior to any other, and the secret exaltation of the divinity immanent in all things found such serenely expressed."

In its Olympian majesty, the Mahesamurti of Elephanta is worthy of comparison with the Zeus of Mylasa or the Asklepios of Melos."

"The principal relief at Mallalipuram is the great rock-carving known as the Gangacatarna "descent of the Ganga". This enormous sculpture is high relief, measuring nearly 30 yards in length and 23 feet in height and entirely covering one face of the cliff, groups a whole world of animals, ascetics, genii, and gods round the cascade in which sports a band of nagas and nagis, symbolic of the sacred waters. What we have before us here is a vast picture, a regular fresco in stone.

This relief is a masterpiece of classic art in the breadth of its composition, the sincerity of the impulse which draws all creatures together round the beneficent waters, and its deep, fresh love of nature. In particular we may draw attention to the ascetic prostrating himself on the left of the cascade; this amazingly realistic figure with its synthetic, rugged, and direct workmanship, at once restless and simple, has all the quality of a Rodin."

Of the colossal war-horse placed outside the Southern facade of the black Pagoda at Konark in Orissa, built about the middle of the thirteenth century by Narsingaha I, art critic E. B. Havell says:

> *"Here Indian sculptors have shown that they can express with as much fire and passion as the greatest European art the pride of victory and the glory of triumphant warfare, for not even the Homeric grandeur of the Elgin marbles surpasses the magnificent movement and modelling of this Indian Achilles, and the superbly monumental war-horse in its massive strength and vigour is not unworthy of comparison with Verocchio's famous masterpieces at Venice!"*

The Konark war-horse, prancing into battle with a massively strong warrior striding beside it, appealed to Havell because it also showed that the Indian sculptor was quite capable of handling martial themes. "Not even the Homeric grandeur of the Elgin marbles surpasses the magnificent movement and modelling of this Indian Achilles, and the superbly monumental war-horse with its massive strength and vigour is not unworthy of comparison with Verocchio's famous masterpiece at Venice."

V. S. Naipaul (1932-) Nobel Laureate, was born in Trinidad into a family of Hindu origin is known for his penetrating analyses of alienation and exile. He has discussed some of his controversial ideas about rewriting Indian history:

> *"I am less interested in the Taj Mahal which is a vulgar, crude building, a display of power built on blood and bones. Everything exaggerated, everything overdone, which suggests a complete slave population. I would like to find out what was there before the Taj Mahal."*

As J D Beglar, the assistant-director of the Archaeological Survey of India (ASI), in his Report for 1871-72, wrote: "It is only after the Mughal conquest of India that Muhammadan architecture begins to be beautiful". Before that the Islamic approach to architecture was barbarous. According to the reading of the invaders, "their religion demanded the suppression of aesthetic feelings".

Hindu art has been incomprehensible to most Western critics, particularly of the colonial era and they often used harsh epithets like 'barbarous', 'ugly', etc. to describe it. But it was not so with Huxley. He found much in Indian art to appreciate even while he used Western standards of judgment.

Aldous Huxley (1894-1963) the English novelist and essayist, born into a family that included some of the most distinguished members of the English ruling class, found:

> *"The Hindu architects produced buildings incomparably more rich and interesting as works of art. I have not visited Southern India, where, it is said, the finest specimen of Hindu architecture are to be found. But I have seen enough of the art in Rajputana to convince me of its enormous superiority to any work of the Mohammedans. The temples at Chittor, for example, are specimens of true classicism." "Mohammedan art tends..to be dry, empty, barren, and monotonous. Huxley also visited the Taj at Agra and he was much disappointed. He found the building expensive and picturesque but architecturally uninteresting. He thought that it was elegant but its elegance was of a "very dry and negative kind", and its classicism came not from any "intellectual restraint imposed on an exuberant fancy", but from "an actual deficiency of fancy, a poverty of imagination". Comparing it with Hindu architecture, he said: "The Hindu architects produced buildings incomparably more rich and interesting as works of art. According to him, its fabulous "costliness is what most people seem to like about the Taj", and that because it is made of marble. But "marble", he says, "covers a multitude of sins." Its costliness makes up for its lack of architectural merit.*

It could be said that art is not Islam's forte as it repudiates it and, therefore, it has not developed. It had little to convey or communicate in the way of deeper spiritual truths. Its God was best satisfied with demolition of the shrines of "other Gods", and it was in that direction that Islam found its best self-expression." It shared this passion of demolition with other iconoclastic religions including Christianity-we forget what it did in its heyday.

Sir William Wilson Hunter (1840-1900) entered the Indian civil service in 1862. He was a man of broad cultural interests and was author of several notable volumes mainly on Indian historical subjects, acknowledges England's debt to India:

"English decorative art in our day has borrowed largely from Indian forms and patterns. The exquisite scrolls on the rock temples at Karli and Ajanta, the delicate marble tracey and flat wood-carving of Western India, the harmonious blending of forms and colours in the fabrics of Kashmir, have contributed to the restoration of tastes in England. Indian art-work, when faithful to native designs, still obtains the highest honours at the international exhibitions of Europe."

Jawaharlal Nehru (1889-1964) first prime minister of free India, says:

"The amazing expansion of Indian culture and art to other countries has led to some of the finest expressions of this art being found outside India. Unfortunately many of our old monuments and sculptures, especially in northern India, have been destroyed by invaders in course of time."

Sir Edwin Arnold (1832-1904) poet and scholar and Author of The Song Celestial, which is a translation of the Bhagwad Gita. His description of the Elephanta caves is very fine. He says of the statue of Ardhanareswara:

"This statue of colossal size, is nevertheless very delicately cut, and the limbs and features possess an almost tender beauty."

In regard to Indian sculpture he writes:

"Everywhere-on plinth and abacus, frieze and entablature-appears the same lavish wealth of work and fancy; for it is characteristic of the Hindu art, which the Moslem also in this respect adopted, to leave no naked plans in the stone."

He speaks of the Meenakshi temple at Madura thus: "Each gopuram looks like a mountain of bright and shifting hues, in the endless detail of which the astonished vision becomes lost. Imagine four of these carved and decorated pyramidal pagaodas, each equally colossal and multi-coloured with fine minor ones clustering near, anyone of which would singly make a town remarkable!"

M. Rene Grousset (1885-1952) French art historian, says: "In the high plateau of eastern Iran, in the oases of Serindia, in the arid wastes of Tibet, Mongolia, and Manchuria, in the ancient civilized lands of China and Japan, in the lands of the primitive Mons and Khmers and other tribes of Indo-China, in the countries of the Malaya-Polynesians, in Indonesia and Malay, India left the indelible impress of her high culture, not only upon religion, but also upon art, and literature, in a word, all the higher things of spirit."

Captain Philip Meadows Taylor (1808-1876) a lieutenant in the Nizam of Hyderabad's army who learned Persian and Hindi. Author of Confessions of a Thug (1839) says of the Ellora caves:

> *"the carving on some of the pillars, and of the lintels and architraves of the doors, is quite beyond description. No chased work in silver or gold could possibly be finer. But what tools this very hard, tough stone could have done wrought and polished as it is, is not at all intelligible at the present day."*

Colonel James Tod, after carefully examining and exploring the temple at Barolli (Rajasthan) exclaims: "To describe its stupendous and diversified architecture is impossible; it is the office of the pen alone, but the labour would be endless. Art seems to have exhausted itself, and we are perhaps now for the first time fully impressed with the beauty of Hindu sculpture. The columns, the ceilings, the external roofing, where each stone presents a miniature temple, one rising over another until the crown, by the urn-like kalasha, distract our attention. The carving on the capital of each column would require pages of explanation, and the whole, in spite of high antiquity, is in wonderful preservation."

"The doorway, which is destroyed, must have been curious, and the remains that choke up the interior are highly interesting. One of these specimens was entire and unrivalled in taste and beauty."

Temple Gods that Display a Shocking Beauty

To the Western eye, these gods and goddesses are, given their sacred function, almost shockingly beautiful. Divinity and sensuous, sexual beauty seem to be inextricably mixed. But the appreciation of a god's physical beauty was one of India's customary approaches to the divine. Perfection of the body was considered a prerequisite for the flow of inner beauty and supremacy of spirit.

If we look at the Goddess Uma, for example, she is portrayed as a slender, seductive and exquisitely beautiful woman. She has a statuesque and graceful figure, her full breasts are softly sculpted and her skirt is slung so low as to reveal the curve of her stomach. Other deities, too, such as the superb Shiva, Lord of Dance, are exquisitely elegant with their perfectly proportioned thighs and legs, plump and supple and decorated with folds of tightly drawn cloth, and their long curved feet and fingers.

These figures are nearly 1,200 years old, yet their details are still remarkably crisply defined. The lost wax method of modelling was done to such high standards, both technically and aesthetically, that it is still used today unchanged.

No wonder Francois-Auguste-Rene Rodin (1840-1917), one of our masters of bronze modelling, whose work can be seen at the Royal Academy, was overwhelmed when he saw the Chola sculpture in 1913.

"There are things that other people do not see: unknown depths, the wellsprings of life," he said.

"There is grace in elegance; above grace, there is modelling; everything is exaggerated; we call it soft but it is most powerfully soft! Words fail me then."

1. *Sindhu-Saraswati Valley Culture:* The highest expression of Indian proto historic culture was the Sindhu Saraswati Valley culture, after its main centre.

In spite of a sense of practicality, the figures displayed on the many seals executed in stone, steatite, ceramics and metal display an advanced aesthetic quality. The copper figure of a dancer and the torsos of figures, are not treated with the rigid and coarse style typical of ancient art, but with a delicate sensitivity of feeling for the graceful movements of the dance and the clear concept of free representation of the human figure.

2. *The Mauryan Dynasty:* The Mauryans left traces of their rule in the great royal palaces of Pataliputra, the modern Patna, the capital of their empire. Megasthenes, the Greek ambassador to the Selecuids to the Court of Chandragupta Maurya, reported that the palace compared in its magnificence with the palace of Darius of Persepolis in Persia. The few ruins that survive appear to confirm this.

The Arts of the Andhra Dynasty: The Andhra dynasty known to itself on inscriptions by the name of Satavahana and by other names, enjoyed favourable political circumstances, gave rise to the finest example of rock architecture, along the northwestern and then on the east coast at Amravati.

The Amravati School: The scenes depicted in Amravati reliefs are generally extremely complex and lively, with characters shown moving freely both in groups and singly, and in a wide variety of stances. In the works at Nagarjunakonda and Amravati, the silpin, or Indian artist-craftsmen, achieve a fusion of metaphysical and tactile reality, thereby attaining a unique balance that gives Indian art a special place in the history of world art. The Indian artist's unique contribution is to have created eternal values that are immediately understood.

The Gandhara School: The school of Gandhara, which was more less contemporary with the schools of Mathura and Amravati, developed and reached its zenith in the northwest frontier zones, especially in Afghanistan and in the area now known as Pakistan.

The Mathura School : Mathura stands on the Jamuna river in western Uttar Pradesh and close to one of India's oldest city. It lay on the main trade routes from north India to the rest of Asia, and by the time of the Maurya and Sunga dynasties (4th to 1st centuries BC). was not only a leading commercial and religious centre and a place of pilgrimage for many different sects, but also the focal point of a highly creative literary and artistic school.

The school of Mathura, with red sandstone sculptures, the material for which was quarried from the Sikri caves outside the city, was contemporary with the Gandhara school.

3. *Gupta and Post-Gupta Arts:* In the realm of sculpture and painting Gupta art marks the highest reach of the Indian genius. Its influence radiated over India and beyond. By the end of the Gupta period the whole region of South East Asia had been deeply influenced by Indian thought and custom especially in Indian religion. Its keynote is balance and freedom from convention. It is thoroughly Indian in spirit and is marked by classic restraint, a highly developed taste and deep aesthetic feeling. Its ideal was the combination of beauty and virtue.

Notable panels such as the Gajendra moksha, Vishnu reclining on Ananta, undoubtedly rank among the best specimens of Hindu sculpture. Samudra Gupta issued no less than eight types of gold coinage of great artistic value. Referring to the coin, which shows Samudra Gupta with the Vina on the observe and Lakshmi on the reverse, Percy Brown says:

> *'the excellent modelling of the king's figure, the skilful delineation of the features, the careful attention to details and the general ornateness of the design in the best specimens constitutes this type as the highest expression of the Gupta numismatic art.*

The Gupta art is famous for Rupam or concept of beauty. The Gupta artists applied themselves to the worship of beautiful form in many ways. They worshipped art in order to awaken a new sense of spiritual joy and nobility. There are many distinguishing features of the Gupta art. We find both refinement and restraint. The Gupta artists relied more on elegance than on volume. Their art showed simplicity of expression and spiritual purpose. Some of the most beautiful images of Shiva belong to this period. They created the Ardhanarishvara form of Shiva where the deity is represented as half male and half female.

The iron pillar near New Delhi is an outstanding example of Gupta craftmanship. Its total height inclusive of the capital is 23 feet 8 inches. Its entire weight is 6 tons. The pillar consists of a square abacus, the melon shaped member and a capital. According to Percy Brown, this pillar is a remarkable tribute to the genius and manipulative dexterity of the Indian worker.

The cultural achievements of the Guptas evoked praise from the historians, both foreign and Indian. According to L.D. Barnett, "Gupta period is in the annals of classical India almost what perclean age is in the history of Greece."

Vincent Smith wrote: "The age of the great Gupta kings presented a more agreeable and satisfactory picture than any other period in the history of Hindu India. Literature, art and science flourished in a degree beyond ordinary and gradual changes in religion were effected without persecution."

Sardar Kavalam Madhava Panikkar (1896-1963) observed: "The two hundred years of the Gupta rule may be said to mark the climax of Hindu imperial tradition."

The poet Kalidasa, was one of the "Nine Jewels" a group representing the best minds of the kingdom, who were gathered together at the court of Chandragupta II, in the 5th century AD. The figurative art of the Gupta period clearly shows that artists had a full knowledge of the best works produced and the most advanced techniques developed in the past.

There was intense commercial and cultural intercourse between Asian mainland, and the influence of Gupta art spread very widely, impressing its iconographical and stylistic tendencies on many foreign artists. Chinese and Central Asian pilgrims came to India to visit the shrines and to study in the best universities in the land.

This was the Golden Age of Indian Art-of splendour and of the most flourishing artistic resurgence to occur in India.

Dr. Ananda Coomaraswamy, regarded Gupta art as the:

> *"flower of our established tradition, a polished and perfect medium, like the Sanskrit language, for the establishment of thought and feeling. Its character is self-possessed, urbane, at once exuberant and formal Philosophy and faith possess a common language in this art that is at once abstract and sensuous, reserved and passionate."*

A.L. Basham made the following observation about the achievement of the Gupta period:

> *"This was surely a period of high civilization in every sense, but especially in the truest sense of the term-an age of equilibrium, when human relations reached a degree of kindliness rare in the history of the world, and the best minds of India expressed the fullness and goodness of life in imperishable art and literature."*

Post Gupta Age: During the six centuries following the Gupta Age (AD 600-1200) the chief interest in the history of Indian art was centred around the evolution of different types of temple architecture. A number of temples were constructed. The grandest example of Orissan architecture is the famous Sun temple of Konark, a symphony in stone, constructed during the reign of Narasimhadeva (1238-64).

The temple was conceived on a gigantic scale and was intended to be an architectural replica of the chariot of the sun being whirled along through the heaven by seven stately horses. Around the basement of the temple are twelve giant wheels with beautiful carvings. At the main entrance are two caparisoned steeds straining to drag the chariot through space. The whole building is ornamented with exquisite sculptures presenting an alluring pageant of sculptured magnificence. No wonder, Abul Fazl was struck by the grandeur of the temple and wrote in his Ain-I-Akbari that "even those whose judgment is critical and who are difficult to please stand amazed at the sight."

Rock Temples and Monasteries: Hindu temples mostly dedicated to Shiva, were carved in the rock at Ajanta and

Ellora. Rock-cut temple, 164 ft. deep, 109 ft. wide, 98 ft. high. Est. 200,000 tons of rock excavated, reputedly using 1" chisels over a span of nearly 100 years. Both as architecture and examples of decoration they were more successful, in their simplicity, than were the Buddhist temples, even though they followed the same general plan. Similar rock cut shrines are also to be found on the island of Elephanta near Mumbai and other places.

In the temples dedicated to Shiva, the images do not usually crowd one upon the other, as they often do in the Buddhist shrines. All is simpler and more sober. The reliefs are placed at much greater intervals, displaying a more mature spatial concept. The walls are decorated with life size figures depicting mythological events, giving an overall effect of monumentality and imposing power.

The Kailash Temple intended to be an earthly replica of Shiva's splendour, the most extensive and most sumptuous of the rock-cut shrines, worthy of being ranked among the wonders of the world.

Philip Meadows Taylor (1808-1876) an Anglo-Indian administrator and novelist, was born in Liverpool, England. He wrote on Ellora:

> *"this carving on some of the pillars, and of the lintels and architraves of the doors, is quite beyond description. No chased work in silver or gold could possibly be finer. By what tools this very hard, tough stone could have been wrought and polished as it is, is not at all intelligible at the present day."*

J. Griffiths wrote: "There for centuries the wild ravine and the basaltic rocks were the scene of an application of labour, skill, perseverance, and endurance that went to the excavation of these painted palaces, standing to this day as monuments of a boldness of conception and a defiance of difficulty as possible, we believe, to the modern as to the ancient Indian character. The worth of the achievement will be further evident from the fact that "much of the work has been carried on with the help of artificial light, and no great stretch of imagination is necessary to picture all that this involves in the Indian climate and in situations where thorough ventilation is impossible."

Richard Lannoy has written: "The Kailash temple at Ellora, a complete sunken Brahmanical temple carved out in the late seventh and eighth centuries AD is over 100 feet high, the largest structure in India to survive from ancient times, larger than the Parthenon. This representation of Shiva's mountain home, Mount Kailash in the Himalaya, took more than a century to carve, and three million cubic feet of stone were removed before it was completed.

In Europe's middle ages, the great cathedrals, including the one of Chartres, rose from the ground upwards to the sky, supported not so much by stone as by the powerful religious symbolism that drove the Christian church. In India, the craftsmen did not build, but removed the earth and stone to discover space in the service of a different religious symbolism, not one identified with any religious monolith, but instead, one to which different religious groups owed allegiance. Here Lannoy is more precise:

"A hollowed-out space in living rock is a totally different environment from a building constructed of quarried stone. The human organism responds in each case with a different kind of empathy. Buildings are fashioned in sequence by a series of uniformly repeatable elements, segment by segment, from a foundation upwards to the conjuction of walls and roof; the occupant empathizes with a visible tension between gravity and soaring tensile strength.

Entering a great building is to experience an almost imperceptible tensing in the skeletal muscles in response to constructional tension. Caves, on the other hand, are scooped out by a downward plunge of the chisel from ceiling to floor in the direction of gravity; the occupant empathizes with an invisible but sensed resistance, an unrelenting presence in the rock enveloping him; sculpted images and glowing pigments on the skin of the rock well forth from the deeps. To enter an Indian cave sanctuary is to experience a relaxation of physical tension in response to the implacable weight and density of solid rock."

Rizwan Salim writes about the beauty of Kailash:

"Gaze in wonder at the Kailash Mandir in the Ellora cave and remember that it is carved out of a solid stone hill, an effort that (inscriptions say) took nearly 200 years. This is art as devotion. The temple built by the Rashtrakuta kings (who also built the colossal sculpture in the Elephanta caves off Mumbai harbour) gives proof of the ancient Hindus' religious fervour. But the Kailash temple also indicated a will power, a creative imagination, and an intellect eager to take on the greatest of artistic challenges. The descendents of those who built the magnificent temples of Bhojpur and Thanjavur, Konark and Kailash, invented mathematics and urban surgery, created mind-body disciplines (yoga) of astonishing power, and built mighty empires would almost certainly have attained technological superiority over Europe."

K. De B. Codrington notes the technical skills of the builders of the Kailash temple at Ellora:

"The monolithic Kailash temple of Ellora, with its stupendous sculptures, is a marvel of engineering, unsurpassed by any in the world..." The Kaislas (very closely resembling in its outlines the Everest Peak, as Havell has demonstrated) has been scooped out of a hill, and stands four-square in a court yard hewn from solid rock, complete with gateways, nandi pavilion, staircases on either side, porches and subsidiary shrines—formed by the chisel, and sculptured from top to bottom without fault!"

Robert Payne (1911) an American critic, and author of the splendours of Asia: India, Thailand, Japan, in the Kailash temple at Ellora, for instance, he sees "nothing less than the mountain of creation. It was here that Shiva hammered out the shapes of men and women of fables and mythologies of universes and eternities." he writes. He is awed by the sweep of imagination, the exuberance and tumult of creation itself, depicted in stone.

About the truth and precision of the work, which are no less admirable than its boldness and extent, J. Griffiths has the following glowing testimony:

> *"During my long and careful study of the caves I have not been able to detect a single instance where a mistake has been made by cutting away too much stone; for if once a slip of this kind occurred, it could only have been repaired by the insertion of a piece which would have been a blemish."*

Percy Brown (1872-1955) has said:

> *"The temple of Kailash at Ellora is not only the most stupendous single work of art executed in India, but as an example of rock architecture it is unrivalled. Standing within its precincts and surrounded by its grey and hoary pavilions, one seems to be looking through into another world, not a world of time and space, but one of intense spiritual devotion expressed by such an amazing artistic creation hewn out of the earth itself. Gradually one becomes conscious of the remarkable imagination which conceived it, the unstinted labour which enabled it to be materialized and finally the sculpture with which it is adorned; this plastic decoration is its crowning glory, something more than a record of artistic form, it is a great spiritual achievement, every portion being a rich statement glowing with our meaning. The Kailash is an illustration of one of those rare occasions when men's minds, hearts, and hands work in unison towards the consummation of a supreme ideal. It was under such conditions of religious and cultural stability that this grand monolith representation of Shiva's paradise was produced."*

> *"The Kailash Temple, it is safe to say, is one of the most astonishing 'buildings' in the history of architecture. This shrine was not constructed of stone on stone, it was in fact not constructed at all: it was carved, sculpted in*

> *toto from the volcanic hillside! A squared, U-shaped trench was first cut into the slope to a depth of close to 100 feet. The 'liberated' mass in the centre was then patiently carved from the living rock to produce a freestanding, two-story Hindu temple of dazzling complexity. The temple, which is dedicated to Shiva, the often threatening god of the Hindu trilogy, measures 109 feet wide by 164 feet long. It stands on an elevated plinth to attain greater presence in its tight surroundings. The complex consists of entry, Nandi (i.e. bull) shrine, open porch, main hall, and inner sanctum. Variously scaled panels, friezes, and sculpture highlight many surfaces."*
>
> *Historian Romesh C. Dutt (1848-1909) writes: "The Kailash is imposing in its solid grandeur."*

Perhaps the most spectacular example is the Kailashanatha temple at Ellora, which is a transition from the rock-cut to the free standing style, wholly cut from the rock of the hillside, to which no further material was added. The plan of a free-standing temple is rigorously adhered to and it is stylistically close to the southern temple.

The Kailash temple is approximately of the same area as the Parthenon at Athens and is one and a half times higher than the Greek structure. The number of stone cutters and workmen employed and the expense involved in cutting the temple must have been immense.

S. Natarajan has remarked: "It is an enormous shrine carved wholly out of an isolated block of stone with a number of sculptures characterized by dramatic pose and beauty of movement, fine modelling and sculptural accuracy in carving. Particularly remarkable is the skill with which different emotions are portrayed.

In the sculpture of Ravana trying to lift the Kailash, the serene calmness of Shiva and the excitement and fear of Parvati as she clings to Shiva for support are quite visible portrayed. In the dread dance of Shiva the principle of universal violence and unrestrained ecstasy in destruction are brought out while the "Relief of the Kiss" portrays the infinite bliss of divine love."

- Says Ernest Binfield Havell:

  "The design of the Kailash remained, for all time, the perfect model of a Shivalinga,-the temple craftsman's vision of Shiva's wondrous palace in his Himalayan glacier, where in his Yogi's cell the Lord of the Universe, the great magician, controls the cosmic forces by the power of thought; the holy rivers, creating the life in the world below, enshrined in His matted locks; Parvati, His other Self, the Universal Mother, watching by His side."

Sculptors had by this time acquired a thorough knowledge of anatomy, and were able to give expression to a great range of movement and gesture. They were able to give material form to the sensuous visions of the poets by their masterly handling of the female shape, creating a form of art un paralled elsewhere. Indian art is rich in representations of the female body, a subject in which Indian artists appear to have excelled since earliest times.

O' artisan, genius of a man!

Look at your lustrous creation.

You speak poetry with your tools,

You give life to a structure of stone!

O' artisan, genius of a man!

You are the pride of my nation!

Hindu artists accepted the sensual and erotic as integral part of life, and death with them accordingly in their carvings, paintings and writing. To some Western eyes, used to Victorian standards, the results may appear offensive, but these have a calm dignity far removed from the more self-conscious efforts of lesser artists.

In classic Sanskrit treatises, the sculptor has been given various names. He is known as the *Sadhak* (Admirer), the *Mantrin* (Wizard), and the *Yogi* (Visionary). This is perhaps explained by the ultimate aim of the sculptor to be primarily spiritual and only secondarily aesthetic. The sculptor was not endeavouring to portray the mere perfection of the physical structure, as with the Greeks. He believed that even the perfect human figure could not fully manifest the higher spiritual values of life, nor contain within itself the attributes and qualities of the divinity.

Therefore, to give expression to such abstract conceptions, the sculptor consciously set for himself an ideal, which was not based on the contemplation of the natural form, but upon meditation of the divine form. Consequently, you would notice a distinctive power of suggestiveness in the sculpted forms. Perhaps their supreme function, the idols and forms suggest attributes and possibilities beyond the range of mortals. But every time the chisel carved a shape, it was based on *Shilpashastras* (axioms of sculpture). Drawing inspiration from the mind, mythology and experiences, the sculptor has left behind an impression that cannot be ravaged even by time itself. Perhaps.

ART OF THE PALLAVA DYNASTY

The Pallava dynasty succeeded the Andhra dynasty in the east Deccan in about the 5th century and endured until around the end of the 9th century. Like that of the Gupta kings, the court of the Pallava rulers was a centre for eminent men of letters and art. It is known from contemporary inscriptions that Mahendra-varman (600-635), who was called the Temple Builder, was a great patron of the arts, particularly architecture. Unfortunately none of his construction have survived.

Arnold Hermann Ludwig Heeren (1760-1842) says: "It is without an involuntary shudder that we pass the threshold of these spacious grottoes, and compare the weight of these ponderous roofs with the apparent slenderness and inadequacy of its support, an admirable and ingenious effect which must have required no ordinary share of abilities in the architect to calculate and determine!" He concludes: "Such are the seven pagodas or ancient monuments so-called, at Mavalipuram on the Coromandel (Cholamandal) coast, of which extraordinary buildings it will be hardly too much to assert that they will occupy a most distinguished place in the scale of human skill and ingenuity."

CAVE TEMPLES, REGAL ARTS AND ARCHITECTURE

Many cave temples were excavated and carved in the same period in the region between Tiruchirappalli and the Krishna estuary. These temples were mostly dedicated to Lord Shiva. King Narasimha-varman (625-645) built the port of Mamallapuram, near Chennai, where he ordered the excavation of many rock temples. He also enriched his citadel with five raths, open air sculptures rather than temples, since they were carved out of isolated rock outcrops to imitate real temples. The five raths at Mamallapuram are named after the Pandavas, the heroes of Mahabharata. The abundant decoration on the upper stories of these buildings gives them a baroque air, an effect which was maintained and elaborated in medieval India. The Gangahara Relief at Tiruchirappalli is a work of remarkable plastic worth and is charged with vitality and expressive force.

The finest sculptured work at Mallapuram, which is also the major achievement of Pallava sculptors, is the Descent of the Ganga, carved out of a granite rock. A split running down the rockface provides the channel for the water representing the sacred river. The subject is taken from an episode in the Kiratarjuniya, by the 6th century poet Bharavi. A whole world of human and divine beings, entire families of animals in the most varied postures, monkeys, elephants and cats, all issue as it were from the living rock to pay homage to Lord Shiva for his miraculous gift to them of the Ganga springing down from the mountain. The work is rich in detail of all kinds, and is completely successful aesthetically, whether looked at as a whole or in detail.

This colossal work achieved a synthesis between Gupta elegance and the lively narrative art of the Amravati school:

"Indian Art "says art critic E. B. Havell "is always super ably decorative.

"The best Indian Sculpture touched a deeper note of feeling and finer sentiments than the best Greek. There

is in this art a depth and spirituality which never entered into the soul of Greece."

Rashtrakuta dynasty who were undoubtedly responsible for a number of cave temples excavated in the rock at Ellora, which was the capital of the early kings of the dynasty. The temple of Dharmanatha at Malwa and the temple of Shiva at Elephanta may also be attributed to them. The most important Rashtrakuta temple is the Kailasnath temple, which was constructed in the reign of Krishna-I (757-83).

The style of the Kailasnath temple is characterized by pyramidal roofs sloping down to great quandrangular pilasters, which are balanced by thick projecting cornices and panels decorated with sculpture. The sculptures on the inner walls of the main shrine show flying spirits in audacious and exciting, but also extremely elegant postures. The reliefs in the sanctuary of Shiva rely on the visual effects obtainable from chiaroscuro, or light and shadow, and broken movement.

The theatrical effect evident 200 years earlier at Elephanta reaches a climactic conclusion in the Kailash where the image of Ravana in one relief panel is actually detached from its background so that the action takes place on a deeply shadowed stone stage. The Kailash is indeed a daring undertaking that speaks eloquently both of the creative genius of the architect and the driving enthusiasm of Krishna-I.

Originally, both exterior and interior of this rock-cut temple carried painted adornment over a thin layer of plaster. In certain areas, three layers of paint are discernible, indicating the continual refurbishment of the mural decoration. Further confirmation of such renewal of the murals come from 16th century Muslim accounts which speak of the Kailash as Rang Mahal or Coloured Mansion.

Chola dynasty ruled from 907 to 1053 in south India. The period was one of comparative peace and prosperity, and saw the production of a considerable amount of notable art. The magnificent temples which were built in south Indian cities were not only religious centres, but also as factors in the economic and social unification of the religion. Temples were built in exaggerated manner, rising up very steeply from the plinth to a lofty pyramidal tower ending in a wide cupola. The temple of Shiva at Tanjore, has a tower of 190 feet high rising from a 180 foot base. The tower is surmounted by a slab weighing eighty tons.

The gopura, or main doors, also assumed great importance taking on a monumental quality under the succeeding Pandya dynasty.

The great temples of South India are marvels of massive construction. All of the southern kingdoms fell before the Moslem invasion of the 14th century. The Muslim invasion in India and their iconoclastic zeal snapped further development of art and gradually choked its perennial flow of inspiration. Because art in all phases thrives only in peace and security. The Meenakshi temple, is a spectacular pastiche of South Indian architecture, the shrine housing the deity dates from the 12th century.

According to the great Indian historian R. C. Majumdar (1888-1980): "Those monolithic temples wrought out of massive stone, are complete with all the details of an ordinary temple and stand today as an undying testimony to the superb quality of Pallava art."

Dr. James Fergusson writes this about the Hullabid Temple:

> *"All the pillars of the Parthenon are identical, while no two faces of the Indian temple are the same; every convolution of every scroll is different. No two canopies in the whole building are alike, and every part exhibits a joyous exuberance of fancy, scorning every mechanical restraint. All that is wild in human faith or warm in human feeling is found portrayed on these walls"*

GRAVITY PILLAR

This temple was built in 12th century AD and is an example of medieval art in India. It took 103 years to complete. The temple's exterior is made of beautifully carved stone with sculptures and friezes. Inside, the temple is decorated with richly carved panels and pillars. There is a tall pillar in the centre of the temple courtyard which is balanced by gravity alone, there is no material cementing it. The 40 foot tall and 20,000 kg stone 'gravity pillar' stands in the courtyard of the Chenna Keshava temple, built by Vishnuvardhana (1110-1140 AD) in Belur.

The engineers made a meticulous study of the wind force, at the place, calculating a height and weight for the stone pillar which could stand for all time. The pillar has been without any hole, hook, peg or cementing of any sort to hold it. There is a channel running from end to end at the base, through which one can pass a stick, proving that the pillar neither fully rests on the platform nor is dug into it.

Speaking of the Halebid Temple, Vincent A. Smith wrote: "One of the most marvellous exhibitions of human labour to be found even in the patient East! The architectural framework, it will be observed, is used mainly as a back ground for the display of an infinity of superb decorations, which leaves no space uncovered and gives the eye no rest."

"Hindu sculpture," says E. B. Havell, "has produced a master piece in the great stone alto-relivo of Durga slaying the demon Mahisha, found at Singasari in Java, and now in the Ethnographic Musuem, Leyden..Judge by any standard it is a wonderful work of art, grandly composed, splendidly thorough in technique, expressing the extraordinary power and concentrated passion the wrath and might of the Supreme Benificence roused to warfare with Spirit of Evil. The student will find in this phase of Indian imaginative art an intensity of feeling-a wonderful suggestion of elemental passion transcending all the feeble emotions of humanity-a revelation of powers of the unseen which nothing in European art has ever approached, unless it be in the creations of Michel Angleo or in the music of Wagner!"

WONDERS OF ELEPHANTA (GHARAPURI CAVES)

A notable achievement of architectural sculpture in Western India during this period are the cave temples on the island of Elephants (Gharapuri) in the Mumbai harbour. There are altogether seven caves on the island. The central one contains some masterpieces of sculpture representing some of the 16 lila-murtis of Shiva as Nataraja, Lakulisa, Andhakari, Gangadhara, Atdhanariswara, Somaskanda, Ravananugraha, etc. But the best representation of Shiva is as Mahesamurti, otherwise known as Trimurti.

Describing the image of Mahesamurti, Francois-Auguste-Rene Rodin (1840-1917) French sculptor has said:

> *"This full, pouting mouth, rich in sensuous expressions, these lips like a lake of pleasure, fringed by the noble, palpitating nostrils."*

According to French art historian, Rene Grousset (1885-1952) who speaks of the Trimurti statue at Elephanta Caves:

> *"Universal art has succeeded in few materialization of the Divine as powerful and also as balanced. He believed that it is "the greatest representation of the pantheistic god created by the hands of man." He concludes with poetic enthusiasm: "Never have the overflowing sap of life, the pride of force superior to everything, the secret intoxication of the inner god of things been so serenely expressed."*

In the words of Rene Grousset, "The three countenances of the one being are here harmonized without a trace of effort. There are few material representations of the divine principle at once as powerful and as well balanced as this in the art of the whole world. Nay, more, here we have undoubtedly the grandest representation of the pantheistic God ever made by the hand of man Indeed, never have the exuberant vigour of life, the tumult of universal joy expressing itself in ordered harmony, the pride of a power superior to any other, and the secret exaltation of the divinity immanent in all things found such serenely expressed."

The giant triple-headed Maheshmurti, is 18 foot high sculpture represents the supreme aspect of Shiva, which embodies not only the creator and destroyer but also the maintainer of the cosmos. The three massive heads have been conceived as a psychological and aesthetic whole, with the central serene face providing a focus for the formal design. The central image of the Great God (Shiva Mahadeva) presents a mood which is detached and other worldly, and represents Shiva in his Tatpurusha aspect, which is the supreme, serene, and beneficent one.

The most outstanding of early caves is located on the small island of Elephanta, outside Mumbai. It is dedicated to Lord Shiva. This is the most elaborate and important large pillared excavation with more than 16,000 square feet of floor space, depicting various aspects of Shiva. He is represented in numerous manifestations, such as the Great Ascetic (Yogishvara), Lord of the Dancers (Nataraja), dual male and female aspect (Ardhanarishvara) and the Descent of the river Ganga (Gangahara). Also impressive among the works are the giant door-guardian figures who stand flanking the four portals to the temple. Unfortunately, these figures, and the majority of the relief panels, have suffered extensive damage, from an early Portuguese military garrison.

The scale and magnificence of the main cave suggests that it was a royal commission. The personal characteristics of the three gods are clearly marked on their faces: they have in common a brooding assurance of their supreme divinity. The sculptor was a master able to combine the three heads into a homogenous bust to create a unique effigy. While the broad shoulders seem to belong to the central face, they also meld convincingly with the other two heads in profile. The caves of Elephanta, with the powerful and subtle Trimurti, date to Gupta period, the Golden Age of India.

Frijof Capra (1939) the famous theoretical high-energy physicist has observed:

> *"A superb sculpture of Shiva in the Hindu temple of Elephanta shows three faces of the god..in the centre the sublime union, of the two aspects in the magnificent head of Shiva Maheshvara, the Great Lord, radiating serene tranquility and transcendental aloofness. In the same temple, Shiva is also represented in androgynous form–half male, half female–the flowing movement of the god's body and the serene detachment of his/her face symbolizing, again, the dynamic unification of the male and female."*

"One of my first excursions in Bombay was to the famous Elephanta (Gharapuri) caves, a magnificent ancient temple dedicated to Shiva with huge stone sculptures representing the god in his many manifestations. I stood in awe in front of those powerful sculptures whose reproductions I had known and loved for many years: the triple image of Shiva Maheshvara, the Great Lord, radiating serene tranquillity and peace; Shiva Ardhanari, the stunning unification of male and female forms in the rhythmic, swaying movement of the deity's androgynous body and in the serene detachment of his/her face; and Shiva Nataraja the celebrated four-armed Cosmic Dancer whose superbly balanced gestures express the dynamic unity of all life." "I had a more powerful experience of Shiva sculpture in the Ellora caves. The beauty and power of these sacred caves are beyond words."

While the iconography of Indian art was uncomprehendingly received as the repository of esoteric wisdom or the outcome of demonic religion, early travellers did not hesitate to reflect on the architectural grandeur of the Hindu temples and the delicate craftsmanship of the surface sculptures on them. They were ready to appreciate the skill involved in the excavations The cave temples near Bombay and Goa, notably Elephanta, Hanheri, and Mandapeswar, thus came to the notice of Europeans.

Initially these temples suffered at the hands of religious zealots as attempts were made to convert them into Christian churches. From G. P. Maffei (1588), the official historian of Jesuit missions, we learn that after purging one of the temples at Elephanta of all previous profanations. Father Antoine had dedicated it to God. Presumably the building was aesthetically pleasing enough to be consecrated to God so long as it could be cleansed of its pagan association.

In the midst of unrelenting hostility there are occasional grudging tributes to Elephanta. Father Gasper reported that many monuments of skill and magnificence were to be seen in India. Maffei himself remarked about temples "which are able to compete in magnificence with the most superb of ancient Rome." Later, the Jesuit historian, Du Jarrie (1608), also praised

'Temples fort sompteux and magnifiques' Garcia da Orta remarked that Elephanta was a fine sight when he first arrived from Portugal in 1534, but was becoming the pasture ground of local cattle, while Diego du Couto lamented the imminent destruction of 'one of the most beautiful things in the world'.

Partha Mitter has written: "After suffering from the depredations of Portuguese soldiers they began to attract men of letters, visitors in the age of Humanism who brought with them certain powers of observation.

The cave temples lend themselves easily to romanticization because of their grand conception and massive scale, of the interplay of light and shadow within and without them and finally on account of the wonderful visual dialogue between the simplicity of the total conception and the richness of decorative details. It was they who spread the news that these monuments were some of the greatest wonders of the world."

The name Elephanta and that to Indians was known as Puri (Gharapuri). The name Elephanta originated from the large sculpture of an elephant that stood at the entrance to the temple, but has now disappeared.

The next visitor to Elephanta was the statesman Joao de Castro, a remarkable man and Renaissance personality with wide-ranging interests and accomplishments. Castro's navigational diary Roteiro de Goa ate Dio reflects a deep feeling of wonder on his part at the sight of the huge and magnificent temple at Elephanta, for he was thoroughly overwhelmed by the great 'boldness' of manner in which the whole edifice was hewn out of the hard, solid rock. A work of such magnitude and artifice, he declared, could not have been produced by mortals and it must be regarded as one of the wonders of the world. Castro was so impressed by the sculptures that he stated that "Indeed the proportions and symmetry with which each figure and everything else is made it would be worth the while of any painter to study it even if he were Apelles."

Diego du Couto whose career spanned a period of fifty years in India during which time he gradually came to appreciate the splendors of the cave temples of Elephanta. He took elaborate measurements of the 'remarkable' and 'stupendous' temple, remarking that it was laid on a north-to-south axis. He took enormous pains to go through the sculptural panels on every single wall in the main temple which were then described with great precision and care.

The elaborate plastic treatment of Shiva's matted hair with beautiful jewels set in it especially fascinated Couto who mentioned it admiringly on several occasions in his seventh Decade of his Asia book. We also learn from Couto, that the Elephanta interior was covered with a fine coat of lime and bitumen composition which 'made the Pagoda (temple) so bright, that it looked very beautiful and was worth seeing.' The colours have faded since in Elephanta, and only Couto's testimony remains to tell us how splendid it looked in the sixteenth century.

The veritable apotheosis of Elephanta came in 1875, when a grand banquet was held in the main cave in honour of the Prince of Wales who was visiting India, 'the brightest jewel in the Imperial crown.'

The Englishman John Ovington (1696) author of "A Voyage to Surat in the Year 1689, "was specially fascinated by the animal sculpture in Elephanta: "Here likewise are the just dimensions of a Horse Carved in Stone, so lively with such a Colour and Carriage and the shape finisht with that Exactness, that many have Fancyed it, at a distance, a living Animal, than only a bare Representation.'

According to the Cambride man, Dr. Fryer, Elephanta too was a 'miraculous Piece hewd out of solid stone; it is supported with Forty two Corinthian Pillars, being a Square, open on all sides but towards the East; where stands a statue with three Heads, crowned with strange Hieroglyphics.' He noted with regret that the Portuguese 'strive to erase the reminders of this Herculean Work, that it may sink into oblivion of its Founders.'

European reaction to Indian Art-Western stereotyping of Indian art and culture.

A failure of Western culture to come to terms with Hindu arts. In the early period of European explorations of Asia, travellers saw Hindu sacred images as infernal creatures and diabolic multiple-limbed monsters. The most famous of all stereotypes was that of monsters, presented in books as authentic portrait of Indian gods. From the earliest date the Christian Church had taught that all pagan religions were invented by the devil. The typical reactions of an early Western travellers were bound to reflect certain prejudices stemming from his Christian background as well as total ignorance of Hindu iconography.

The friar Odoric of Pordenone, who visited a number of places in south India between 1316-1318, gave a much fuller report of India and its inhabitants and their customs than did Marco Polo. He was the first traveler to leave a description of a monstrous idol in the form of half-human and half-ox. Odoric took the colossal Buddha figure in the Khotan area to be the devil.

Ralph Fitch, travelling between 1583-1591, was the first Englishman to report that the Hindu idols in Bijapur looked like the devil.

This is was when the British Raj embarked on a reconstruction of India's past in an effort to cope with the complexities of the conquered territories. After all, the secret of political control lay in a sound knowledge of the subject people.

The British writing suffered from being imprisoned with the Victorian framework. Their unwillingness to accept Indian art on its own terms was certainly due to the puritanical norms of the Victorian times.

Few were capable of understanding the supreme abstraction of Hindu philosophy. What they overlooked was the fact that Hindu art belonged to an entirely different world of imagination, one that did not correspond to the classical ideals. In early travel accounts Hind gods masquerade as pagan monsters. These travellers had been taught by the Church that all non-Christian religions were demonic. William Finch, who followed him in the years, 1608-1611, described the temples as, "pagoda, which are stone images of monstrous men fearful to behold."

Most travellers followed the medieval traditions in calling Hindu gods the devil. After all, had not the Church Fathers taught that all pagan gods were demons and devils?

A good deal of hostile or unsympathetic western criticism of Indian civilization has been directed in the past against its aesthetic side and taken the form of disdainful or violent depreciation of its fine arts, architecture, sculpture and painting. This aesthetic side of a people's culture is of the highest importance and demands almost as much scrutiny and carefulness of appreciation as the philosophy, religion and central formative ideas which have been the foundation of Indian life and of which much of the art and literature is a conscious expression in significant aesthetic forms. The Indian mind in its natural poise finds it almost or quite as difficult really, that is to say, spiritually to understand the arts of Europe, as the ordinary European mind to enter into the spirit of Indian painting and sculpture.

Alfred Maskell wrote about Indian art in his book Ivories

"We feel that the artist has been ever bound and enslaved by the traditions of Hindu mythology. We are met at every turn by the interminable processions of monstrous gods and goddesses, these Buddhas and Krishnas, Vishnus and Ramas, these hideous deities with animals' heads and innumerable arms, these dancing women with expressionless faces and strange garments. In his figures the Hindu artists seems absolutely incapable to reproduce the human form.."

This is ignorant and childish rodomontade is here quoted only because it is typical. Perhaps the easiest way to show its true value would be to ask you to imagine similar words spoken by an Oriental, who should substitute the word "Christian" for the word "Hindu": "Enslaved by the traditions of Christian mythology, interminable processions of crucifixes, and Madonnas"-would not this be an idle criticism of medieval European art?"

European reaction to Hindu art was obviously negative. Even today non-European societies are held by the grip of European cultural values.

The indifference in England towards Hindu art was particularly marked. For all its impressive accumulation of information archaeological scholarship had been inadequate for appreciating Indian art.

This early attitude may not be entirely expected; what is remarkable is that the attitude persisted even into the modern period.

The gods and goddesses were frequently portrayed with multiple arms, which prompted early European travellers to speak of them as 'monstrosities'. Certain writers, speaking of the many-armed images of Indian arts, have treated this peculiarity as an unpardonable defect. "After 300 AD." says Mr. Vincent Smith, "Indian sculpture properly so-called hardly deserves to be reckoned as art.

In spite of a great deal of contact between India and the West, very little has changed in the last 700 years since the first written accounts of Indian culture appeared in the writings of the travellers to India. The early writers had to resort to narrow Christian medievalism for their distorted vision of India, and more recently, to myopic rationalism and pretentious scholarship—all of which have contributed to the total "failure" in the Western interpretation of India. The main problem seems to be that Westerners do not have an appropriate framework to objectively assess and appreciate the pluralistic themes and the rich textures that Indian art and culture represent. This lack of understanding exposes Western (especially American) superciliousness that continues to plague the Westerners' intolerance for other cultures.

The idea connected with sex symbolism in Hindu art and ritual are generally misinterpreted by those who take them out of the environment of Indian social life. In the Upanishads sexual relationship is described as one of the means of apprehending the divine nature, and throughout oriental literature it is constantly used metaphorically to express the true relationship between the human soul and God. The words of Sir Monier-Williams are very applicable to the whole question of sex symbolism in Indian religious art: "In India the relation between the sexes is regarded as a sacred mystery, and is never held to be suggestive of improper or indecent ideas." Few aspects of Indian culture are so often, perhaps so wilfully misunderstood as this sex-symbolism in art. Sir Monier-Williams, when in referring to the presence of many words of erotic significance in his Sanskrit Dictionary, he says that "in India the relationship between the sexes is regarded as sacred mystery, and is never held to be suggestive of improper or indecent ideas." As much could hardly be said of Europe. In such an idealization of life itself there lies the strength of Hinduism, and in its absence the weakness of modern Christianity.

India is wont to suggest the eternal and inexpressible infinites in terms of sensuous beauty. The love of man for woman or for nature are one with his love for God. Nothing is common or unclean. All life is sacrament, no part of it more so than another, and there is no part of it that may not symbolize eternal and infinite things. India draws no distinction between sacred and profane love. All love is a divine mystery; it is the recognition of Unity. Indeed the whole distinction of sacred and profane is for India meaningless, and so it is that the relation of the soul to God may be conceived in terms of the passionate adoration of woman for her lover.

DENIGRATION BY MARXIST HISTORIANS

According to so called "Eminent Historians" of India (Romila Thapar and co) "Lord Indra is "rowdy and amoral." The God Krishna has a "rather questionable personal record." Lord Shiva is just "a development of phallic cult." Bhakti is just the reflection of "the complete dependence of the serfs or tenants on the landowners in the context of Indian feudal society."

That they should see nothing but questionable conduct in Krishna, that even a foreigner-Stella Kramrisch-should see such an effulgence in the concept of Shiva and this eminent historian (refer to D. N. Jha, Ancient India, An introductory outline p. 18) just the extended phallus, that he should see nothing more in bhakti than a reflection of feudalism-what telling evidence of the success of Maucaulay, the Missionaries and Marx! While our eminent historians try to belittle the achievements of Indian art and architecture in the ancient period-by insinuating that it was derived from other countries, by seeing only a reflection of the life of the privileged classes-Soviet historians talk of the high standards the Indians attained in these spheres. They talk of its high originality. They talk of "the true masterpieces of Indian world of art" as exemplified by the Ajanta caves." So, the gods of the Hindus are "rowdy and amoral," with a "rather questionable personal record," they are just developments of primitive cults-animism, fertility, and the rest, specially the phallic cult!

These (Indian) intellectuals and their patrons have worked a diabolic inversion: the inclusive religion, the pluralist spiritual search of our people and land, they have projected as intolerant, narrow-minded, obscurantist; and the exclusivist, totalitarian, revelatory religions and ideologies – out to be the epitomes of tolerance, open-mindedness, democracy, secularism!

At the academic level, Indian Marxists are welcomed in American seminars as privileged commentators on "Hindu communalism." It is ironic as well as disturbing that a movement which still swears by Lenin (whose October 1917 coup d'etat deposed the first democratic Russian Parliament) and Stalin, is hailed in Western universities as the guardian of a civil polity against the encroaching barbarism of Hindu revivalism."

Thus, Romila Thapar and R. S. Sharma are quoted at some length as representatives of Indian Marxist thought in A Dictionary of Marxist Thought-By Tom Bottomore. Harvard University Press. December 1983. ASIN: 0674205251.

Dr. Ernest Binfield Havell (1861-1934) states: "This Shiva's emblem symbolizes the reproductive power of nature."

Art of a Hindu is a manifestation of God as has been aptly pointed out by Pandit Jawaharlal Nehru "Art is intimately associated with the Indian religion and philosophy that it is difficult to appreciate it fully unless one has some knowledge of the ideas which govern the Indian mind for in Indian art there is always religious urge, a looking beyond.."

Dr. Karan Singh has called Lord Shiva: "The great primeval lord and a powerful symbol representing the creative force behind all manifestations. The magnificent image of Shiva dancing represents one of the high water marks of Human art. The magnificent monolithic sculpture of Trimurti on the Elephanta island is one of the world's great artistic creations, this massive sculpture shows clearly the three aspects integrated in a single, divine entity."

Annie Besant (1847-1933) wrote: "Indian Art is a blossom of the Tree of the Divine Wisdom, full of suggestions from worlds invisible, striving to express the ineffable, and it can never be understood merely by the emotional and the intellectual; only in the light of the Spirit can its inner significance be glimpsed."

Rizwan Salim has wisely observed:

"From the earliest surviving Gupta period temples of the fifth century to the grand Mughal monuments and Rajput palaces, Hindustan has more than a thousand year old tradition of stunningly beautiful and awe-inspiring architecture. Yet so lacking in cultural pride have Indian architects been, that after 1950 they eagerly adopted the European Leftwing architects' Bauhaus style, the architecture of ugly concrete boxes. Now they slavishly follow the currently fashionable West "Post-Modern" style that developed out of the Bauhaus. There has been no authentic Indian architecture now, structures replicating shapes and forms, motifs and decorative elements of ancient Hindu temple and Mughal and Rajput palace art."

Stella Krimrisch: "The mystery of Shiva has left its imprint over the millennia on the resilient matrix of the Indian mind."

Jawaharlal Nehru has said:

"It is not some secret doctrine or esoteric knowledge that has kept India vital and going through these long ages, but a tender humanity, a varied and tolerant culture and a deep understanding of life and its mysterious ways. Her abundant vitality flows out from age to age in her magnificent literature and art, though we have only a small part of it with us and much lies hidden

or has been destroyed by nature or man's vandalism. The Trimurti in the Elephanta caves might well be the many-faced statue of India itself, powerful, with compelling eyes, full of deep knowledge and understanding, looking down upon us."

H. H. Wilson also says: "Whatever may have been the origin of this form of worship in India, the notions upon which it was founded, according to the impure fancies of European writers, are not to be traced in even the Shaiva Puranas."

Ananda K. Coomaraswamy has rightfully observed:

"It is impossible to treat of art as an isolated phenomenon apart from the spiritual and physical life of the people who gave it birth. Indian art cannot be understood by those without sympathy for Indian culture; and this is still a rare thing. The orthodox Christian, the materialist, and the Imperialist are all, in so far as they are what these names imply, constitutionally unable to sympathize with the ideals of Indian civilization. Indian art is essentially religious; and those who are entirely ignorant of and hopelessly out of sympathy with Indian religions, as well as those who in the name of Puritanism would secularize or abolish art entirely, have not in them a capacity of understanding."

The Master of the Dance-(Nataraja)

Hollier-Larousse, author of World Mythology has written:

"As destroyer and renewer, Shiva determines the rhythm of the worlds. Thousands of years before scientists discovered the similarity of structure between the atomic nucleus and the solar systems, the Hindus asserted that the same rhythm must of necessity be found at all stages of creation and in all domains. That is why ideas about rhythm and density-play a role in Hindu thought comparable to that which we associate with weight and shape, which are merely manifestation of them.

Now what in the eyes of man is the purest manifestation of rhythm, if not dancing? So Shiva is the supreme dancer, the king of dancing Nataraja. And he is frequently depicted as such, in a pose of perfect harmony, in the midst of a vast crown on which myriad sparks alternately flare and die again. Even so worlds appear and disappear. Prostrate beneath his feet, Tripurasura, the demon of the three towns, of the three worlds, obligingly offer to act as his stool. And Shiva makes use of him, for his triple universe is the entire reason for his dance.

Better than any words, the dance could in fact evoke the supreme and perfect rhythm of this dynamic and triumphant joy in which the individual is at one with great 'interplay' of the world (lila). 'He whom no sign could describe is made known to us by his mystic dancing," says a Shivaist poet from Southern India."

Dr. Ernest Binfield Havell has described the statue of Shiva Nataraja at the Elephant Caves:

> *"is a majestic conception and an embodiment of titanic power: "Though the rock itself seems to vibrate with the rhythmic movement of the dance, the noble head bears the same look of serene, calm and dispassion which illuminate the face of the Buddha."*

Sharada Srinivasan, a Fellow at National Institute of Advanced Studies, Bangalore writes:

> *"Fritjof Capra catapulted Nataraja into a modern-day scientific icon when he euphorically stated in his book of 1974 The Tao of Physics that:*

"the dancing Shiva is the dancing universe, the ceaseless flow of energy going through an infinite variety of patterns that melt into one another".

It has been argued that the Nataraja metal icon can be viewed as a human or anthropomorphic representation of dynamic cosmic phenomena. Indeed, texts such as Naisadhiyacharita poetically describe the scattering of myriad stars in the sky by Shiva's dance and splintering of rocks and crystals of Mount Kailash while the Vadnagar Prasasti speaks of Shiva playing newly created planets as if they were crystal balls.

A close examination of the symbolism evident in Chidambaram—the temple by the sea coast of Tamil Nadu dedicated to the worship of Nataraja—shows that the ancient seers' revelations encompass concepts which are at once both mystical and tantalizingly scientific.

Chit is consciousness and ambaram refers to the cosmos and a literal translation would be the cosmic consciousness. The shrine to Nataraja at Chidambaram architecturally and conceptually links the cosmic realms and the inner consciousness through Shiva's dance—the anandatandava or dance of bliss—where Shiva is described by the Tamil poet, Umapati of Chidambaram, as sachchidananda; that is, 'being, consciousness and bliss'.

The Chit Sabha or the golden-roofed 'Hall of Consciousness' in the Chidambaram temple is the only shrine where the Nataraja metal icon is worshipped inside the innermost sanctum, the garbhagriha. Instead, inside the Chit Sabha, by the side of the Nataraja bronze, is the enigmatic Chidambara Rahasyam or the secret revelation of Chidambaram, wherein Shiva is worshipped as the formless akasa lingam. It symbolizes the sky, represented, aptly, by a curtained empty space. The curtain represents the aroopa or formless manifestation of Shivakami or Shakti, the primordial feminine energy who inspires and witnesses Shiva's cosmic dance.

This presages an intuitive understanding of concepts such as the wave-particle duality of quantum physics, with matter and energy being sides of the same coin.

The Tatvaryastava stotra, a hymn on Nataraja at Chidambaram, describes Shiva as sky-clad and Chidambaram as the sacred spot for the element, sky, where Shiva, as Lord of the universe, is both the universal dancer and the witness of his own dance, who creates and removes maya before finally ensuring emancipation.

Maya, represented by a black curtain behind Nataraja in the Chit Sabha, can be interpreted as a 'measure of reality' with the Mayamata being an ancient text on architectural measurements. Therefore, not only is Shiva's dance cosmic, but Shiva can also be identified with the sentient universe, as well as with the consciousness within, which creates and destroys notions of reality.

These ideas hint at quantum mechanical paradoxes such as observer-created reality inherent to Heisenberg's Uncertainty Principle. They also bring to mind the ideas of 'quantum consciousness' and 'the infinite brain' theorized by physicist Roger Penrose who strove for a grand unified theory of the forces of the universe encompassing quantum consciousness in his book The Emperor's New Mind. Indeed, the profound concepts symbolized by the Chidambaram temple are a humbling reminder of our sheer insignificance and transience in the gigantic universe that we, so often self-indulgently and haughtily, inhabit.

In Shiva's Temple, Stone Pillars Make Music—An Architectural Rarity

Shiva is the Destroyer and Lord of Rhythm in the Hindu trinity. But here he is Lord Nellaiyappar, the Protector of Paddy, as the name of the town itself testifies — nel meaning paddy and veli meaning fence in Tamil. Prefixed to nelveli is tiru, which signifies something special—like the exceptional role of the Lord of Rhythm or the unique musical stone pillars in the temple. In the Nellaiyappar temple, gentle taps on the cluster of columns hewn out of a single piece of rock can produce the keynotes of Indian classical music. "Hardly anybody knows the intricacies of how these were constructed to resonate a certain frequency. The more aesthetically inclined with some musical knowledge can bring out the rudiments of some rare ragas from these pillars."

The Nelliyappar temple chronicle, Thirukovil Varalaaru, says the nadaththai ezhuppum kal thoongal—stone pillars that produce music—were set in place in the 7th century during the reign of Pandyan king Nindraseer Nedumaran. Archaeologists date the temple before 7th century and say it was built by successive rulers of the Pandyan dynasty that ruled over the southern parts of Tamil Nadu from Madurai. Tirunelveli, about 150 km south of Madurai, served as their subsidiary capital.

Each huge musical pillar carved from one piece of rock comprises a cluster of smaller columns and stands testimony to a unique understanding of the "physics and mathematics of sound." Well-known music researcher and scholar

Prof. Sambamurthy Shastry, the "marvellous musical stone pillars" are "without a parallel" in any other part of the country. "What is unique about the musical stone pillars in the Tiruelveli Nellaiyappar temple is the fact you have a cluster as large as 48 musical pillars carved from one piece of stone, a delight to both the ears and the eyes," The pillars at the Nellaiyappar temple are a combination of the Shruti and Laya types. This is an architectural rarity and a sublime beauty to be cherished and preserved.

SRI AUROBINDO AND INDIAN ART

According to Sri Aurobindo: "A good deal of hostile or unsympathetic western criticism of Indian civilization has been directed in the past against its aesthetic side and taken the form of a disdainful or violent depreciation of its fine arts, architecture, sculpture and painting. The Indian mind in its natural poise finds it almost or quite as difficult really, that is to say, spiritually to understand the arts of Europe, as the ordinary European mind to enter into the spirit of Indian painting and sculpture.

For the Indian mind form does not exist except as a creation of the spirit and draws all its meaning and value from the spirit. This characteristic attitude of the Indian reflective and creative mind necessitates in our view of its creations an effort to get beyond at once to the inner spirit of reality it expresses and see from it and not from outside.

A great oriental work of art does not easily reveal its secret to one who comes to it solely in a mood of aesthetic curiosity or still less as the cultivated and interested tourist passing among strange and foreign things; but it has to be seen in loneliness, in the solitude of one's self a sense which modern Europe with her assault of crowded art galleries and over-pictured walls seems to have quite lost..-have put their temples and their Buddhas as often as possible away on mountains and in distant or secluded scenes of Nature and avoid living with great paintings in the crude hours of daily life.

Indian architecture especially demands this kind of inner study and this spiritual self-identification with its deepest meaning and will not otherwise reveal itself to us. The secular buildings of ancient India, her palaces and places of assembly and civic edifices have not outlived the ravage of time; what remains to us is mostly something of the great mountain and cave temples, something too of the temples of her ancient cities of the plains, and for the rest we have the fanes and shrines of her later times, whether situated in temple cities and places of pilgrimage like Srirangam and Rameshwaram or in her great once regal towns like Madura, when the temple was the centre of life. It is then the most hieratic side of a hieratic art that remains to us. These sacred buildings are the signs, the architectural self-expression of an ancient spiritual and religious culture.

Indian sacred architecture of whatever date, style or dedication goes back to something timelessly ancient and now outside India almost wholly lost, something which belongs to the past, and yet it goes forward too, though this the rationalistic mind will not easily admit it, to something which will return upon us and is already beginning to return, something which belongs to the future. An Indian temple, to whatever godhead it may be built is in its utmost reality an altar raised to the divine Self, a house of the Cosmic Spirit, an appeal and aspiration to the Infinite.

Indian sacred architecture constantly represents the greatest oneness of the Self, the cosmic, the infinite in the immensity of its world-design, the multitude of its features of self-expression, laksana, (yet the oneness is greater than and independent of their totality and in itself indefinable), and all its starting-point of unity in conception, its mass of design and immensity of material, its crowding abundance of significant ornament and detail and its return towards oneness are only intelligible as necessary circumstances of this poem, this epic or this lyric-for there are smaller structures which are such lyrics-of the Infinite.

The western mentality, except in those who are coming or returning, since Europe had once something of this cult in her own way, to this vision, may find it difficult to appreciate the truth and meaning of such an art, which tries to figure existence as a whole and not in its pieces; but I would invite those Indian minds who are troubled by these criticisms or partly or temporarily overpowered by the western way of seeing things, to look at our architecture in the light of this conception and see whether all but minor objections do not vanish as soon as the real meaning makes itself felt and gives body to the first indefinable impression and emotion which we experience before the greater constructions of the Indian builders. The Indian vision of the world and existence was vaster fuller than Shakespeare's, because it embraced not merely life, but all being, not merely humanity, but all the worlds and all Nature and cosmos.

Terror and gloom are conspicuously absent from the feelings aroused in it by religion, art or literature. The very goddess of destruction is at the same time the compassionate and loving Mother; the austere Maheshwara, Rudra is also Shiva, the auspicious, Ashutosha, the refuge of men.

The Indian thinking and religious mind looks with calm, without shrinking or repulsion, with an understanding born of its age long effort at identity and oneness, at all that meets it in the stupendous spectacle of the cosmos. And even its asceticism, its turning from the world, which begins not in terror and gloom, but in a sense of vanity and fatigue, or of something higher, truer, happier than life, soon passes beyond any element of pessimistic sadness into the rapture of the eternal peace and bliss.

Mark the curious misreading of the dance of Shiva as a dance of Death or Destruction, whereas, as anybody ought to be able to see who looks upon the Nataraja, it expresses on the contrary the rapture of the cosmic dance with the profundities behind of the unmoved eternal and infinite bliss. So too the figure of Kali which is so terrible to European eyes is, as we know, the Mother of the universe accepting this fierce aspect of destruction in order to slay the Asuras, the powers of evil in man and the world. There are other strands in this feeling in the western mind which seem to spring from a dislike of anything uplifted far beyond the human measure and others again in which we see a subtle survival of the Greek limitation"

Ideals of Indian Art—Excerpts

It is prima facie incredible that a highly developed civilization, spreading over thousands of years and over a vast area like India, which has produced a splendid literature and expressed lofty ideals in building materials, should have lacked the capacity, or found no occasion, for giving them expression in sculpture and painting. Nevertheless, this was the general opinion of European savants and art critics.

Sir George Birchwood, author of the official handbook to the Indian section of the Victoria and Albert Museum, ridiculed the Indian artist's divine ideal. He and other Victorian critics, held that "the unfettered and impassioned realization of the ideals kindled within us by the things without us" was beyond the capacity of the Indian craftsman. Indian art to him meant no more than a pretty chintz, a rich brocade, or gorgeous carpet, fantastic carving, or curious inlay; and an ancient architecture fascinating to the archaeologist and tourist with its reminiscences of bygone pomp and splendour, but an extinct art useless for the needs and ideals of our prosaic and practical times.

Viewed from the secularist and pseudo-scientific angle, Indian art will always be unattractive and incomprehensible. But the Indian artist is not really blind to the beauties of Nature. He can be realistic in the European sense, though realism for him has a different meaning to that which we attach to it, for the philosophy which inspires him regards all that we see in nature as transitory, illusive phenomena, and declares that the only Reality is the Divine Essence or Spirit. Thus while modern European art hardly concerns itself with the Unseen, but limits its mental range to the realm of Nature and thus retains, even in its highest flights, the sense and form of its earthly environment, Indian art is always striving to realize something of the universal, the eternal, and the infinite.

European art, since the so-called Renaissance, has, as it were, its wings clipped: it knows only the beauty of earthy things. Indian art, soaring into the highest empyrean, is ever trying to bring down something of the beauty of the things above.

The Indian artist had an entirely different starting point. He considered that the perfect human animal was an inadequate symbol for the beauty of the divine nature which comprehended all human qualities and transcended them all. It was only by meditating on the Ultimate Perfection that the artist's mind could perceive some glimmer of the beauty of the Godhead. Mere bodily strength and mundane perfections of form are never glorified in Indian art. Indian art is essentially idealistic, mystic, symbolic, and transcendental. The artist is both priest and poet. In this respect Indian art is closely allied to the Gothic art of Europe–indeed, Gothic art is only the Eastern consciousness manifesting itself in a Western environment. But while the Christian art of the Middle Ages is always emotional, rendering literally the pain of the mortification of the flesh, the bodily sufferings of the Man of Sorrows, Indian art appeals more to the imagination and strives to realize the spirituality and abstraction of a supra-terrestrial sphere.

Indian mysticism has its philosophic system, the Yoga-shastra; Yoga was not and is not practiced merely as a spiritual exercise leading to the beatific vision. It claims to be a psychological process of drawing into oneself the dynamics or the logos which controls the universe and to be adaptable for all kinds of mental and physical activity. It inspired the artist, poet, and musician as well as the mystic who sought spiritual enlightenment. It gave the craftsman his creative skill and the soldier perfect control over his weapons, the statesman his far-seeing vision, the seer and inspired thinker his super-natural powers.

In all Indian poetry, art, and mythology, the sublime nature of the Himalayas has always been regarded as a special revelation of divine beauty and as a fitting shrine for all the gods. On Mt. Kailash, the temple's glorious pinnacle, sits the Divine Thinker in His icy cell, controlling the Universe by the power of Yoga. Here Vyasa, says the Mahabharata, taught the Vedas to his disciples.

Here is the heavenly staircase by which Buddha and many other avatars descended to be born on earth, and here the heavenly Ganges falls in seven torrents over the mountain's crest. The sacred lake, Manasarovara, (the most excellent Lake of the Mind) fed by Kailash's snows, is the legendary source of the four world-rivers which water the four great continents, or the four petals of the World Lotus, another pregnant symbol in Indian art. The wild geese (hamsas) which drift thither with the monsoon winds, are to the pious Hindu symbols of the human soul wringing its way to its heavenly resting-place.

Indian artist for many centuries shrank from the thought of depicting for the common crowd the Yogi's vision of the Divine Form: like the secret lore of the Vedas it was a sacred mystery revealed to none but the elect. From the seaports of her eastern and western coasts streams of Indian colonists and craftsmen, poured all over Southern Asia, Lanka, Burma, Siam, Sumatra, Java, and far-distant Cambodia. Through China and Korea, Indian art entered Japan about the middle of the sixth century.

Hindu iconographic art, like modern cubism, joins mathematics with aesthetics. In the yantra it shows the impersonal form of the Godhead developing mathematically from a central point. (Bindu). Hindu philosophy thus clearly recognizes the impossibility of human art realizing the form of God.

It therefore creates in Indian painting and sculpture a symbolical representation of those, milder, humanized, but still superhuman, divine appearances which mortal eyes can bear to look upon. A figure with three heads and four, six or eight arms seems to a European barbaric conception, though it is not less physiologically impossible than the wings growing from the human scapula in the European representation of angels– an idea probably borrowed from the East. But it is altogether foolish to condemn such artistic allegories a priori, because they many not conform to the canons of the classic art of Europe.

All art is suggestion and convention, and if Indian artists by their conventions can suggest divine attributes to Indian people with Indian culture, they have fulfilled the purpose of their art. It is the unfortunate tendency of modern European education to reduce art to mere rules of logic or technique anatomy or perspective, style or fashion, so that the creative faculty on which the vitality of art depends is drowned in empty formularies of no intellectual, moral, or aesthetic values.

In the cave-temples of Elephanta, Ellora, and Ajanta Indian sculptors played with chiaroscuro in great masses of living rock with the same feeling as the Gothic cathedral builders, or as Wagner played with tonal effects, hewing out a colossal scale the grander contrasts of light and shade to give a fitting atmosphere of mystery and awe to the paintings and sculpture, which told the endless legends of the Buddha or the fantastic myth of the Hindu Valhalla.

Art will always be caviere to the vulgar, but those who really learn and understand it should begin with Indian art, for true Indian art is pure art stripped of the superfluities and vulgarities which delight the uneducated eye. Yet Indian art, being more subtle and recondite than the classic art of Europe, require a higher degree of artistic understanding, and it rarely appeals to European dilettanti who, with a smattering of perspective, anatomy, rules of proportion and design, aspire to be art critics, amateur painters, sculptors, or architects, and these, unfortunately, have had the principal voice in deciding administrative questions which vitally affect India's artistic life.

So the question whether Indian art is still a vital force, revealing India's spiritual self, seems to be less important than the question of taste – or whether from the European standpoint India's spiritual self should be allowed to reveal itself in art which the European and the Anglicized Indian do not appreciate or understand.

Europe of the present day has far more to learn from India in art than to teach. Religious art in Europe is altogether lost: it perished in our so-called Renaissance. In India, the true spirit of it still lives.

Bhakti is the moving spirit of all great religious art, in the West as well as the East. It is bhakti that keeps Indian art alive: it is the lack of it which makes modern Western art so lifeless. Anglo-Indians have always ascribed the artistic triumphs of the Indian Mughal dynasty to the superior aesthetic genius of Islam; but this is quite untrue reading of Indian art-history. The art of Fatehpur-Sikhri and of Jahangir's great palace at Agra are essentially Hindu art. Abul Fazl, writing with full appreciation of contemporary painting, says of the Hindus: "Their pictures surpass our conception of things. Few indeed in the whole world are found equal to them." Even in the Taj Mahal, the typical masterpiece of what we call Mughal art, many of the principal craftsmen were Hindus, or of Hindu descent; and how much Persian art owed to the frequent importation of Indian artists and craftsmen is never understood by European art-critics.

All the great monuments of Saracenic art in India surpass those of Arabia, Turkey, Egypt, and Spain, in the exact measure by which they are indebted to Hindu craftsmanship and inspired by Hindu idealism.

The inspiration of the Taj Mahal came not from its Muslim builders; it was the spirit of India which came upon it and breathed into it the breath of life.

Saracenic art flourished in India just as long as the Mughal emperors were wise enough to observe perfect impartiality between Muslims and Hindus. When the bigot Aurangzeb expelled all the Hindu artists and craftsmen whom his father and grandfather had attracted to the service of the state, the art of Mughals in India was struck with a blight from which it never recovered.

Every national art is an expression of national character and when we compare the devout and reverent outlook upon Nature shown in these sculptures with utter vulgarity of modern India....India, vulgarized by modern education and by the sordid ideals of modern commercialism, will never compensate humanity for the passing of India with its love of beauty – the perfect law of Nature, in which science and art are one.

But my main objective is to help educated Indians to a better understanding of their own national art, and to give them that faith and pride in it without which the wisest measures that any Government could devise will always be thrown away. Even if, for Europeans who think like Macaulay, all Indian art should be worthless, it will always remain a priceless boon to Indians, offering them something which the best European art can never give them. Let Indians of the present generation, who through Macaulay's narrow and short-sighted policy have never enjoyed this precious heritage, see that their children are put in possession of it.

Havell saw Islamic architecture as one of rapid capitulation to the superior indigenous art of India.

Akbar was not the exception but the classic example. His wholesale adoption of Hindu styles and his patronage of Indian craftsmen marked the end of a brief experiment with non-Indian forms (Tughluk's tomb for example), and the beginning of one of the greatest periods of purely Indian building. Taking the bull firmly by the horns, Havell turned to the classical age of Mughal architecture, the reign of Shah Jehan (1628-58), and in particular to none other than the Taj Mahal. His first point was that whatever its inspiration, 'there is one thing which has struck every writer about the Taj Mahal and that is its dissimilarity to any other monument in any other part of the world.' Outside India there was Humayun's tomb in Delhi, or the other two white marble tombs, those of Itimad-ud-Daula in Agra and Salim Chishti at Fatehpur Sikri, were so inferior as to be unworthy of comparison.

There was no precedent in the strictly non-representational art of Islam. If the inspiration for the building was to be sought in sculpture rather than architecture, then it must be sought in Indian sculpture. The purity of line and subtlety of contour which characterized it were precisely the qualities that distinguished the Mathura Buddhas or the Khajuraho apsaras. The hint of effeminacy in the Taj Mahal could only have been done by an Indian artist with his purely conceptual approach that was so blatantly seductive. Besides, the records showed that the inlay artists employed on the Taj were all Hindus.

Havell had studied the silpa-shastras – the traditional manuals of the Hindu builder – and he believed that even the bulbous dome conformed more closely to Indian ideals than those of Samarkand. There was even a sculptural representation of such a dome in one of the Ajanta cave temples. Moreover, the internal roofing arrangement of four dome grouped round the fifth, central dome conformed exactly to the 'panch-ratna', the five jewel system so common to Indian buildings of all sorts.

Painting

Vincent A. Smith in History of Fine Art in India and Ceylon says: "The remarkable success attained by Hindu Art, both plastic and pictorial, in the treatment of plant motives and the representation of indigenous animals is unsurpassed."

Dr. Ernest Binfield Havell says: "Among Rembrandt's pen and ink studies collected in the British Museum, the Louvre, and elsewhere, a number have been identified as copies or adaptations of India miniatures, and it has been shown that from them chiefly, Rambrandt derived the Oriental atmosphere for his Biblical subjects!"

Ananda K. Coomaraswamy said of miniature paintings in general that they conjure a magic world in which the men are always heroic and the women always beautiful.

In classical Sanskrit literature painting is considered an occupation not unworthy of princes. It is evident from early Sanskrit records that painting was closely associated with popular festivals and with civic life in ancient India. There are many allusions to them in Sanskrit literature. The Ramayana describes Ravana's palace in Lanka, where

Gay, blooming creepers clothed the walls,
Green bowers were there and picture-halls,
And chambers made for soft delight.

A chitrasala, or gallery of mural paintings, was an indispensable annex to a Hindu palace until quite modern times, or until Indian art fell into disrepute and it became fashionable for Indian princes to import inferior European oil-paintings and European furniture. These chitra-salas were quadrangular cloisters surrounding one of the palace gardens or pavilions, sometimes reserved for public resort. Paintings are easily destroyed by natural causes or deliberate injuries;

and what remains of Indian painting cannot be the hundredth or even the thousandth part of what once existed. We cannot, however, doubt that the art was continuously practiced from pre-Buddhist times to the present day. The paintings of Ajanta though much damaged, still form the greatest extant monument of ancient painting and the only school except Egyptian in which a dark-skinned race is taken as the normal type. They belong to the same courtly religious culture as that which finds expression in the works of Kalidasa, and show the same deep understanding of the hearts of men and women and animals that has given to Shakuntala her immortality.

Krishna and Radha under a Tree in a Storm

artist unknown. 1750-1825-The Brooklyn Museum

Abdul Fazl, the Mohammedan historian, wrote of Hindu painters: "Their pictures surpass our conception of things. Few indeed in the whole world are found equal to them." (source: Blochman's Ain-i-Akberi. Volume I p. 108)

Writing on the technique of the Ajanta paintings, Mr. Griffiths, who superintended the copying of them by his students in the Bombay School of Art, says truly:

"The artist who painted them were giants in execution. Even on the vertical sides of walls, some of the lines, which were drawn with one sweep of the brush, stuck me as being very wonderful; but when I saw long, delicate curves drawn without faltering, with equal precision, upon the horizontal surface of a ceiling where the difficulty of execution is increased a thousand fold it appeared to me nothing less than miraculous!" "The Chinese Schools owe their inspiration originally to the art of India. In the early centuries of the Christian era the traditions of Indian religious art had been taken into Turkistan and China by Indian Buddhist missionaries and craftsmen, and by Chinese students taught in Indian Universities."

CONCLUSION

The Western artists see nature with his eyes and judges art by intellectual and aesthetic standards. The Indian seeks truth in his inner consciousness, and judges of its expression by metaphysical and imaginative standards. Art for him is not to please, but to manifest."

Art in India has always been considered a path of realization of the Ultimate Reality. It is spiritual in outlook, idealistic in expression and sublime in interpretation.

It is not merely a matter of sensuous enjoyment, not a luxury to be enjoyed by the leisured rich class of people or state rulers, not something to amuse oneself with. It has a deeper basis and a more exalted aim It was considered to be as vital for human progress as Devotion or Knowledge of Love. God was considered to be the fountain of all Beauty as He was considered to be the source of all Knowledge, Power and Wisdom. God as Absolute Beauty is one of the basic ideas of Ancient Hindu Culture.

Rukhmini addresses Lord Krishna as Bhuvana Sundara (the most beautiful in the universe), Madhusoodana Saraswati, the great advaitic scholar, describes Shri Krishna as Soundaryasarasarvaswa (the entire essence of Beauty). But for His Beauty how can there be anything beautiful in creation?

In ancient India Art went hand in hand with Religion. In one sense we may say, Art turned inward is Religion and religion turned outward is Art. Temples have been repositories of all arts; they have enshrined not only idols of deities but art treasures as well.

The Indian imager approached his work with great solemnity, invoking the god whom he would represent. In the Agni Purana, he is told, the night before undertaking a great work, to pray: "O thou Lord of all gods, teach me in dreams how to carry out all the work I have in my mind."

The artist tries to bring Godhead nearer to us by working along the line of the Beauty aspect of God. Man is a miniature God, he has in himself potentially all the Divine faculties. He may have only a little knowledge now, but he will become a great knower in due course. So art is verily a path to the Supreme; it is a Yoga, Soundarya Yoga, so to say. Artists are, at any rate ought to be, great yogis in their own way. Great

Rishis and devas have been great artists; the authorship of some of our art traditions is traced to great sages.

The very names given to some of the Deities show how much emphasis was laid upon this aspect of Art. Nataraja is the arch-dancer, Ranganatha means the stage manager. All art expressions in India have a spiritual background. Unlike the narcissistic and eccentric modern artists, Indian art is not made by a named artist, but by the artist, incarnated in numerous nameless individual.

Huston Smith has said: "In Hinduism, art is religion, religion is art. To inform and transform us – what we might truly be.

No figure in all art is better loved that this dancing Shiva– lord of dances – the cosmos is his theatre–he dances ceaselessly in twirling stars, circling seasons–the rhythm of the human heart timelessly, effortlessly–his rhythms gather time and timeless. India was addicted to sculpture–perhaps because it tokens to timelessness and eternity–chiselled in rock we are presented with the relief map of the world as it would have eyes to see its mystery and promise. The invisible reality to which art points to. Indians saw no point in carving replicas that we usually see ordinary, pedestrian, prosaic, art's opportunity is to see deeper than we usually do–to see the infinite stirring in things, warming to bust their buds–so everything in these shapes in. The images are ones awakened and for our awakening–we who are still asleep–to understand is to be reborn."

Ananda K. Coomraswamy thinks:

> *"The Greek sees the aim of art as the faithful reproduction of nature; but it failed in the greatest qualities because the religion expressed in it was in no sense transcendental. The great cat-gods of Egypt, the sublime Buddhas of Java, the four-handed gods of India, even the great Chinese dragon, are greater imaginative art, belong more in the divine in man, than do the Hermes of Praxiteles or the Venus of Milo."*

Indian architecture shows the combination of massiveness and soaring upwardness which is the soul of Indian Art in general. Indian sculpture and ichnography depend on Yogic vision and not on mere artistic manipulation. Thus Hindu art is best expressed as "Emotion recollected in tranquillity." It excels in idealism, creativeness, suggestiveness, and evocation of emotion. It is born in bliss and expresses itself in bliss and enkindles bliss.

In the chapter on the "Inspiration of Indian Art" in his great work "Indian Sculpture and Painting,: Mr. Havell, after describing the spiritual character of the Hindus, and the meaning they understood of the winds which swept through the forest trees, the waters which poured down from the Heaven-built Himalayas, the power and beauty of the rising and the setting sun, the radiant light and heat of midday, the glorie of the Eastern moonlit nights, the majestic gathering of th monsoon clouds, the fury of the cyclone, the lightning flash an thunder and the cheerful dripping of the life-giving rain, says

> *"From this devout communion with nature in all the marvellous diversity of her tropical moods, came the inspiration of an art possessing richness of imagery and wealth of elaboration which seem bewildering and annoying to our dull Northern ways of thinking."*

Comparing the European and Hindu art, Dr. Ernest Binfield Havell says:

> *"European art has, as it were its wings clipped: it knows only the beauty of earthly things. Indian art, soaring into the highest empyrean, is ever trying to bring down to earth something of the beauty of the things above."*

Speaking in 1908 of the influence of Indian Art on the art of Europe and Asia, Mr. E. B. Havell says:

> *"In the early centuries of the Christian era, and from this Indian source, came the inspiration of the great school of Chinese painting, which from the seventh to the thirteenth centuries stood first in the whole world...The influence of India's artistic culture can be clearly traced, not only in Byzantine Art, but in the Gothic cathedrals of the middle Ages. Europe is very apt to dwell upon the influence of Western Art and Culture*

upon Asiatic thought, religion and culture upon the Art and Civilization of Europe is rarely appraised at its proper value....From the seaports of her Western and Eastern coasts, India at this time sent streams of colonists, missionaries and craftsmen all over Southern Asia, Ceylon, Siam and far-distant Cambodia. Through China and Korea, Indian Art entered Japan about the middle of the sixth century. About AD 603 Indian colonists from Gujarat brought Indian Art into Java, and at Borobudur, in the 8 and 9 centuries Indian Sculpture achieved its greatest triumphs. Some day when European Art criticism has widened its present narrow horizon, and learnt the foolishness of using the art standards of Greece and Italy as a tape wherewith to measure and appraise the communings of Asia with the Universal and the Infinite, it will grant the nameless sculptors of India an honourable place among the greatest artists the world have ever known."

"Europe of the present day has in art far more to learn from India than to teach!"

8

The Real Hindu Art

Hinduism is a conglomeration of a wide variety of beliefs and Infact, it is unique in its tolerance of diversity. Roots of this religion have been since 4000 years in India, and as it developed it absorbed many beliefs and practices of various kinds of people. Assimilation happened differently for different parts of India.

The Hindu religion is a great repository of heterogeneity of beliefs. Worship of different kinds of deities is a very personal choice, and that aspect of Hindu practice is reflected in the number of different Hindu temples and their sculptural beliefs.

A man who has no knowledge of music, literature, or art is believed to be no better than a beast. Hindu's always believed art to be a key to salvation or ultimate release that is sought by all good Hindus. There is a kind of a holistic feel about Indian art; it is a unity of many forms and artistic experiences.

DIFFERENT FORMS OF HINDU ART

Art rules every part of Indian life, and is found in every reference of ancient Indian Civilization. Indian art is considered a disciplined style of worship and self-restraint. Hindu art can also be thought of as India's oldest indigenous science.

Sometimes lord Shiva, is visually represented as "King of Dance" or Nataraja. This form of Shiva is considered as the most remarkable symbol of divine powers, which was ever created by Indian artistic genius.

Indian artists have frozen the beauty of human bodies in various shapes with the help of stone and bronze for around

5,000 years. It is difficult to name only a single person or persons among the geniuses who brought gods to life in places like the Ellora, Ajanta, Elephanta and Karli caves.

The transition from cave excavation and carvings on the Hindu temples are depicted dramatically and powerfully at Ellora. Ellora is an entire mountain which has been literally shaped out over many centuries by devoted artists. These artists created and "extracted" Lord Shiva's Mount Kailash temple within that enormous rock dome.

Ellora's Kailash cave temple is still one of the few beautiful monuments of art and Hindu devotion. The carvings on some of the walls and pillars is magnificent. No other work on stone or in any other material are as fine. But still what remains a mystery is what tools have been used to make the very hard and tough stone as it is to be seen on the present day.

Indian art is related to Hindu religion and philosophy. It is hard to appreciate the Indian art unless one has insight into the ideals that govern the Indian minds. In the Indian art there is mostly a religious element, a looking beyond.

The beautiful carvings of the Hindu temples, the beautiful wall paintings of Ajanta, or the intriguing art of cave sites and the sophisticated temple building tradition, the Indian Hindu culture offers a good visual feast.

THE SPIRITUAL PATH

The purpose of life, including our human life, is the evolution of consciousness. The aim of our human existence is to become as fully human as possible, to realise or make real the full potential inherent in the human condition. This applies to all levels of being human, to the biological, the emotional as well as the mental level.

Instead of seeing yourself as just a personality with a mind and a body, imagine yourself as part of an individualised life-stream that flows eternally towards increasingly higher levels of consciousness. This life-stream builds itself different personalities as vehicles for its flow of consciousness. You are one of these temporary vehicles. Your personality is temporary, the present cutting edge of your life-stream as perceived in our space-time. The aim of your life-stream at this level is to develop a vehicle that allows the full expression of your soul suitable for travel beyond the human condition. When this is accomplished, no further personalities are needed. As an ascended being the life-stream can now traverse the trans-human conditions of consciousness.

SPIRITUAL AWAKENING

This evolution of consciousness normally is a slow process and most personalities are not aware that they are part of an evolutionary growth. However, as the personality comes closer to perfection, it does become aware of its purpose and it begins to long for spiritual unfoldment. Before this spiritual awakening, the personality may already have believed in God and followed a religious faith in the traditional way. But there is a difference. In the traditional religious life the believer may try to follow the doctrines of his faith the best he can, but he basically remains on the same slow evolutionary path of consciousness.

With the spiritual awakening, spiritual growth becomes the main focus of this personality. The slow evolutionary process now becomes a spiritual revolution, not only in regard to the speed of the growth of consciousness but also in regard to the overthrow of established values. This spiritual revolution may take place within the confines of an established religion or it may happen outside a religious faith. Within a religion, these awakening spirits will sooner or later come in conflict with established doctrines. They may try to revolutionise or restore their church to its highest ideals and eventually become mystics or saints or martyrs or just start their own church or sect. Most established religions had at best an uneasy relationship with their mystics and (later) saints.

In any way, whether the awakening and subsequent spiritual growth takes place within or without an established religion, the awakening personality will begin to follow the spiritual guidance that comes from within rather than the established rules and doctrines of church and society. Spirituality is no longer something that one does on Sunday mornings or other established times and according to established rules, but rather it becomes the central purpose and focus of life. With this, we may say that the personality is now on the spiritual path.

VARIETIES OF SPIRITUAL PATHS

While the real goal of the spiritual path is the same for all, there are many different roads that one can travel and one may even travel without a road. Also the goal may be described in different terms without always recognising that it is the same goal. This is so because we all have different starting points and different preferences and opportunities. Many spiritual travellers will not expect to reach their goal in their present lifetime, while others may realise that they do not really need to travel anywhere.

Some of the better-defined roads are the different forms of Yoga, the Tao, the Gnostic teachings, the Rosicrucians and various ancient and modern Mystery Schools. While the Mystics are generally regarded as a distinct group, they really travelled each on his or her own individual path. At present Ascension teachings through books and channelled guidance attract many followers. These teachings are largely individualised outgrowths from the writings of the Theosophical Society since the end of the nineteenth century.

Looked at from a different perspective, we may say that there are two different approaches that often intermingle in each individual spiritual path. One is the path of the Doer or the Magus, while the other is the path of the Knower or the Mystic. The Doer mainly works in the world as a healer, alchemist or white magician, trying to master the non-physical energies and forces. The Mystic, on the other hand, follows mainly the inner path, seeking Union with the Divine Self and in the process becomes a Knower and a teacher. However, ultimately Knower and Doer both become one.

The Path of the Mystics

The recorded experiences of the many mystics in all religions is of particular interest because we can learn from these what the spiritual path looks like when it is not guided by specific verbal or written teachings. Most of these individuals in past centuries did not know that there was such a thing as a spiritual path and that others had travelled the same or a similar route. They just felt a longing to come closer to God and to feel at one with Him, to melt into Divinity like a drop of water becomes one with the ocean.

Each of them had different experiences and many of them walked only part of the way, but by constructing a composite picture from a large number of their writings we can discern a distinct pattern of the typical mystical path. Few mystics seem to have travelled all of this 'typical' path, but this may be because we can see only one life-time of a multiple-life-time journey. This typical mystical path may best be described as a five-stage journey and we may easily see its relationship to contemporary spiritual practises.

1. *The Awakening:* The spiritual awakening is the beginning of the mystical path and also of the spiritual path in general. It may be sudden or gradual. Often it comes as an emotionally overwhelming 'mystical experience', possibly ending a period of great emotional torment and suffering. Another frequent setting is during a spiritual initiation ceremony, such as presently during water baptism for 'Born-Again Christians'.

   Others may have this awakening experience during an especially intense prayer or meditation or drift gradually onto the path by attending workshops or reading spiritual books. The latter as well as others coming to the path because of philosophical considerations turn out to become like the 'mental mystics' as compared to the 'emotional mystics' who had their mystical experiences mainly at the emotional level.

   This initial peak experience may last for hours or days with gradually declining intensity. Commonly it is a combination of deep feelings, such as universal love, with profound spiritual intuition or insight, although depending on the personality traits the emotional or the mental component may dominate. Also psychic phenomena are frequently involved in the form of visions and voices.

2. *Purification:* After the awakening the individual does not only want to repeat the mystical experience but really wants to live in a permanent state of grace close to God. However, the aspiring mystic realises that he is not yet worthy, he becomes acutely aware of his imperfections, of the impurity of his thoughts and feelings. He starts to cleanse himself of all selfish or impure desires. Commonly this is combined with periods of fasting or food denial. Medieval mystics tended to be very severe with themselves in order to 'mortify' the body and with it the unruly senses and the desires of the flesh. Worldly pursuits no longer hold any interest. Periods of prayer and meditation are greatly extended. While this process of purification requires strong willpower and causes much self-inflicted pain, it is also increasingly interspersed with beautiful and uplifting mystical experiences that spurn the seeker on to greater sacrifices for the sake of more rapturous experiences. This purification process continues for many years. Instead of turning the spiritual energies released by the awakening experience inward to purify, it may also be directed outwards. These individuals then become religious fanatics and may remain at this level for the rest of their lives.
3. *Illumination:* After the Self has been sufficiently cleansed or purified and the mind remains fully focused on the presence and the qualities of the Divine, a state of illumination may unexpectedly arise. This will be similar to the experience of awakening but even more intense and longer lasting. Again, it may be predominantly emotional with feelings of indescribable Divine love, being at one with 'All That Is' and combined with visions and voices, or it may be predominantly mental with profound insights and states of pure knowing. Commonly the initial peak experience is combined with perceiving an intense or blinding inner white light. For many months these deep feelings and insights will keep flowing in, but gradually settle into a state of a permanently raised and more intuitive

consciousness. The illuminated mystic will now always remain aware of the Divine presence in everyone and everything and radiate a presence of love and goodwill. Intuitive abilities will be greatly increased. Commonly, one will receive a spiritual gift with the illumination. This may be the ability to heal or to see or to know. By developing this ability one will become a great healer, seer or spiritual teacher.

The perception of mysticism as being incomprehensible to normal, unenlightened humans is due to the fact that most mystical writings were composed by the emotional type of mystics. They focused on emotional states of being and perceived and described their visions and experiences with emotional metaphors that remained incomprehensible to the uninitiated. This is similar to the present descriptions of reality given by quantum physicists.

Life in this state of illumination is easy and full of joy, a permanent state of great happiness and contentment. It is like living in a state of grace that can never be lost again. But sometimes it is being lost.

4. *The Dark Night of the Soul:* There is a saying that he whom God loves most, will be given the severest tests. This certainly seems to be true of the few mystics who continue to travel further along the spiritual path even after illumination. During the long and difficult purification process the aspiring mystic gave up most of his sense attachments, the pleasure of eating, of sexual union, of bodily comfort and of pleasant company. Instead all the energies were focused only on what was perceived to be transcendental and divine.

   But there was still one thing left that had not been surrendered, that is the will, the central part of the Self. To give up the will, the innate instinct for personal happiness had to be surrendered. This is called the 'mystical death' or the spiritual crucifixion. During illumination the mystic seemed to walk hand in hand with God and sunned himself in eternal Divine bliss.

This makes the contrast even greater to the feeling of having lost all the former grace and glory and being totally abandoned by God to a life in abject misery. However, gradually the Self begins to accept total surrender. It gives up itself, its personality and individuality, asks for nothing and desires nothing. Now there is total passivity and acceptance of whatever God has ordained or whatever comes. Now the mystic is finally ready for the last stage of his earthly journey.

5. *The Unitive Life:* Finally, by giving up everything, the mystic has gained everything. By being completely passive, he is able to be filled with the Divine Spirit. No longer does he experience the strong mood swings between divine bliss and utter desolation, he has now settled into a feeling of constant peaceful and love-filled union with the Divine. However, this is not the goal of his long journey, just a by-product. The real achievement is that the mystic is now an ideal tool or instrument of the Divine Will to be used for manifesting the Great Plan on earth.

While now the mystic still lives in the world, he is no longer of the world. He may be a great reformer, healer, inventor, statesman, educator or spiritual teacher but whatever he does is never for any small or selfish interests, instead it is always for the greater good of All That Is. He now lives a life of service. Whatever he does, he is now a spiritual master, even if that is not always apparent to the outside world. After his passing, he will be an ascended being, not needing to return to earth.

Comments on the Mystical Path

In this description it is easy to draw comparisons to the life of Jesus of Nazareth and see in it a symbolic enactment of the mystical path. The baptism symbolises the spiritual awakening, the 40 days in the desert correspond to the period of purification, followed by illumination (the transfiguration on the mountain) and selfless service in the form of a healing and teaching ministry. The experience on the cross and the events leading up to it are his dark night. While the unitive life is cut short, it is signified by the ascension and the following teaching period in ascended form.

It may also be mentioned that the described states of the mystical path do not necessarily follow one after the other but some may occur simultaneously, such as enlightenment and the dark night of the soul or purification, enlightenment and selfless work. These may coexist or alternate, causing emotional extremes over short periods. Coexistence is possible because we do not need to be perfect to reach illumination and, therefore, continue with our purification on deeper levels.

Furthermore, these extremes and the perceived sufferings are mainly the lot of the emotional type of mystics while the mental type follows a much smoother path. Both have the difficult task of giving up their attachments to gratifying the senses and surrendering their will, it is just that the emotional mystics are so much more sensitive and take things very much to heart. It also must be understood that it is not necessary to give up things, only the attachment to things but that was not always understood by those leading a life of extreme asceticism.

Ascension Teachings

The ascensicn teachings are a New Age phenomenon and largely based on channelled teachings. These started with Madame Blavatsky and led to the foundation of the Theosophical Society late in the nineteenth century. The aim of these teachings is to present a greatly accelerated path to ascension.

Ascension is highlighted as the main aim and achievement of the spiritual path. Ascension means that we are no longer in need of experiences at the human level. For our continuing progress towards higher levels of consciousness we develop a spiritual light body through our ascension work. Presently ascension teachings focus mainly on guided imagery to open, balance and extend the chakra system and build a light body.

A key feature is a system of initiations as a measure of progress on the spiritual path. These initiations are to take place in our higher energy bodies and may or may not be remembered with our normal body consciousness. While there are some variations in the way of counting, the basic requirements for passing the five initiations before ascension may be described as follows.

1. Spiritual Awakening.
2. Purifying the body, learning to work with the energies and controlling the etheric body.
3. Purifying and controlling the emotions as well as developing a higher emotional body.
4. Purifying and controlling the mind as well as developing a higher mental body.
5. Submitting the will to Divine Guidance.
6. Selfless work for the greater good of humanity.
7. Ascension.

While formerly initiations in the physical body took place in the form of tests and rituals within secret societies, presently they appear to be incorporated as special situations in our normal life. As an example the third initiation requires us to have good control of the mental, emotional and etheric forces. In ancient Egypt an appropriate test might have been for the disciple to demonstrate that he can control an untamed lion with his mind and the lion obeying him. At the slightest sign of fear the lion would kill him.

A modern equivalent might be a diagnosis of advanced and incurable cancer. To overcome this without much outside help, one needs to use the mind constructively to guide the emotions in a positive way, release all negativity, especially be free of the fear of death and also learn to direct the life-force energies as in guided imagery. While only a small percentage of sufferers of advanced incurable diseases may have been given their disease as an initiation test, most of those who did recover from near-terminal conditions reportedly had profound spiritual experiences.

Ascension and the Mystical Path

The relationship of the ascension initiations as portrayed above to the divisions of the mystical path are quite obvious. Starting with the spiritual awakening in both, the first three initiations are related to the mystical period of purification. In contrast to the yoga system of purification, which concentrates strongly on controlling the etheric energies, the mystical path does not address the etheric or life-force body directly. However, this level is purified indirectly by removing emotional energy blockages and by learning to control the emotional energies, which in turn direct the etheric life-force energies.

Illumination is the first major initiation and is the result of purifying and learning to control the mind and developing a higher mental body as the requirement for the third initiation. The fourth initiation will be passed after waking from the dark night of the soul and the fifth initiation is the result of the unitive life.

The ascension teachings portray largely a magical or doer path in contrast to the knower-based mystical path. A combination of both may in some ways be easier to follow than either one of them on its own. The severity of the mystical path can be greatly eased and progress speeded up by suitable guided imagery, while the present ascension teachings seem to neglect the purification and control of the emotional and mental bodies that feature so prominently in the mystical path.

An Integrated Spiritual Path

Presently travellers on the spiritual path have two important advantages as compared to those in former centuries. We now have published information on the nature and variety of spiritual pathways so that we no longer need to find our way alone in the darkness of ignorance. Furthermore, with the information explosion in recent decades and the learning of technical skills, our capacity to understand and communicate has greatly increased. What formerly could only be expressed as incomprehensible mysticism, can now be understood and presented in rational and scientific terms. This makes it much easier for us to come to the stage of illumination instead of being bogged down for long time spans in emotional misery, which formerly was the lot of most mystics.

In the following, I want to give some helpful information on the various stages of a modern spiritual path and on the different components and tools that you may incorporate into your individualised approach. There is now so much information available on ascension, the path of yoga, working with energies, healing the emotions and the mind and so forth that your problem is not to find information, but to develop the ability to discern and know what is right for you. You can do this by keeping your highest goal in mind and asking your inner or higher guidance for help.

Beware of getting sidetracked by psychic abilities or happenings. Developing psychic abilities can be fascinating, but is no more spiritual than material, emotional or mental activities. However, psychic activities can be more deceptive than other activities. Most psychic happenings take place on the astral level or open us to astral influences. Spirit entities operating on this level commonly are less spiritually developed than someone on the spiritual path and often give misleading or mischievous information. They also love to imitate or pretend being a high spiritual entity or even God.

Churches, sects and cults commonly have astral counterparts that feed on the devotion of their followers and try to lure potential recruits just as much as commercial advertisers. But these astral entities are more dangerous because they are usually hidden from our awareness and their intentions and methods may not be clean.

Already St. John of the Cross, a highly respected mystic of the sixteenth century, advised his followers to be wary of visions and voices as these commonly come from a lower level and tend to lead the spiritual seeker astray. They will disappear when moving the consciousness higher into more spiritual regions. The only thing that protects us from being used or misled by lower spirits but at the same time remaining open to contact with truly high spirit beings is the purity of our consciousness.

Awakenings

Do not worry wondering whether you had already a spiritual awakening and are now on the spiritual path or not. Just start or continue searching for spiritual information, reading interesting books and visiting spiritual web sites. You will be doing the right thing. By always keeping your goal in mind, you will quite naturally be attracted to what is important and right for you.

While in the beginning it is helpful and necessary to read quite a bit from different sources to get a good overview, later it is better to read as little as possible. By continuing to read a lot you remain at the intellectual level and that hinders the development of intuitive abilities.

One of the early sidetracks on the spiritual path are the many interesting books now available. If you do not control yourself, you can easily become addicted to reading and spend the rest of your life reading interesting books on spiritual and related matters instead of really doing what needs to be done. Therefore, move quickly through the information phase and start the real work. Whenever you really need additional information, your spiritual guidance is likely to let you unexpectedly find it.

If you are a practising member of a religious denomination, you do not need to be concerned that the spiritual path may be incompatible with your religious beliefs. Instead, you may expect that it will increase your faith. If you discover a contradiction or incompatibility here or there, put it on the shelf for the time being. Remember, the spiritual path does not have any doctrines. Any writings about it are personal opinions that you do not need to accept. On the contrary, walking the spiritual path means finding your own insights and personal relationship with your God.

Purification or Cleansing

The purification period does not need to be a time of misery and suffering as it was for the mystics. Instead, it can be a time of adventure and discovery. The greatest adventure is to discover yourself. By removing biological, emotional and mental blockages, you will become healthier and happier. Life will become emotionally as well as mentally more satisfying. What could be better? The main fun of the spiritual path is not the arrival at the end, but the whole long and interesting journey of getting there. You do not need to make a sharp distinction between working on the biological, the etheric, the emotional and the mental level. They are all closely related. It is just easier to write about one level at a time. You may concentrate on one level, say the emotional, which also affects all the other levels at the same time, although the greatest impact will be directly on the emotional level. It is also easier to start with concentrating on the body or biological level and then proceed to the etheric, emotional and mental level in turn.

In addition to purifying, we also aim to strengthen and balance each level to achieve an overall inner as well as outer harmony. We may say that we move to sanitise and spiritualise all aspects of our Self.

The Biological Level

While many great spiritual teachers have not placed much emphasis on the body, they nevertheless purified it just as a side effect of their spiritual quest. See for instance the 40-day fast of Jesus of Nazareth in the desert, or the Buddha fasting until the imprint in the sand where he was sitting in meditation looked like the hoof print of a camel. The Buddha is also quoted as telling his monks: "if you want to be healthy, eat only one meal a day". Of course, that was in India, in colder climates more food is required. Furthermore, in previous centuries all food was organic, and air and water were still unpolluted. We have to work hard on purifying our bodies to get to the point where previous spiritual seekers started. Therefore, it has advantages for the later work on the higher levels if we start with sanitising the biological level. For this I recommend:

- The Basic Cleanse. This may be repeated from time to time, especially if you want to lose weight, also any other cleanse that you may prefer.
- Test for food allergies and chemical sensitivities at the end of the Basic Cleanse, see Allergy Testing in Healing Foods.
- Adopt a predominantly raw-food diet with plenty of fresh green and purple juices, see the High-Quality Diet in Healing Foods.

- Select your food according to your metabolic and blood type as explained in Healing Foods.
- Regular physical exercises and outdoors activity, yoga, stretching, shaking, walking and swimming.
- Sanitise your teeth, bedroom and workplace.

The Etheric Level

The main features of the etheric level are the etheric body, the etheric part of the chakra system and the acupuncture system. For a basic understanding of this level see the articles in the section on 'Energies' at this web site. This level determines directly the basic health of our body and how energetic we are. This is not only the energy of life and of the etheric blueprint of our body, but also the energy of healing and manifestation.

In order to manifest something, be it our own health or healing someone else or manifesting a physical or social condition, we need to do energy imagery: hold a clear visualisation or other form of guided imagery of the desired situation, fill it with etheric energy and expect it to manifest in your reality. This is the basis and the principle of all genuine magic. An important part of our work at the etheric level is learning how to accumulate and direct etheric energy.

The most important principal to understand is that energy follows thought. However, mental and etheric energies exist on vastly different density levels and do not affect each other directly. Therefore, they require the assistance of the emotional or feeling level, which is sandwiched between the two. For learning to accumulate and direct etheric energies I recommend that you practise the exercises described in Cultivating the Energy and also in The Love Cure. When you are able to feel the energy flows, you may also try using them in guided imagery for healing and other manifestations.

Furthermore, by practising The Love Cure you automatically improve any weaknesses and imbalances in your chakra system. This, in turn, will have favourable effects on your health, on healing your emotional level and building your light body. If you are so inclined, you may in addition also acquire and use any of the various guided ascension and chakra meditations available on tape or CD from New Age outlets. For improving your acupuncture system see the article on Meridian Therapy, and use mainly mental tracing after you have learned to feel the energy flows. For more practical information on working at the etheric level you may see the various books on Kahuna Magic such as the pioneering books by Max Freedom Long ('The Secret Science Behind Miracles' and 'The Secret Science at Work') and the more recent 'Kahuna Healing' by Serge King and 'HUNA-A Beginner's Guide' by Enid Hoffman.

The Emotional Level

For most travellers this will be the most difficult and possibly painful level to sanitise but it will also be the most rewarding. To start with, I suggest that you read the articles in the section on HEALING OUR EMOTIONS, and especially the main article 'The World of Feelings and Emotions'.

The important steps in healing our emotions are:

1. Removing emotional blockages and traumatic body memories.
2. Overcoming addictions and cravings.
3. Learning to freely feel and express our emotions without hurting others.
4. Using meditation and guided imagery to develop a higher emotional body by surrounding ourselves with positive and uplifting feelings and emotions.
5. Using appropriate beliefs and mental awareness to react positively to daily events.

1. *Emotional Cleansing:* Experiment with the methods described in Mind Tools, especially emotional release, regression and the Emotional Freedom Technique. These are best practised in Healing Groups as described in the article on 'Healing Social Relationships'. Also rebirthing may be used if you have the opportunity.

   An excellent way of healing the emotional level as part of a total healing on all levels in the context of our spiritual development is the system of Body Electronics devised by Dr. John Whitman Ray.

Similar to Reichian Therapy and Bio-energetics, Body Electronics works mainly on the body, using sustained pressure to release memories of emotional events that have been built into muscle structures. Body Electronics is best practised as a group activity, possibly after an initial assessment by a practitioner. Reichian Therapy and Bio-energetics, on the other hand, are mainly practitioner based.

A relatively simple way to contact and release past emotional traumas is by using present emotional upsets. If something strongly affects you emotionally, try to feel into yourself, possibly combined with a relaxation or meditation exercise, to discover why it upsets you. Most likely some old forgotten memories come up about a similar incident in your younger years. Whatever the method, when an emotional event from the past is made conscious, it either ceases its detrimental effects on its own or can now be dealt with in a rational way.

Some of the main hidden emotions that we need to uncover and release are fear, guilt and resentments. These block the flow of life-force energies and make us susceptible to lack of energy, diseases and aging. The main remedies, after making a suppressed emotional memory conscious, are unconditional love, understanding and forgiving ourselves and all others.

On this level you do not need to clean out all hidden negative emotional memories that would probably be impossible. However, you should aim to uncover and remove all those factors that interfere strongly with the flow of life-force energies in your body, with your emotional health and enjoyment of life and also with your ability to make clear and impartial decisions.

The most important emotional event to discover and release is commonly our last death experience. This often is at the root of our present health or social problems. To discover and overcome this try regression therapy as described in Mind Tools.

2. *Overcoming Addictions and Cravings:* For many, overcoming their addictions and cravings may seem to be the hardest task of the spiritual path. Addictions to certain foods, drugs and stimulants are best overcome with a combination of Emotional Freedom Technique, guided imagery, prayer, affirmation and cleansing periods with a very high fluid intake. Also homoeopathic doses of the addictive agent can be helpful.

   In addition, we may also be addicted to or have cravings for certain activities or objects, such as sex, gambling, entertainment, expensive dresses, jewellery or antiques. Again, the activity or object is not the problem, but rather the attachment to it, the desire for it that controls us rather than we controlling it. The most important step is in acknowledging that we have a problem in this area. Apart from prayer, meditation, guided imagery and affirmations, the most helpful approach would be to live for a sufficiently long period in a simple way in natural surroundings.

3. *Free-flowing Emotions:* Freely expressing our emotions for most of us is contrary to our upbringing and social conditioning. A first step is in learning to feel our emotions when they arise instead of suppressing them because the time or situation is not appropriate. Then we may decide to express them immediately in a harmless way or re-enact the situation at a later time. We can then in our imagination relive the situation and may kick or punch a pillow or do or say, possibly in front of a mirror, what we felt like doing at the earlier time. Nevertheless, it is preferable to develop the skills to react appropriately whenever the situation arises because then we can also be an example to others.

   Marriages and other close relationships are ideal opportunities to learn communicating. If free expression is not always possible, then arrange a fixed time at the end of the day or once a week when you each can freely express your thoughts and feelings. It is important that only one speaks without interruption until he has said everything he wants to say and then the other replies also without interruption.

4. *Generating Positive Feelings:* After emptying ourselves of negativity and learning to acknowledge and express our feelings and emotions, it is equally important to fill and surround ourselves with positive and uplifting feelings. Ideally this will come as a naturally by-product of habitual meditation and through focusing on spiritual feelings during our daily activities. In this way we develop a higher emotional body as a precondition for the second initiation.

   In addition, it will be beneficial to practise feeling exercises as explained in the article on The Love Cure or in the Love Meditation. Another possibility is to look at a beautiful or impressive object, such as a tree, a flower, a cloud or a landscape and send feelings of appreciation, admiration, joy and love to it. You can do the same by thinking of an individual whom you like or love. After sufficient practise also send feelings of forgiveness, appreciation and love to anyone whom you may have hurt or who may have hurt you in the past.

   Finally, learn to carry the loving feeling that you can now generate in special situations over into your normal daily activities. You can do this by training yourself to carry this loving or joyful feeling in your heart wherever you go or whatever you do. Whenever you see or meet someone, you can embrace that individual with the warm feeling in your heart. This is especially important and effective for improving relationships with people who do not seem to like or appreciate you.

   As another useful exercise you may try learning to change one feeling into another. You can start with any emotional feeling that you may experience at the time or you may just generate a warm feeling by breathing into the abdomen or you may generate an emotional feeling by imagining an appropriate situation. Intensify the feeling as much as possible, but then imagine how another emotion might feel. In this way you may experimentally convert love into anger and then back into love. This will show you that you do not need to be at the mercy of emotions arising as a reaction to outside events but that you can make a mental decision how you really want to feel.

5. *Reacting Positively:* After learning to remain centred in the self-generated positive feelings of our heart, we still need to learn to react positively and appropriately to the many frustrations of our daily lives. This can come only by letting ourselves be guided by a spiritual belief system. After adopting a spiritual philosophy of life it will be much easier to see everything that happens to us as a test of our progress on the spiritual path.

Every day we have many little tests. It is alright to feel a burst of anger if we break a valuable item, but we may also just laugh about our clumsiness or look for an inner or outer reason why it happened. It does not matter too much how we react, as long as it is appropriate. If we do feel a burst of anger, then it is appropriate to feel it and not try to rationalise it away. But after having felt the anger, we should not remain stuck in it but use our mind to get out of it, either by seeing the funny side of it if that is possible, or by trying to learn from it. However, it would not be appropriate to suppress any stirring of anger by quickly switching to one of the other modalities.

It is similar with our reactions in relationship to others. The basic rule is to feel and express whatever emotion comes up, but then to modify it according to our understanding of the situation from a spiritual point of view. Our emotional reactions are a reflection of our beliefs and the more spiritual these become, the more positive will be our reactions. The ideal is that we can express our feelings naturally in a way that is a positive example.

The Mental Level

Our mind is the most important level to heal because here we make the conscious decisions that affect all other levels. For an overview see the article 'Healing the Mind'. As with the other levels, our aim is to free ourselves of negativity and developing positive aspects instead. A well developed higher mental body is a precondition for the third initiation. We build this higher mental body by practising abstract creative and intuitive thinking such as by thinking about the purpose of life or existence or the nature of God.

In order to free yourself of negative beliefs and thoughts, you must first recognise them when they occur. A recommended way is to develop the habit of having a small part of your awareness in the background as an observer. Whenever you have a negative thought, your observer will ring an alarm bell and you realise what you have done. Then, as a mental exercise, find the corresponding positive thought.

As an example, you may watch someone passing by and observe that she is rather overweight. If you notice having a critical thought about her weight, mentally apologise to her and either send her a mental compliment about some other aspect of her appearance or just wish her well. It is alright to observe, just refrain from uninvited judgments, especially of a negative kind. However, the habit of critically evaluating others is the opposite to an invited critical and constructive assessment in order to help someone.

Another important aspect in controlling our mind is to refrain from talking about other people, especially about common friends, relatives or acquaintances, except when exchanging some relevant factual information. Anything more is gossiping, judging or criticising and would delay progress on the spiritual path.

The Law of Manifestation

Any kind of worry is negative, whether you worry about your finances or your health or about a child or someone else. Worry or concern is a form of fear and that is the opposite of positive expectations and faith. To a large degree we shape our own future by what we expect. Our inner self tries to manifest what we expect. Our expectation acts like a magnet to attract and draw the expected event into our outer reality. If we worry about anything, we expect a negative outcome and help to make it come true.

Therefore, our key lesson to learn at the mental level is to know what we want and then without wavering expect it to manifest sometime in the future. Except where timing is essential, it is best not set a definite time limit. If we want to use magic to help our expectation to manifest, we can use energy imagery as mentioned earlier: visualise or imagine the desired result and fill it with emotional and etheric energy. The critical factor then is our unwavering faith until the expected event appears.

This brings us to the next important step, to know what to manifest. It is said that we should be very careful with our wishes because they might come true. That means that we are usually ignorant about the hidden implications of a fulfilled desire. Often there is a spiritual or karmic price to pay. We may delay our spiritual progress or even take on a karmic burden of another individual whom we try to help. We may still have certain karmic obligations to fulfil in this lifetime and it would be detrimental to our spiritual progress trying to delay or avoid their consequences.

Often an incarnation with the specific purpose to reach ascension in this lifetime starts already with a severe handicap and is intentionally filled with difficult and possibly tragic karmic events. These tests need to be passed before reaching the high goal. The greater the handicaps, the greater the victory if we are able to overcome them. When we are progressing on the spiritual path bad things do not just happen to us by accident. Therefore, we really do not need to worry; whatever happens to us is good in that it helps us to reach our goal.

Every adverse event, whether karmic or not, gives us a chance to proof ourselves. We need to pass tests on every step of the way to make sure that we have learned our lesson; otherwise the lesson has to be repeated over and over again. To come close to such a worthy goal as illumination or ascension, we must be able to pass the lion test in one form or another.

What all this means is that it is not advisable on the spiritual path to use magic that is our mind power, lightly to avoid obstacles and make ourselves an easy life. If we are successful, we may just have evaded a test and will have to wait for another test to be arranged. Another way of saying this is to go with the flow of your life and do the best you can, rather than always trying to make things happen according to a preconceived plan.

Pure Motive

Another thing to watch out for is the motive for our actions. While it is important that we try to do the right thing, it is even more important that we have a pure motive. Being pure at heart means having pure motives. Therefore, another job for our inner observer is to watch over our motives and warn us if there is any doubt. In case of important decisions we may meditate and contemplate about our motive and make sure that it is sufficiently pure.

A method that helps us to be fair in all situations is to see a problem from all sides, especially from the side of someone who disagrees with us. Usually everyone in a disagreement has a valid point and we have to learn to understand all these opposing views and find the common ground that is fair to all.

With all this focus on purity and doing the right thing, it is easy to fall into the old habit of suppressing what we perceive to be negative within us rather than transmuting and overcoming it. Suppressing creates new blockages and brings us back where we started. Rather we have to acknowledge and integrate all parts of our personality into a single conscious unit. Only when we are fully conscious of our negative parts can we successfully transform them.

Acting like a Master

A good way of overcoming our weaknesses and reaching spiritual mastership is by acting as if we have already reached it. With every doubtful or important decision we may ask ourselves what a spiritual master would do in this situation and then just do it.

Remember the advice given to Jonathan Livingston Seagull by his teacher? In order to be instantly in another place just imagine that you are already in that place! If you habitually act like a spiritual master, then you are a spiritual master.

Never mind a few mistakes or wrong decisions. Nothing better then our own mistakes to learn from. You still have many years ahead of you to learn doing the right thing most of the time.

Actually, when you have reached a level where your motives are basically unselfish, then you do not need to be too concerned about making the right decision. Just trust your intuition or inner guidance. Whatever you choose will usually be right.

It will be like going on a camping trip or bush walk and you have four choices of getting to the selected camp site: a high track over the top of the hill, a much longer level path, a shortcut across a stream through an overgrown valley or you can simply sit in a bus or car to get there. Each of these choices will give you a different experience. Depending on your preference at the time you may choose the high road or the low road, adventure or comfort, it does not matter, there is no wrong choice, only different experiences.

However, the concept of right and wrong still exists in relationship to our intentions or goals. If it is your intention to reach the camp site in the most comfortable way, then obviously the bus or car is the right choice and the other choices are wrong. Right and wrong only disappear if you look at life or your path as a fascinating adventure and do not mind what it brings you, if you are not attached to outcomes.

Mind Tools

Prayer, meditation and studying holy Scriptures were the basic original mind tools on the spiritual path, especially in the West, while in the East visualisation or guided imagery and mantras were commonly used in addition. All of these are still very useful now. For an introduction to some of these methods see Mind Tools. In addition you will find some of the more modern techniques very helpful, especially regression therapy, relaxation, affirmations and centring.

You may gradually develop a routine where you combine several of these methods in a daily programme. This may, for instance start with prayer and/or affirmations, followed by relaxation, then guided imagery and finally meditation. During the day practise centring. A good way to remain centred is to use a silent mantra. A Hare Krishna devotee might use "Hare Krishna" as mantra while someone raised in the Christian tradition may mentally repeat "Jesus Christus" or "Your Will Be Done".

At the same time we may focus part of our consciousness on the heart or forehead chakra. We can do this whenever our mind is reasonably idle without the need for concentrated thinking. When we have to focus our attention we temporarily interrupt and afterwards start again with the mantra. After some time of practise it will be easy to do this automatically whenever the mind is idle.

A powerful exercise is to imagine being purified by a violet flame. There are different versions of this exercise.

In addition, you may make an effort to become and remain more and more aware of your God Presence, at first in meditation and as guided imagery, but gradually also in your daily life. Imagine your God Presence as shown in the picture of The Magic Presence in the introduction to the Spirituality Section. Instead of a figure, you may just visualise an intense white light over your head or feel or sense a protective and loving presence.

Initially imagine sending an offering of love or devotion through the top of your head straight up to your God Presence or if lying down send it up through the forehead or from the heart centre. Then imagine a strong beam of white light together with an intensified feeling of love and protection entering your top centre and proceeding through the forehead and throat centres to the heart centre. At the same time feel and possibly see your whole body surrounded by intense white or yellow, rose and purple light as depicted in The Magic Presence. Connect with your God Presence in this way especially before any prayer or healing work.

The classical text on the mystical path is 'Mysticism' by Evelyn Underhill, first published in 1911. The teachings of 'A Course in Miracles' may be studied as part of the purification process, especially at the mental level. The theoretical part may be difficult to understand, especially if you are more of an emotional than a mental type. However, it will be beneficial for developing your higher mental abilities.

The Science of Spirituality

One of the main aspects of the spiritual path is the development of a higher mental body or the capacity for abstract, creative and intuitive thinking. This is the tool for opening and developing the forehead chakra and may be seen as a precondition for the third initiation or illumination. With this, wrestling with fundamental spiritual questions in order to gain a deeper understanding not only helps to develop our higher thinking but frequently is a trigger for illumination experiences.

One of these fundamental problems is to reconcile our scientific understanding of the world with our spiritual experiences and beliefs. There must be a unity at a higher level despite the outer appearances to the contrary. Try if you can find this understanding of the unity of all that is. What is matter, energy, spirit, consciousness, time? In the The Science of Spirituality I have outlined my answers to these questions, see if you can come up with a different or better explanation. Then learn to apply these principles to interpret and understand social phenomena or your own professional or scientific area. There is a good chance that this can lead to an illumination experience if you are otherwise ready.

Remember, the real purpose of reading or studying 'The Science of Spirituality' is not to gain any knowledge or to make a judgement about believing or not believing the theory, instead it is all about developing your own ability of abstract creative and intuitive thinking in order to develop a higher mental body.

Selfless Service

Selfless service or service to others is the practical expression of our spiritual consciousness. The degree of our inner disposition to serve is an indicator of our level of consciousness. However, just looking at the action itself may not show whether it is a service to others of to oneself. Working as a healer, or writing a self-help book, or working as a carer for a disabled person, or giving money to charities may either be done out of compassion to help others, or it may be done for a self-serving purpose, or it may be a mixture of both.

There is nothing wrong with helping others and at the same time expecting or receiving a benefit for oneself. However, the purer our motive, the more we act out of a feeling of universal love or compassion rather than for personal gain and the more is it an expression of genuine spiritual consciousness.

The importance of selfless service is highlighted in the Ra Teachings of the Law of One. According to this, the main criterion for moving from the human condition to the next higher level of consciousness is the degree of our service to others. To get to this higher or trans-human level, our interaction with others in thought, word or deed needs to result in at least 51% of our actions being selfless or in service to others.

Outlook

We know that we make good progress on the spiritual path if in our daily life and especially in difficult situations we display more and more the spiritual qualities of compassion, devotion, faith, forgiveness, harmony, high ideals, joy, kindness, openness, patience, self-responsibility, serenity, tolerance, unconditional love, understanding, wisdom and a gentle love for All That Is.

Another way of assessing our progress is by how well we are able to unite opposite characteristics within our personality and manifesting each characteristic as the situation requires. For example, are we able to be a good leader as well as a good follower, a master as well as a servant? Can we display the male characteristics of assertiveness, aggressiveness and power as well as the female qualities of gentleness, kindness and yielding? Do we know how to be strong in our beliefs but also open to change?

After years of diligently working to purify and improve yourself you may be wondering when you will have your mind-blowing illumination. However, that is counterproductive. The illumination experience is an act of grace, a gift of your spirit that will come when you least expect it. It may be during a meditation or in the middle of city traffic. Waiting for it is a sure way of postponing it because patience is one of the early virtues we have to learn. When it finally does happen, enjoy it.

The same applies to ascension. Presently it is fashionable to regard the various initiations rather like university examinations for which one has to work hard by doing plenty of guided imagery and meditation. I see this as counterproductive as well. Guided imagery and meditation are helpful but should not remain the main or only tools. I see the most important part of ascension work symbolized by the rose and the cross as used by the Rosicrucians. The rose symbolizes the opening of the heart chakra to universal love and the cross a life of service to overcome suffering. Therefore, the real ascension work is a life of loving service.

You do not need to actively look for good deeds to do or for your future field of loving selfless service. Just continue doing whatever needs to be done at each moment and especially continue purifying yourself at deeper and deeper levels. At the right time your mission will be revealed to you. By now you become increasingly competent to handle anything life throws at you or to play any role that you choose or are obliged to play.

Looking back on the path that you travelled so diligently, you may ask yourself "What Path?" and wonder if there ever was a path or only a figment of your imagination. In reality there was nowhere to go and nothing to do to get there. All you did was to change your perception and your attitude. You know now that you are a great spirit having a temporary experience in a body.

Nothing really changes by gaining or losing a body. As a spirit you can always choose to be joyful or sad, peaceful or loving or anything else you want to be. That is spiritual mastership. There is a Buddhist saying: 'Before enlightenment he gathered wood and carried water; after enlightenment he gathered wood and carried water.'

9

Hindu Ethics

Souls and Matter are only the body of God. Creation is a real act of God. It is the expansion of intelligence. Matter is fundamentally real and undergoes real revelation. The Soul is a higher mode than Matter, because it is conscious. It is also eternally real and eternally distinct. Final release, that comes, by the Lord's Grace, after the death of the body is a Communion with God. This philosophy believes in liberation through one's Karmas (actions) in accordance with the Vedas, the Varna (caste or class) system and the four Ashramas (stages of life), along with intense devotion to Vishnu. Individual Souls retain their separate identities even after moksha. They live in Fellowship with God either serving Him or meditating on Him. The philosophy of this school is Sri Vaishnavism, a branch of Vaishnavism.

INTERPRETATION OF MAHAVAKYAS

All Vedantic schools need to substantiate the meaning espoused by Mahavakyas which occur throughout Upanishadic literature. The interpretation of these *Grand Pronouncements* serve as the cornerstone for establishing each school of thought. The most significant among them is: Translated literally, this means *All this is Brahman*. The ontology of Vishishtadvaita system consists of:

1. Ishvara is *Para-brahman* with infinite superlative qualities, whose substantive nature imparts the existence to the modes.
2. Jivas are *chit-brahman* or sentient beings (which possess consciousness). They are the modes of Brahman which show consciousness.

3. Jagat is *achit-brahman* or matter/Universe (which are non-conscious). They are the mode of Brahman which are not conscious.

Brahman is the composite whole of the triad consisting of Ishvara along with his modes *i.e.* Jivas and Jagat. Hence, "all this is Brahman" denotes the triad of entities.

1. sarvam khalv idam brahma from Chandogya Upanishad 3.14.1
2. ayam atma brahma from Mandukya Upanishad 1.2

Translated literally, this means the *Self is Brahman*. From the earlier statement, it follows that on account of everything being Brahman, the self is not different from Brahman.

3. Tat tvam asi from Chandogya Upanishad 6.8.7

Translated literally, it means *Thou art that*

that here refers to *Brahman* and *thou* refers to *jiva*

The vakya establishes the identity of the jiva and Brahman. The issue here is if the identity involves establishing a unique identity or a universal identity. The difference is as follows:

1. *Unique Identity:* Atman is Brahman; Nothing else is Brahman; Brahman is reality and therefore everything else is illusion
2. *Universal Identity:* Atman is Brahman in the same way as everything else is Brahman.

Ramanuja chooses to take the position of universal identity. He interprets this passage to mean the subsistence of all attributes in a common underlying substratum. This is referred to as *samanadhikaranya*.

Thus Ramanuja says the purport of the passage is to show the unity of all beings in a common base. Ishvara (*Parabrahman*) who is the Cosmic Spirit for the pan-organistic body consisting of the Universe and sentient beings, is also simultaneously the innermost self (Atman) for each individual sentient being (Jiva). All the bodies, the Cosmic and the individual, are held in an adjectival relationship (aprthak-siddhi) in the one Isvara.

Tat Tvam Asi declares that oneness of Isvara.

When multiple entities point to a single object, the relationship is established as one of substance and its attributes.

For *e.g.* in a statement:-

Jack is a tall and intelligent boy

The descriptors *tallness*, *intelligence* and *boy-ness* all refer to a common underlying *Jack.*

Similarly, when the upanishads declare Brahman is the Universe, Purusha, Self, Prana, Vayu, and so on, the entities are attributes or modes of Brahman.

If the statement tat tvam asi is taken to mean as only *the self is brahman*, then *sarvam khalv idam brahma* will not make sense.

Understanding Neti-Neti

This is an upanishadic concept which is employed while attempting to know Brahman. The purport of this exercise is understood in many different ways and also influences the understanding of Brahman. In the overall sense, this phrase is accepted to refer to the indescribable nature of Brahman who is beyond all rationalisations. All descriptions of such an entity will necessarily have to be partial or fall short of the actual.

The typical interpretation of Neti-Neti is *not this, not this* or *neither this, nor that.* In Vishisht Advaita, the phrase is taken in the sense of *not just this, not just this* or *not just this, not just that.* This means that Brahman cannot be restricted to one specific or a few specific descriptions. Consequently, Brahman is understood to possess infinite qualities and each of these qualities are infinite in extent.

PURPOSE OF HUMAN EXISTENCE

The purpose or goal of human existence is called as Purush Artha. According to the Vedas, there are four goals namely Artha (wealth), Kama (pleasure), Dharma (righteousness) and Moksha (permanent freedom from worldly bondage). According to this philosophy, the first three goals are not an end by themselves but need to be pursued with the ideal of attaining Moksha.

Moksha

Moksha is a state where the jiva achieves oneness with Brahman in terms of all knowership and possessing qualities free from all worldly evils and defects. The jiva however doesn't possess the power to manifest/create and unmanifest/destroy. Neither does it have the power to grant Moksha.

The union of Atman and Brahman is likened to a situation where tiny lamps come under the blaze of the Sun. The lamp and Sun are still identifiable as different sources of light and yet the light arising from them is indistinguishable.

Moksha doesn't involve destruction of the self ("I") consciousness of the jiva.

COMPARISON WITH WESTERN NON-DUALISM

Baruch Spinoza, the 17th century rationalist philosopher, in his magnum work Ethics establishes the nature of GOD. Spinoza's pan-organistic God (*i.e.* God revealed as orderly nature) is comparable to Brahman (having the individual selves' and Universe as its body)

Spinoza makes the following propositions on the nature of God, in his work "Ethics". These positions closely reflect the Vishist Advaitic position on the nature of Brahman:

PROPOSITION XI. God, or substance consisting of infinite attributes, of which each expresses eternal and infinite essentiality, necessarily exists.

PROPOSITION XV. Whatsoever is, is in God, and without God nothing can be, or be conceived.

PROPOSITION XVII. God acts solely by the laws of his own nature and is not constrained by anyone.

PROPOSITION XVIII. God is the indwelling and not the transient cause of all things.

PROPOSITION XIX. God and all the attributes of God are eternal.

PROPOSITION XXX. Intellect, in function finite, or in function infinite, must comprehend the attributes of God and the modifications of God, and nothing else.

VISHISHT ADVAITA AND SRI VAISHNAVISM

The Absolute Supreme Reality referred to as Brahman, is a Transcendent Personality with infinite superlative qualities. He is Narayana, also known as Lord Vishnu. He is also the other two members of the Trimurti, namely, Creator Brahma and Shiva, the Lord of Deluge.

A man who has discrimination for his charioteer and holds the reins of the mind firmly, reaches the end of the road; and that is the supreme position of Vishnu.-1.3.9 Katha Upanishad.

Beyond the senses are the objects; beyond the objects is the mind; beyond the mind, the intellect; beyond the intellect, the Great Atman; beyond the Great Atman, the Unmanifest; beyond the Unmanifest, the Purusha. Beyond the Purusha there is nothing: this is the end, the Supreme Goal.-1.3.10,11 Katha Upanishad.

In terms of theology, Ramanujacharya puts forth the view that both the Supreme Goddess Lakshmi and Supreme God Narayana together constitute Brahman-the Absolute. Sri Lakshmi is the female personification of Brahman and Narayana is the male personification of Brahman, but they are both inseparable, co-eternal, co-absolute and are always substantially one. Thus, in reference to these dual aspects of Brahman, the Supreme is referred to in the Sri Vaishnava Sampradaya as Sriman Narayana.

CONCLUSION

Vishishtadvaita conclusions may be briefly summarised as below:

> *Narayana is the Absolute God. The Soul and the Universe are only parts of this Absolute and hence, Vishishtadvaita is panentheistic. The relationship of God to the Soul and the Universe is like the relationship of the Soul of Man to the body of Man. Individual souls are only parts of Brahman. God, Soul and Universe together form an inseparable unity which is one and has no second. This is the non-duality part. Matter and Souls inhere in that Ultimate Reality as attributes to a substance. This is the qualification part of the non-duality.*

Vishishtadvaita philosophy provided the philosophical basis for the establishment of Sri Vaishnavism and gave Vedantic backing to the brimming devotion of the Alwar saints and their composition of wonderful poetry and devotional songs in praise of Lord Vishnu. The succession of great Master-Expositors and spiritual giants of Vishishtadvaita school starts with the twelve Alwars, who left behind an imperishable legacy of Tamil devotional poetry in the form of 4000 songs, now called the Nalayira divya prabandham.

The Hinduism—Legends and Customs—Lord Brahma

We all think we know the world we are living in Jet, we all know in through our own culture's eyes, and it is a known thing that culture is strongly influenced by religion. And one of the oldest religions of this world is the Hindu religion.

In Hinduism, everything begins, ends and it is included in ohm,, which is a sign representing the trinity of God. Like the Christians, the Hindu God is divided in 3 different gods, which are one and the same person at the same time. It's the same way a person can be somebody's brother, somebody's father and somebody else's husband, but being at the same time one single person. The gods Brahma, Vishnu and Shiva represent the Hindu trinity.

Lord Brahma is the Generator, the creator of earth and everything there is: animals, plants and humans. Even being the generator of all things, he isn't worshipped because he married his sister.

Lord Vishnu, the most worshipped one, is the Operator. He is one that makes all the rules of the society, the one that makes things move. He usually uses material thing to persuade people to do the different things he wants them to do. Lord Vishnu is the most handsome one and he is usually represented like a beautiful young man with 4 arms or like a normal beautiful young man that has the *shakra* in his right hand and a snail shell from which it flows sand in the left one. The snail shell and the sand represent the flow of the time.

Lord Shiva is the Destroyer, the most important of the 3 gods. He is the one who will arise the *Divyajyoti*, the Hindu "apocalypse", the end of the world. Hindus believe in reincarnation, so the ones that will go to haven and the ones who will go to hell are the ones who made good deeds and bad deeds during their life until the *Divyajyoti*'s time when there will be too much sin on this world. When this will happen, he will open his third eye, and the world will burn. He is represented usually in the meditation position, with his third eye opened that he gained through meditation. That's why Hindu's wear a coloured dot between their eyes. It represents worshipping the intellect, the power of reason and will. Lord Shiva has an eye instead of a dot because he took the meditation to such level that a third eye opened, the eye of the mind.

Actually, it is with his third eye that he killed *Kaam Dev*, the god of love, because it was affecting him too much.

There are many gods in the Hindu religion. Everything that exists has it own got. There are about 63.000 gods. Some of the most known are *Varun Dev*, the god of air, *Arun Dev*, the sun god, *Agni Dev*, the god of fire and *Kaam Dev*, the god of love, who was killed by lord Shiva. It is useless to pray to him because he's dead. Still, there is a mantra that can invoke *Kaam Dev* into one's life and ask for his help. Mantras are prayers addressed to different gods.

There are many legends in the Hindu mythology and many of them have similarities with the ancient Greek myths. One of them is when devils attacked the haven, the way the titans attacked Olympus. When this happened, *Indra*, the king of haven, went to ask Shiva what to do because the world was in danger. And Shiva told him that only by throwing into the devils with the bones of a holly man the devils would die. And this holly man vas *Dadhichi*, the yoghin. *Indra* left to find *Dadhichi* and the found him meditating. His level of meditation was so high that he was able to make his soul leave his body. So, the gods could take his bones and throw them into the devils, thus saving the world, thanks to the old man's sacrifice.

It is a known thing that the woman is seen as the most fragile and delicate thing is all the societies of the world. Still, within the woman lies a great power. A power big enough to save the world, as Hindus say. When the world is in real danger, the 3 divine powers: the Generator, the Operator and the Destroyer, *Brahma*, *Vishnu* and *Shiva*, join together, thus generating 4 powers. That take the shape of 4 women, 4 goddesses: *Durga*, *Kali*, *Saraswati* and *Lakshmi*. Goddess *Durga* is the enemy of all the evil and the bad things in the world. The ones who worship *Durga* never forgive their enemies. *Kali* is the some like *Durga*.

She is the enemy of all the evil in the world and she is a destroyer, like *Shiva*, but she only destroys the evil. She's represented as being completely black, like the earth, whose rage she represents, wearing a garland of human skulls and she has her tongue always outside her month. She can also be invoked in black magic practices, but she is one of the 4 powers that can save the world in time of need. When the mother earth is angry, she takes the shape of goddess *Kali* to revenge herself. The image of *Kali* presented in the movie "Indiana Jones and the Temple of Doom" is completely fake and it has nothing to do with goddess *Kali*. Actually, the Indian people took the movie as in insult and it was forbidden in India. *Saraswati* is the goddess of intelligence and knowledge. Anybody who is student or learning something should worship *Saraswati* and ask her to make them keep their intelligence in their heads, unless it will vanish. They should ask her for the power of the concentration and of learning.

And finally, *Lakshmi*, who is the goddess of wealth and money. These are the 4 women, the 4 powers generated by the union of the 3 divine lords: *Brahma, Vishnu* and *Shiva*.

Unlike other religions, Hindus are born into Hindu religion. In Christianity, we baptise our children in the church of Jesus. Muslims and Jews circumcised their children in order to make them members of the Muslim or Jewish religious society. Unlike these, Hindus are born into their religion. They are members of the religious society strait from birth. They don't need a consecration like we need the baptise. All the children, regardless of sex, receive their mother's name until she decides to give them a name around the age of 4 years when the legal papers are completed as well. The marriage ritual is also very different. There are 3 types of ceremony: in the jungle, in the society and in the temple. The ceremony that takes place in the jungle, is secret, only the bride and the groom know what happens. It is forbidden now and considered illegal because it is thought to be a devil's ceremony, due to its secret nature.

The most common one is the social marriage but the rituals are very different depending on religions. India is a very big country and big countries mean many different traditions. It is the girl's parents that go to ask the boy's hand in marriage from his parents. The ceremony has 3 stages, which happened during in a night. In the first phase, the girl is taken from her house where she waits for the groom to come for her. She stays on a throne, wearing a red dress.

During the night, the bride, the groom and the bride's parents can't eat anything. When they arrive at his place, she changes her dress and wears a yellow one. A wood fire is set in the house. The girl's parents put her hand into the groom's hand, they are tied, and they surround the fire 7 times. Each time they surround the fire they take an oath. The first 4 times, the man is leading the woman and he takes the first 4 oaths. Than the last 3 times, the woman leads the man and it is her who takes the last 3 oaths. He swears always to protect her, to take all responsibility of her, never to let her cry, and she swears to let death take her first and also to make him happy, and take care of him. Than there is a feast with food and music and dance where everybody participates and she wears a red dress again.

Finally the ritual of death. If the one who dies is a child, a single girl or a single boy, or somebody who died because of a snakebite, he or she is drowned into a sacred river. All the rivers are believed to be sacred because all of them have their own god. If the one who died was married he or she is dressed as a groom or a bride and they are burned on a pyre. When the hair has burned and they can see his skull, they break it with a stick named *copalcria* to release the soul of the dead from its body. Women are not allowed to witness the ceremony. If the dead is a man, the one who will release the soul is his father, his eldest son or his brother. If the dead is a woman, it will be her husband or her eldest son. After the body is burned, there is 13 days ceremony. After 10 days, the men of the family shaves their heads in order to purify the house which isn't pure any more because of the presence of the dead's soul. They say that the soul of the dead stays around the house until all the 13 days ceremonies performed. In the 13th day, the family organises a feast for the *Brahmas*, and after this, the ceremony is completed and the soul is free to go.

The *Brahmas* are the upper class of the Indian society classes that are in number of 4: *brahma*, *shatria, veshia* and *shutra.* In the ancient times, people could change their cast if they had the necessary skills, but nowadays this isn't possible any more: the cast you are born it is like your identity card and you can not change it. The *brahmas* are the scholars, the ones that have the knowledge, the ones that have to teach the people. *Kshatriyas* are the warriors, the ones that fight to protect the country. *Veshias* are the traders, while *shutras* are the lower cast, the ones that serve the upper ones.

Hindus also have their holly days. Actually, each day is a different celebration. But there are four very important: *Holy, Rakshbandhan, Dusshera* and *Diwali.*

Holy is celebrated in March, depending on the position of the moon. It is the festival of colours, and it signifies the victory of love over hatred and the victory of good over evil. They say that once there lived a devil named *Hiraneakashiap* and in his kingdom nobody was allowed to worship God. But his son, *Prahalad*, was a great worshipper of God. His father was so upset with his son, that he tried to kill him. *Prahalad* had an aunt, his father's sister, whose name was *Hulika* and she was also a devil. She had a magic shawl that protected against fire. They tried to set a trap for *Prahalad* and *Hulika* stood in the middle of the fire, with her shawl on. But, by God's will, the shawl passed into *Prahalad*'s hand and the one who died in the fire was *Hulika*. *Hiranyakashyap* tried to kill his son again and again, until one day he put him inside a column and asked him: "where is your God now?". The devil was protected by a magic that he couldn't be killed by an animal, a human or a god, not on earth and not on air. So, when he asked:" where is your God? I can see no God here?", God came as a creature, half human, half lion, a sphinx. He put the devil on his knees, leaving his feet on the ground. He ripped him apart with his claws from his waste. So, no animal, no god and no human killed him, on the earth and not in the air, 'cause he was both on the earth and in the air, and at the same time not on the earth and not in the air. The name of the festival, *Holy*, comes from *Prahalad's* aunt, *Hulika*.

Rakshabandhan is the festival of brothers and sisters. It is in august and it is the most important Hindu festival. The sisters tie a silk band on the wrest of their brothers, and the brothers swear to protect their sisters of everything that's bad in the world. The wife of *Indra*, the king of heaven first performed the ritual, when the heaven was attacked by devils.

Dusshera takes place in September, October and November, depending of the position of the moon. It is the victory of good over evil. Its meaning is the victory of prince *Rama,* the incarnation of *Lord Vishnu* over the devil *Ravana.* He killed the devil and freed his wife and his kingdom, Lanka.

The last one of the four festivals is *Diwali* festival, the festival of light. It takes place nineteen days after the *Dusshera* festival. After prince *Rama* conquered Lanka and freed *Ravana's* wife, when he arrived back to whose own kingdom, after nineteen days, the people of his city enlightened the town with oil lamps in his honour. The main idea of Hinduism is that we have to do what we think is right, to work to live a good life, the way the holy books teach us and don't expect anything and not think about the consequences of our deeds. We should leave the rest to God, accept his wish and accept our destiny.

Bibliography

Aurobindo, Sri: *Vyasa and Valmiki*, Acharya Press, Pondicherry, 1956.

Bose, D. N.: *Dharmashastra: Their Philosophy and Occult Secrets*, Kali Press, Calcutta, 1965.

Collier, Richard: *The Great Indian Mutiny*, MacMillan, New York, 1963.

Frauwallner, Erich.: *History of Indian Philosophy*, Motilal, Delhi, 1973.

Grant, G. P.: *Philosophy in the Mass Age*, Copp Clark, Toronto, 1959.

Harman, William: *The Sacred Marriage of a Hindu Goddess*, Indiana University Press, Bloomington, 1989.

Jain, Jyoti Prasad: *Jain Sources of the History of India*, Bhagawati Press, Delhi, 1964.

Keith, Arthur Berriedale: *The Religion and Philosophy of the Veda and Upanishads*, MacMillan, Delhi, 1925.

Levy, John: *The Nature of Man According to Vedanta*, Routledge & Kegan Paul, London, 1956.

Munshi, K M.: *Glory that was Gurjaradesa*, Rawat Press, Bombay, 1955.

Ramakrishnananda, Swami: *Life of Sri Ramanuja*, Sai Kalyani Press, Madras, 1959.

Satyapal Verma: *Role of Reason in Sankara Vedanta*, Parimal Publication, Delhi, 1992.

Thomas, P.: *Kama Kalpa or the Hindu Ritual of Love,* D. B. Taraporevala Sons, Bombay, 1965.

Vable, D.: *The Arya Samaj. Hindu without Hinduism*. Vikas Publ., Delhi, 1983.

Wendy Doniger: *Siva: The Erotic Ascetic,* Oxford University Press, Delhi, 1998.

Index

◆◆◆